Take

a

Lesson

Take
a
Lesson

*Today's Black Achievers on
How They Made It and
What They Learned along the Way*

CAROLINE V. CLARKE

John Wiley & Sons, Inc.

Published by John Wiley & Sons, Inc.
Published simultaneously in Canada.

This publication is designed to provide accurate and authoritative information in regard
to the subject matter covered. It is sold with the understanding that the publisher is not
engaged in rendering professional services. If professional advice or other expert
assistance is required, the services of a competent professional person should be sought.

Kevin Clash Photo: Mark Husmann.
Johnnie L. Cochran, Jr. Photo: Leroy Hamilton.
Spike Lee Photo: David Lee.
William M. Lewis, Jr. Photo Courtesy of Wagner International.
Joan Parrot-Fonseca Photo Courtesy of Joseph Daniel Clipper.
Robin Roberts Photo: Steve Fenn/ABC.
Ruth Simmons Photo: Jim Gipe.
Terrie Williams Photo: Dwight Carter.

ISBN 0-471-37825-9 (cloth : alk. paper); ISBN 0-471-20989-9 (paper : alk. paper)

Printed in the United States of America

10 9 8 7 6 5 4 3 2 1

*Dedicated with love, admiration, and gratitude
to my greatest teachers and
the best parents a child could have,
Vera and Robert Clarke*

A little learning, indeed, may be a dangerous thing, but the want of learning is a calamity to any people . . .

— Frederick Douglass
Abolitionist, Orator, Journalist

Acknowledgments

❖

In late December 1993, Fate seated me next to Carole Hall at dinner in Vail, Colorado. We didn't know each other well, but as we discussed our plans and resolutions for the coming new year, we hit it off. Knowing that I was a journalist, she suggested that I write a book. Knowing that she was in book publishing, I shared my idea for this one. She loved it and said, "Go for it," before our conversation shifted to other topics.

Vacation ended and we both returned to work in New York. More than a year went by. Then, out of the blue, she invited me to lunch.

Carole's follow-up on that dinner conversation resulted not only in this book, but in *Black Enterprise Books*, a series in which this is our sixth offering. She is a skilled and insightful editor. She is also a steadfast supporter of *Black Enterprise*, and a caring and generous friend. I thank her for it all.

I must also thank former John Wiley & Sons editor Ruth Mills, who, with patience and humor, pushed me to begin this project, and my current Wiley editor, Airié Dekidjiev, who enthusiastically nudged me to completion.

My deepest gratitude goes to all 27 of the subjects of this book, who paused overloaded schedules to sit awhile with my trusty tape recorders and me. I must especially thank Joe Moniz, who allowed me to interview him when this was nothing more than a sketchy idea in my head. His chapter, which accompanied my book proposal, won the publisher over completely. Also, unbeknownst to them, Ruth Simmons and Kenneth Chenault were the first subjects who agreed to do the book once it was official. They did so without hesitation and without knowing who else would sign on. Being able to mention their participation (which I did at every opportunity), no doubt helped pave the way for others to follow.

To my *Black Enterprise* family, thanks for your constant encouragement and support, and for staying committed to the B.E. mission. To my loving "bosses," Earl and Barbara Graves, thanks for this and so many opportunities, and for showing me again and again how to not just do it, but to pull out all the stops, and do it right.

Finally, I've been blessed with an amazing extended family and true friends who always cheer me on. I am deeply grateful for them and to them. To my extraordinary parents, thanks for giving me roots and wings and a family full of sterling examples to emulate, especially your own. To my children, Veronica and Carter, who amaze, delight, and teach me new lessons every day: You are the best part of my life. And to my husband, Johnny: You inspire me to be the best I can be, to look for my deep purpose in life and be about it. You encourage me to try, then try again if need be and, through it all, you keep me laughing. I love you. I'm so proud of you. And I thank you for reciprocating in full.

Note to the Reader

❖

The passing on of information and history from one person to another to another has always served us well. Ours is an oral tradition.

Long before the term *mentor* ever existed, griots [African musician-entertainers] would hold court in tribal communities across Africa, imparting wisdom by telling stories that would be passed, like precious heirlooms, down through generations. Through our preachers and poets, storytellers and musicians, grandparents and parents, it continues on to this day.

In keeping with that custom, this book is a collection of first-person interviews conducted with 27 contemporary African American achievers. They represent a broad variety of industries from investment banking and entertainment to aviation and politics. Their personal backgrounds, too, are incredibly diverse.

What they have in common is that all have achieved groundbreaking successes; all have at least one "first black" distinction; all are extremely concerned about their role in helping to pave the way for other African Americans to succeed; and all are over 40 (due to my belief that you have to live a while to have not only knowledge, but perspective, worth sharing). It is also important to note that they are successful not merely because they have achieved social or economic status, or because they are leaders in their fields—although all that is true. They are also successful in the sense that they are passionate about what they do and they have chosen their own paths, consciously and not without risk, rather than allowed themselves to be pushed and pulled along in life by the whims of circumstance or expectations of others.

In candid, intimate interviews, they tell their own stories in their own way. Some share the lessons and landscapes of their childhoods. A few focus on the people who most influenced their approach to the world. Others reveal the pivotal moments that changed their lives and outlooks forever. Each talks about the specific experiences that shaped who they are, and they each answer a central question: What are the greatest lessons you've learned?

I shaped and edited their responses, but the words you'll read in each chapter are theirs alone. My hope is that as you read, you will hear the rise and fall of their voices, sense the depth of their emotions, and feel their presence as vividly as if you were sitting with them in my place. I also hope you'll do more than absorb the lessons these women and men share. Take them to heart. Use them. Pass them on.

Contents

❖

Take
a
Lesson

Introduction

❖

The best thing about being a journalist, in my view, is that it gives you license to ask people questions that you would otherwise never ask. I'm not talking about plumbing the depths of a subject's personal life, or digging for dirt and demons. Rather, I'm referring to those questions the answers to which truly reveal who a person is; what drives them; what moves them; where they derive their courage and strength; how they handle adversity and change and, even, success, because success comes with its share of challenges as well.

Those are the answers, when they are thoughtful and honest, that cut through the rhetoric of life straight to the heart of it. Those are the answers that can help the rest of us resolve the questions we struggle with in our own lives.

From the moment I did my very first interview more than a decade ago, it occurred to me that I was asking questions of my subject that I had never thought to ask my own parents or best friends. As a result, I learned things about that person that I didn't know about most of the people to whom I was closest.

As my career progressed, I realized that I wasn't just learning *about* the people I interviewed. I often learned *from* them. The experiences they recounted, and the added value that their hindsight perspective gave to those experiences, was often helpful to me. On occasion, they made an indelible impact.

Such was the case with the first magazine feature I ever wrote. It was for *Black Enterprise* in 1988. At the time, I was a novice newspaper reporter, just one year out of Columbia University Graduate School of Journalism and about as green as green gets. Already in my second full-time job since graduating, my main ambitions were to become a staff writer at a respected magazine and to reach an annual income that would equal my age (23 at the time) in thousands. I hoped the freelance work at B.E. would inch me along toward both goals.

My assignment was to profile Clifton Wharton, chairman and CEO of Teachers Insurance and Annuities Association-College Retirement Equities Fund (TIAA-CREF). With more than $50 billion in assets at the time, TIAA-CREF was the nation's largest pension fund and Wharton was the first African American to head a Fortune 500 company (a fact that is repeatedly overlooked today as the general media notes the rise of several other African Americans to top corporate slots).

In preparing for our interview, I learned that Wharton's life was a model of rare privilege and astonishing achievement. He was born the only child of the first black career officer in the Foreign Service to reach the rank of ambassador and, in addition to his pioneering appointment at TIAA-CREF, his own list of first-black accomplishments filled an entire page. He was the first black to graduate from the School of Advanced International Studies at John Hopkins University; first black Ph.D. in Economics from the University of Chicago; first black to become a director on the boards of a major life insurance company (Equitable Life) and automobile manufacturer (Ford Motor Co.); first black to become president of a predominantly white university (Michigan State) or chancellor of a university system (State University of New York). Wharton had also chaired the Rockefeller Foundation and, shortly before our interview, had become the first black elected a fellow of the American Agricultural Economics Association. That is just a sampling of his accomplishments.

Given all this, to say that I was anxious as I was led down a gleaming corridor toward Wharton's spacious office in midtown Manhattan would be a fantastic understatement. I was flat-out panicked. Here I was, a kid, basically, about to attempt a meaningful dialogue with a man who was in the throes of reorganizing one of the nation's largest yet most troubled financial institutions. TIAA-CREF was at a do-or-die moment in its long history, the pension funds of 890,000 account holders hung in the balance, and Wharton held the reins. Needless to say, he had more important things to do than be interviewed.

My worst fear was that he would take one look at me and despair that he had committed an hour of his workday to a rookie journalist the sum of whose knowledge about big business could free-fall through the eye of a needle. But I soon discovered that I needn't have worried at all, which is far more a measure of his grace in this situation than of mine.

Wharton was focused, responsive, respectful, and more generous with his time than I was led to expect. If he was ambivalent about my degree of experience or expertise, he never showed it. We talked in depth about the forces that shaped his childhood, his mentors, his consistent efforts to groom others for like success, his concerns about the chilling effect of racism in the corporate world and—his favorite topic—his wife, Dolores, and her own outstanding work. Of course, he also talked with passion and in great detail about his vision for TIAA-CREF, the progress made, and problems faced in executing that progress.

From that interview, I got all of the information I needed to write a profile that, thankfully, I can still read without embarrassment. But, more important, I walked away from that meeting with new insight into the heart and mind of a great leader. Two of the more lasting lessons I took from Wharton's example that day were to value every encounter and to discount no one. As he has noted himself, "Doing wonderful things for the bottom line is fine, but without a sense of genuine compassion, leaders will fall short of greatness. Great leaders do not lose their humaneness nor forget what it was like when they started at the bottom." For obvious reasons, Clifton Wharton was one of the first people I interviewed for this book.

I also learned that day that a genuine thirst for information and an innate ability to connect with people are two of a journalist's most valuable tools. The know-it-alls among us sometimes forget—or refuse—to ask the most basic questions, and it's those questions that sometimes yield the most telling responses.

As an editor at *Black Enterprise* for several years now, it has been my responsibility and great privilege to interview scores of entrepreneurs, professionals, and corporate executives. Whether they were building their own companies or sculpting careers, whether they were little known strivers or prominent Wall Street tycoons, the common thread among them has been this: They long for mentorship from other African Americans. No matter where they were on the ladder of success, they bemoaned the fact that they were often isolated—within their industries or their firm, or their department, or even socially.

Generally, high achievers keep a tight lid on their feelings of loneliness and frustration. After all, one of the most fundamental tenets of success is that you focus on the pros, not the cons; the solutions, not the problems; what you can control, not what you can't. And you certainly don't uncap your well-masked inner conflicts in the presence of a reporter. But, as I have conducted one-on-one interviews over the years, that lid has typically blown off, resulting in a degree of candor that often surprised my subjects and me.

As much as I'd like to think people have opened up to me because of some skillful ingenuity of mine, I know that, in part, they were just happy to be talking to a black reporter from a black publication about their experiences in a way that only another black person can fully appreciate.

It was also important for them to be able to tell members of their own community (in the form of *Black Enterprise* readers) what it's really like to strive for success in an environment that neither encourages, supports, nor even respects those ambitions in the same ways it does for whites.

Wherever you are now in your life and career, I'm sure you know the feeling. This book was designed to help fill that void. The 27 women and men who fill these pages may not be able to mentor you personally, but in this book they offer you the next best thing.

The context of our experiences is at times as significant as the experiences themselves. These subjects don't just spout the seven secrets of successful people, they know what it is to put all those time-tested principles into play and still get mistaken for a messenger or mail clerk. Like you, they have armed themselves with everything we're taught is needed to become successful and happy—a great education, a positive outlook, and a commitment to excellence—and yet, on a daily basis, they still operate within a culture that undercuts their potential, their performance, and, at times, their very right to the American Dream.

What they focus on here, though, is not that common framework of our lives but how they have learned to function and prevail within it, which is not to say that they swagger through each chapter full of vainglory and self-congratulation. Quite the contrary. Our greatest lessons most often stem from our darker times. So, in excavating those lessons, these women and men — all best known for their triumphs in life — frequently recall their brushes with defeat, self-doubt, and personal tragedy. In so doing, they become more than role models; they become *real* models.

One by one, they tell you precisely what they had to go through to reach their goals, how they made it, and what they learned along the way. For example, how did poor Texas sharecroppers imbue their twelfth child with what it takes to become the first black president of one of the nation's most elite colleges? Smith College president Ruth Simmons tells you how.

Why would one of the few African Americans to ever be made partner at one of Wall Street's premiere investment banks opt to leave and start his own small firm? Provender Capital Management founder Fred Terrell tells you why.

Is there one (hard-driving, anal-retentive) personality type that holds the key to high-level corporate success? Absolutely not, says Time Warner's Dick Parsons, who lauds the attributes of his own Type-B personality in his chapter.

How does it feel to ride a 30-year wave of corporate stardom, then find yourself unemployed? Girls, Inc. CEO Joyce Roche and Avis Group CEO A. Barry Rand lay it all out.

Too often, we view people with great titles or status or wealth as somehow different from us. We assume they were born to their dazzling fates or we believe they were plucked from the crowd by some omnipotent benefactor — that they were, in effect, handed their success or merely destined for it, whether deserved or not. The people featured in this book prove all that untrue.

Each of them has taken chances, made tough choices, hit rough spots — even fallen and failed — only to rise again having learned from the experience. Those lessons, clearly articulated in each chapter, are as distinctive and highly personalized as the individuals conveying them. But there was one message that each expressed: "It's an old Christian value: Know thyself." So said Sy Green, the first African American managing director at the insurance giant Chubb & Sons, and so said all who share their lives' experiences in these pages.

The single most critical key to success, based on their collective view, is that *you must know who you are*, stand firm in that, and be comfortable with it. Then, when the tides turn (as they inevitably will) at work or in your personal life, you will float. You may be tossed around a bit, and get bruised and confused in the process, but that most fundamental crumb of knowledge about your values and motivations, about what you want and what you won't accept, about your very essence and capabilities, will enable you to right your course.

Ultimately, that's what this book is about: helping you to right your course; stay on course; get on course; find your course.

David Crocker, a former executive who rose from the depths of IBM's massive 1980s downsizing to become a terrific motivational speaker, is fond of responding to the old saying, "Experience is the best teacher," with the notion that there is in fact one better: *Other people's* experience. This book offers you the invaluable benefit of exactly that.

CHAPTER ONE

Kenneth Chenault

CEO, American Express Co.

Perched high atop one of the World Financial Center's gleaming towers, Ken Chenault's spacious office has a panoramic view of Manhattan that is framed on one side by the majestic Hudson River and punctuated with the Statue of Liberty. It is, in a word, breathtaking. So much so that it's hard to imagine staying focused on the enormous task of running a $20 billion business in such a room.

But Chenault is no daydreamer. In his 20 years with American Express, the New York native has made a name for himself as a clear-headed strategist with a special knack for steering through the chaos of corporate transition. Now, in one of the most highly anticipated successions in corporate history, Chenault, 49, has become Chief Executive Officer of this respected global empire.

With a record of high ahievement and leadership that dates back to high school, Chenault seemed destined for greatness. But even this proven strategic planner wouldn't have predicted it on this plane. As a Bowdoin College student, Chenault set his sights on a career in social service, although his peers envisioned him in politics. "There weren't many African Americans in business for me to be exposed to," says Chenault, who also graduated from Harvard Law school, "so business just wasn't in the frame." Chenault is married and has two sons.

There's an African parable that I often include in the speeches I give because I think it starkly illustrates the challenges we face. It goes like this: *Every morning in Africa, a gazelle wakes up. It knows it must run faster than the fastest cheetah, or it will be killed. Every morning in Africa, a cheetah wakes up. It knows it must outrun the slowest gazelle, or it will starve to death. It does not matter whether you are a cheetah, or a gazelle. When the sun comes up, you'd better be running!*

To western minds, this epitomizes type-A behavior. It's a shortcut to a coronary; the paranoid vision of a dog-eat-dog world, where only the top dog survives. But if you have seen the plains of Africa—even if only in your heart—it conveys a different, more subtle meaning.

At any given moment, running fastest may be essential to existence because behind you may be a hungry predator. This is the reality of life. But running fastest is also the ultimate expression of freedom. It can be a celebration of the essence of life. So, what I take from that parable is that at any moment, no matter who you are, you must be prepared to give your best.

Growing up, there was a strong expectation in our house to do your best, and there was a great emphasis on manners and integrity. My mother was very realistic and practical. She always said, "It's a tough world we live in. You need to face reality. But, at the end of the day, you need to overcome it."

My father always stressed focusing on the things you can control. He said, "Your own performance you can control; no one can take that away from you." That's one reason my father chose to be a dentist. He really valued independence and determining his own fate. He told me, "You need to determine what constitutes success for yourself and not determine it based on what other people think." His advice has served me well.

How do you achieve success? How do you "run fastest?" Through my career, I have distilled some principles that have guided me.

First: Personal integrity. My earliest lesson about this is still clearly etched in my memory. I think I was in seventh grade. I was taking the advanced math course they had for kids in our district, and there was a summer basketball tryout at the exact same time. I think my father knew what I would be tempted to do, and he said to me beforehand, "Sometimes you need to make trade-offs. . . ." That's all he said. I decided to trade off the math class and go to the basketball tryouts.

It was a situation in which if you did well at the first tryout, you went to the second stage, then the third, and so, I had missed the math class for about three days. Then one afternoon — you know how you sort of *feel* somebody's presence? — I was in a game, doing very well, and then I just felt it. I looked up and saw him watching me from the stands. Ordinarily, he would have called out, "What is the deal?" and pulled me out of the game. He did not do that.

He waited until the game was over, then he called me over and said, "You played very well, but you've really disappointed me. One reason is that you intentionally went against what I said. More importantly, you made a trade-off that made sense in the short term, not the long term. What you don't even see is that, ultimately, you could have done both."

He went on to say that it was all about character, and that I really needed to think about the fact that I was able to operate like that for three days. And there was, of course, punishment. I was grounded for two weeks or more. But he was so disappointed, and that really hit me very hard.

Personal integrity is a very big thing with me. Don't sell yourself to the highest bidder. If you don't believe in the product or ideals of a company or organization, don't accept the job. Dedicate yourself to a core set of values. Without them, you will never be able to find personal fulfillment, and you will never be able to lead effectively.

Second, always try to associate with the best and brightest people. Don't allow yourself to be intimidated by someone's reputation for being hard and tough. A professor or boss who demands excellence from you will generally be a fair person. Believe in yourself, and never be afraid to challenge yourself. In other words, stay away from stupid people.

Third, don't overestimate the importance of networking. Whether in school or in business, your main focus always needs to be on completing the job at hand. Having a good set of friends in the classroom will not help when the bluebooks are passed out. If you're already in your career, don't expect a network of strangers or acquaintances to lay the path to your success.

Execution — performance — is the bottom line measure for everything we attempt to do. To be successful, our EQ, or execution quotient, must equal our IQ. This is something I stress to American Express employees around the world. Network off of your performance.

Fourth, although security is nice, don't shy away from organizations in chaos. In business, the greatest opportunities often lie in companies experiencing rapid growth and in those companies forced to reinvent themselves because they are in bad shape.

For African Americans, I think this is especially important, because a company undergoing crucial change is more willing to promote on merit than to hold back to serve old prejudices. American Express is a company that has absolutely thrived on rapid—even aggressive— change. Does it make things more difficult? Yes, at times. But it can also make the environment, and your role in it, far more stimulating.

Fifth, recognize that being one of the only blacks—whether in a classroom, in a department, on a workteam, in an organization, or just in a meeting—automatically makes you very visible. Use this to help yourself. Look at it as an opportunity, and leverage that opportunity by making a visible contribution.

My first job at Amex, in strategic planning, offered me an opportunity to attend meetings with senior management. Many folks would have dropped everything for a chance to meet with the CEO, but often, I passed up the opportunity. I decided to attend only meetings where I was reasonably confident that I could make a contribution. I knew that, as a very visible employee, having the boss see me meant nothing. Having him see me solve his problems meant everything.

Sixth, remain open to life's possibilities. I was actually fine when I was practicing law and, if you had asked me at the time if I was going to continue practicing law, I probably would have said yes. Then, I had some interviews with this consulting firm, Bain & Co., and I started to feel a level of excitement that, even at the time, I didn't realize was missing from the legal experience.

Just two and a half years later, when a search firm called me and asked if I'd be interested in coming to American Express, I said I didn't think I had a strong interest in working for a large company. I thought, if anything, I was going to go into venture capital because I liked the analysis and deal-making aspects of it. But after meeting with [former CEO] Lou Gerstner, who also came from a consulting background, I was enticed by his emphasis on change and accountability.

Seventh: In my late 20s, I started to do something that made a major difference for me. It's something I learned from my mother: Active listening, to be really open about different perspectives and to always go through the pros and cons. Whenever I think about an issue, I always argue the opposite side of it. So, when I ultimately decide on a course of action, I've already been through all the conceivable scenarios, and I'm going to go for it.

Eighth, wherever you are, whatever challenges or opportunities you face, *know who you are.* Approach your career and conduct your business in a way that makes it clear that you do. This seems like a simple concept. But I've seen many people too often lose sight of it, and suffer as a result.

For me, nowhere was that better illustrated than at Harvard Law School. My experiences there taught me how to deal in an environment where my initial view was that everyone was an incredible superstar. It was one of the very first things that struck me. It was not a fear of whether I belonged, but more, where do I stand with this group?

What I see as the danger in any high-powered school—or highly competitive situation—is that you can very quickly be made to feel that you are inadequate. That can happen in the classroom; it can happen socially. It can happen repeatedly as you advance in a career.

At Harvard, there were so many people who professed that they knew exactly what they were going to do. If you go into a situation and you don't have that singular focus, it sets you off balance. At the end of the day, very few people essentially have that, but those who do can really start to dominate the environment. I saw too many people who allowed themselves to be distracted by the attitudes and reactions of the people around them.

And so, what I got from Harvard that has been very, very helpful throughout my career is the importance of having a strong sense of self. Without it, not only can you not lead, you risk being consumed by all sorts of elements that don't reflect what you're about. If you lose that, you will not be able to radiate the self-confidence that rallies people to a winning message. You will not have the inner strength to carry your ideas forward, no matter what your place in the corporate hierarchy.

Part of being a leader is pulling people from disparate backgrounds together. If you're not clear about who you are and what you represent, you will not have the ability to do that.

You have to maintain your sense of balance and perspective. I look at other people who have been in prominent positions. From what I've seen, some of the hardest challenges they face are how to maintain balance; how to keep to certain values; and how to prevent what is happening in their careers from engulfing them.

More and more over the last five to eight years, I've tried to make sure I keep in balance what my beliefs and values are. I do this in a variety of ways. One is to try to stay close to my roots, which are defined as family and some of the friends I knew back when. Human nature is human nature, and once you're very successful, even those people will treat you differently, but they will still speak some of the truth to you. And they will generally give you their perspective—not necessarily on what you're dealing with professionally—but on life in general.

Also, I try to seek out nonbusiness experiences and people who are outside the business realm, to get a different perspective. And, especially over the last year, I frankly just try to fight for some time when I can step back and think a little bit.

People can compartmentalize, and everyone does that, but there is an uncertainty about what's going to happen in your personal relationships and in your family that is both thrilling and scary. It doesn't matter how successful you've been or how much money you've made, there are things that can happen, such as illness and death. I think recognizing how precious the family experience is, and that it can be taken away at any time, helps to keep me grounded.

Finally, we, more than others, must give back to help our community and to ease the way of those who will follow. I believe very strongly in the power of an individual to bring about change, but then I also believe in the influence of events. Sometimes you get the right timing, and match the individual with the event, and amazing things result.

It doesn't take much to make a great change in a community. You can do it by reading to a child. You can do it by volunteering at a soup kitchen. You can do it by visiting an older shut-in. You can do it by cleaning up a neighborhood. You can do it by mentoring, getting involved, setting an example, having a positive impact on a child's life.

As a teenager, some things just came naturally to me, like the ability to motivate people, to get them moving in a certain direction. But what really fed my self-esteem was that teachers, friends of my parents, and even kids I grew up with, kept sort of reinforcing the idea that I had a lot of potential and that by staying focused, I was going to be able to do a lot.

Too many children have no direction. No one tells them why it's important that they do their homework, or takes them to a ball game or to a museum; no one says to them, "I love you." No one says to them, as people said to me, "I know you will do your best. You're going to be able to do a lot."

It is easy for successful people to become self-absorbed. To some, life is about spending money, acquiring things, restricting their social circle, celebrating themselves. Their only effect on others is envy and cynicism. If our best become self-absorbed, if our most successful look out only for themselves, then the difficult lessons of the old millennium will haunt us forever.

I've always been really fascinated by history. I can vividly remember, when I was five years old, my parents used to get these *Life* magazine Books of the Year, and I would look through them and really try to imagine what it was like to deal with those situations. That's how I learned to read.

To this day, history just fascinates me, especially in the form of biographies. We can learn a great deal from those who went before us, who broke down barriers so that we could step forward.

Frederick Douglass said that the destiny of the black in America is the destiny of America. At long last, America is beginning to show signs of recognizing that. As barriers against us fall, we must not fail to move forward.

I happily extend my hand to the young people who will follow me and outachieve my efforts. I really do believe that the future is theirs for the taking.

CHAPTER TWO

Kevin Clash

Principal Puppeteer, Jim Henson Company

Before Teletubbies, or Barney or Arthur the bespectacled aardvark, there was *Sesame Street*'s beloved Elmo, and you don't have to live with a preschooler to know exactly who this furry, little red monster is.

In the last five years, Elmo has almost become an industry unto himself, starring in major motion pictures and videos, as well as an enchanting new segment of *Sesame Street* dubbed "Elmo's World." And who can forget the Christmas crush a few years back when Tickle Me Elmo topped every child's wish list?

What you may not realize, in spite of Elmo's prominent place in kiddie culture, is that his creator and Emmy award winning alter-ego is Kevin Clash. In fact, Clash, who nurtured his craft as a kid in Baltimore, will tell you that the best thing about being a master puppeteer is that you can become fabulously successful and wealthy and still remain virtually unknown.

On some days, though, that can also be the worst thing. Says Clash, 40 (whose talents have also spawned television's once-popular Alf and Baby on the show *Dinosaurs*, as well as a Mutant Ninja Turtle or two): "The work definitely comes with its own rewards, and I love what I do. But everybody wants to be appreciated, and in this end of [show] business, we get discounted and taken for granted a lot. I entertain and educate our kids. What could be more important than that?" Clash, who is divorced, has a daughter.

I love the reaction I get when people realize I'm Elmo. If we're doing a show, like *The Rosie O'Donnell Show*, the audience will see me go up on stage and get down on the floor behind a chair, and they'll just think, oh, he must be plugging in wires or something. Then, during the performance, they'll forget anyone's there.

When it's over, and they see me get up, I see the looks on people's faces. They can't believe it, and I'm thinking, yes, it's true: Elmo is a black man.

I guess if there's one lesson you could take from my life and work, it would be about what can happen when you recognize that you have a gift or a passion, and you just go after that, even if it takes you in a different direction from everybody else.

As far back as I can remember, I was always really intrigued by puppets. At 10 years old, I was illustrating and building them, just playing around with them a lot. I grew up in Baltimore and my father was the handyman for the area that we lived in. I got to go around building sheds with him and stuff, so I learned something about building from him, but I never went to school for any of this.

From the beginning, I designed the puppets, built them, made their clothes, their hair, their props. And I never really thought about how I did it or how difficult a certain idea would be to execute. I just did it. So, I'd have to say it was really a gift, but it was always one I worked hard at. You know, it's not enough to have a talent or a dream. That gives you a great start, but it's working at it, learning more about it, perfecting it that makes you a success. The gift alone doesn't get you there.

So, I started working at it when I was very young, and by 15, I knew this was it for me. This was what I wanted to do.

I watched every show with puppets in it that came on television: *Kukla, Fran and Ollie, Captain Kangaroo*. There was a special in the 1970s called *Of Muppets and Men* and a local show in Baltimore called *Professor Cool's Fun School*. I was into all of it and, of course, I was into *Sesame Street*.

My first big turning point came when I was in the tenth grade. One day, my social studies teacher said to me, "You know, you're going to fail this class, because you're not interested in it. We have to do something to get you into it or else you're not going to make it." He knew I was into puppets because I performed in talent shows at school, so he came up with this project where he paired all of us off, and got each couple to pick a country. We had to learn everything we could about the place and then present what we learned to the class.

My partner and I got Russia. We did our research and came up with this presentation where my partner played a reporter and I performed with this puppet I built called Arnie. Arnie was supposed to be Russian and could change into a male or female for different interviews with the reporter. We put on this show explaining about the culture and the country and we got an A. In fact, it worked so well that they had us do it at a big assembly for the whole school.

The principal's secretary had a friend who worked at the local newspaper on a section called *Young World*. She told him about me and he came over to my parents' house and watched me put on a show for my mother's daycare kids. He took photographs and did a story that ended up on the cover. From that, I started getting jobs around the Baltimore area doing shows. That was the real beginning of my career.

I started doing live shows in the city at what was then the Inner Harbor. The area that we lived in had a Heritage Fair every year. A guy named Stew Kerr, who did *Professor Cool's Fun School* at the CBS affiliate, saw me perform my puppet variety show there. At the time, Jim Henson was doing a TV show called *Sam and Friends* in which he was taking the music of his era, like Louie Prima and Danny Kaye, and having his puppets perform that stuff. In our community, Minnie Ripperton and Earth Wind and Fire were big. So, I would have my puppets singing "Fire" and doing the bump and the robot. I would also spoof commercials that were on at the time. Like I'd have a mummy puppet dance around and sing the jingle, "I am stuck on Band-Aids, 'cause Band-Aids stick on me."

My shows were hosted by a puppet based on a friend of mine, Tony Bartee. (The characters we create always come from aspects of us or people we know. Elmo is based on my mother's daycare kids.) Stew Kerr saw me and told me to come in and audition for his show. I auditioned using Bartee and I got on the show. I would shoot the shows on Friday evenings and would build the puppets during the week, after I did my homework for school. It was hard work, but it got me into the habit of that, which was a good thing, because later it got even harder.

All this was happening at a time when everybody else in the neigh-

borhood was into hanging out at the recreation center all day, playing basketball and football. I did that stuff too, and I was good at it, but I wasn't
passionate about it. There's a feeling you get when you are really into
something. You shouldn't ignore that—it could lead you to places you
never even dreamed about. At least, that's what happened for me.

Thankfully, my parents were very supportive. They never said "You
should be a doctor, lawyer, teacher," whatever. They were saying, "You
should find something that you enjoy doing." I clearly enjoyed performing
so they encouraged me. But I don't think my mom thought I would really
go onto performing professionally, partly because I was so shy. I used to
walk down to the grocery store and if I saw people hanging out, I would
walk all around rather than go past them, because I didn't know what to say.

What helped most to break me out of the shy thing was probably the
need to negotiate fees. I didn't have an agent, and I had to get paid. To
get paid enough, I knew that I had to talk to people, I had to make them
understand that there was a value to what I was doing. Eventually I got
into the actors union where there was a certain base you'd get paid, but
prior to that I would just come up with a fee and hope to get it.

It was interesting, because when I started doing live shows, I wouldn't
have a problem getting a certain fee—the right fee—from white people,
but black people would typically say, "Oh, that much?" It wasn't discrimination. It was lack of appreciation. It's kind of sad, but white people
were more accepting of it as a real talent, something with real value. My
own people—outside of my family—didn't take it as seriously. They
thought it was fun, they appreciated it in that sense, but I don't think
they really valued it.

Even today, I've won Emmys—the top award you can win in television, and I've won some other great awards—but I've never been recognized by my own people. Part of me knows that shouldn't matter. I was
told a long time ago that, in this occupation, you're not going to be
known like a Denzel Washington. And in certain ways that's good for
you. I'm okay with that. I don't need my face to be known. But I do want
to be recognized for what I contribute, and it would mean so much more
coming from my own.

It would also send a message to young kids about the value of creative choices or choices that are just different. I love my work, but it's
also turned out to be very lucrative and full of a wide variety of opportu-

nities—directing, producing, recording, toy manufacturing. Our children — black children in particular—should know that they don't have to be either a sports personality or a movie star or a musical artist. There are so many ways to excel, but if we only glorify a few things, they'll only aspire to be those few things. That's so limited, and so much talent gets wasted with that mindset.

I know it sounds corny, but a lot of what we all should learn in life, we could learn from *Sesame Street,* and I'm not talking about the ABCs. *Sesame Street* teaches children how to believe in themselves and each other; it teaches them how to cooperate and share and be friends. But I think that the most important thing *Sesame Street* teaches kids is how to celebrate everything—especially differences.

It teaches tolerance and respect and kindness. But then it goes even further and teaches you to *celebrate* tolerance and respect and kindness. And, while you're at it, celebrate every race, every talent, every skill, every choice. *Celebrate everything!* We don't do that enough. We don't celebrate each other's differences and accomplishments enough, and I can't categorize that as black or white. That's about a culture that's geared to celebrity worship and seeing the differences between us as dividers that separate us.

On *Sesame Street,* everybody is celebrated. It's not just the message of the show, it's how we work as a crew on the show. We're an ensemble cast, there is no one star. We all have our own strengths and when we bring it all together, it works wonderfully. Everybody's role in that is important. Everybody gets their moment to shine.

All of this grows out of the mind and wonderful example of [the late Muppets founder] Jim Henson. With Jim, not only was the sky the limit as far as creativity goes, he was an incredibly good person. He taught me an incredible amount about puppeteering, but he taught me even more about how to be a good person. Jim was a multi- multi- multimillionaire, but he still liked to have fun with us. He never came off like the boss. He and his whole family were just very respectful of all people. Race was never any type of barrier with him at all.

Here's a perfect illustration of how unconscious Jim was of race: There is this Swedish Chef muppet and his face is light—you know, he's supposed to be Swedish—but his hands are live hands. Whoever's performing him has to put their own hands in the chef's sleeves so they can throw food and stuff around. One day, we were talking about casting a scene with the chef and Jim said, "Well, let Kevin do it." The others said, "He can't." And Jim said, "Why not?" He had to think for a minute before he was like, "Oh, right. Wrong color hands." Race as a barrier was never something that he focused on.

Jim was a hero of mine long before I knew that about him. I met him through a guy named Kermit Love. I first saw Kermit on *Call It Macaroni*, a TV show that would have a young boy or girl spend the day with a professional. One day, I watched this show (it was in my senior year of high school) and saw Kermit build a puppet with a kid and go out to Central Park and put on a show. I found out that Kermit helped Jim design [the muppets] Big Bird and Snuffy and I really wanted to meet this guy.

My mother called the show and got in touch with him. He said if I was ever in New York, I should come by. So I went on a school trip up to New York and took one of my puppets to show him. He liked it and he became like a grandfather to me. He started to send me bits and pieces of work and eventually he introduced me to Jim Henson.

When the producers of *Sesame Street* first asked me to do some guest spots, they had me come up to New York for a week to observe, and then I went back home. This was Jim [Henson], it was the Muppets, this was a very big deal to me, but it didn't happen. It turned out that they really didn't need anybody else at that point. I was crushed. Just totally crushed. Then, several months later, I got a call to do some guest spots. That was the beginning.

By then, I was doing *Captain Kangaroo* and the *Great Space Coaster*, so I was literally working 24 hours a day. I'd do *Captain Kangaroo* in the morning, *Space Coaster* in the afternoon, fit *Sesame Street* in when they needed me, and I'd build puppets at night. It was a good thing I was young, because I could do that. Eventually, I hired a guy to help me build the puppets.

It was physically very demanding, but it was a lot of fun because there was so much variety. Some shows had more music than others and so there was so much creativity involved. I was enjoying it so much, it didn't feel like work. But it wasn't all fun either.

At one point while I was juggling *Sesame Street*, *Captain Kangaroo*, and *The Great Space Coaster*, I had some problems with *Sesame Street*. They weren't giving me as much work as the other two, but they would give me specific dates when they wanted me there and there were conflicts in the dates. I had already signed a contract and it was a pay or play type of deal where if I walked away I wouldn't get the money but if they walked away, I would still get paid. So I asked my lawyer to work out the conflicts.

When I told this *Sesame Street* rep that I was going to send my lawyer to work it out, she said, "We don't talk to lawyers. Since you can't do these days, you won't get paid." I could have fought about it, but I let it go because I knew that at some point I was probably going to work there full-time, and I didn't want to close that door. But it was a really difficult time. To be successful, you have to learn from the positive and the negative.

You also have to let an opportunity pass sometimes, believing you'll get another shot. The first time I got called to do a movie, I had to say no because I just had no time, but I knew in my brain and in my heart that they would call me again. And lo and behold, they did. Eventually *Captain Kangaroo* got cancelled and *Space Coaster* went off the air and Jim's wife, Jane, called and asked me if I'd be interested in doing *Sesame Street*. I jumped at it, and right away, a movie came up.

Labyrinth was my first movie, and it was the most unbelievable thing. I had never been out of the country before, and we shot in London, so that experience was phenomenal. I worked with [rock star] David Bowie—I think I was 25 at the time—and this was just amazing.

Really from the time I was in high school, every new opportunity that came up, I jumped at. New shows, new projects like the movies, travel to new places – all of it excited me. I wasn't intimidated by any of it, even at that age. You can't be. You have to just jump into it. There's no other way to keep moving forward but to go, go, go. Take a chance.

I was confident, but also, it was just what I wanted to do and I was doing it. Whatever I didn't know, I knew I would learn, and people with more experience have always been so willing to teach me. I try to do that now. To be generous with your skills or experiences should always be a part of what you do. Jim Henson taught me that. Kermit Love taught me that. Working on *Sesame Street* taught me that. You don't learn just from being a student; you can learn a lot from teaching others.

Excellence is everything. There have been so many projects where I was only supposed to do the physical part of the work, not the voices, but I ended up doing both because the producers just liked what I did. Especially with movies, a lot of times producers want to get voice people to do them, but I almost always do my own. On *Teenage Mutant Ninja Turtles*, again, they were considering getting someone else to do the voices, but they loved the way I did it, so they kept it. Knowing that they didn't plan to use my voice, I could've blown off that part of it, but by doing it well, I changed their plans.

Because of that, I'm a perfectionist. I always want things to be the best they can be; I don't compromise on that, and lately I have a lot less patience with people who don't have the same standards. I'm at a point in my career now where I'm producing and directing. It's my job to make sure that everything is as right as it can be. What's nice is having that ability and the power to do that for the betterment of the project, not just for the betterment of me. But for all the work I do at that level, I still love getting out there and doing my own puppets.

We got a call from a social worker a while back who said there was a little girl who didn't have long to live, and her dream was to meet Elmo; could she come on the set? So, she came, in a wheelchair, this beautiful little girl. She and her mother were so happy. We knew she was very sick, but to look at her you wouldn't know it. It was the coolest thing. It was great.

I didn't set out to do things like that. I just did what I loved doing, something that I was passionate about and good at. I never could have imagined that it would lead to where it has, financially or emotionally, like with this little girl. I have a daughter. I could identify with that mother. That experience, for me, was as great as performing with David Bowie or Maya Angelou. That's what it's all about.

It's interesting, doing what I do really [neutralizes] the race thing, because puppets come in every color, size, and shape and that's actually one of the reasons people *like* them. I mean, Elmo is just this sweet, little furry red monster who is loved by millions of people, not just kids. That sick little girl or the most narrow-minded bigot doesn't necessarily care what color the guy who created him is — they just love Elmo. If you think about it, that's a pretty powerful thing. We ought to learn from that.

CHAPTER THREE

Johnnie L. Cochran, Jr.

Partner, The Cochran Group
Schneider, Kleinick, Weitz, Damashek & Shoot

Passionate, committed, and deeply religious, Johnnie Cochran is a man who defines his profession but is not defined by it.

The nation's best-known litigator built his Los Angeles-based career first as a successful prosecutor who nailed the LAPD in several police brutality cases, then as a zealous trial lawyer advocating for such diverse clients as Michael Jackson and Reginald Denny, the white truck driver attacked in the aftermath of the Rodney King verdict. So he was already a newsmaking, precedent-setting attorney when he took on his most visible role to date: lead defense lawyer for ex-football hero O.J. Simpson, on trial for murder.

Cochran's controversial and successful defense of Simpson made his a household name from coast to coast. Cochran, 63, went on to host his own talk show on Court TV following the trial. While the show positioned him as provocative and confrontational, one-on-one he is actually softspoken and contemplative.

Today, he continues to rack up newsworthy victories in his vital law practice and is a highly sought after orator, lecturer, and legal consultant. Cochran is married and has three grown children.

When you pick beneath the surface, I think you will find that most well-rounded people are made up of a bundle of contradictions. I have been shy basically all my life. Even though I could be outgoing at times and I've always loved to joke around, I really was shy.

In high school, I did things like playing football—I was even a quarterback—yet I was also a scholar. Even to this day, when I've hosted my own television show and repeatedly faced crowds of reporters and big audiences at speaking engagements and so on, even though I am very comfortable in those situations, I'm just as comfortable in a one-on-one situation over in a corner. In fact, although I love doing some public show in front of a jury, I am more content when I'm at home, when it's quiet and I can sort of retreat and go within. But that preference has never prevented me from getting out there and doing the other, especially since that's a big part of my job.

I am one of the lucky ones who can honestly say that I am doing with my life exactly what I always wanted to do. I can remember my mother early on started to talk about my becoming a doctor, but I always wanted to be a lawyer. I loved to talk, argue, persuade, and be an advocate. I didn't know any lawyers—particularly any black lawyers—when I was a child. But I knew about Thurgood Marshall, and, to me, becoming a lawyer was about bettering yourself.

My father had been at the top of his class, but when he was 14, just after entering high school, his father died and he had to leave school to go to work and support his family. I think he attached a lot of his dreams to us. And, knowing what had happened to his dreams, I willingly took a lot of that on. I wanted him to be able to look at my life and think, "Dream fulfilled." Now, when my mother found that I wanted to go into law, she was disappointed. But she said, "Well, just promise me you'll be the best that you can be." So I did, and she accepted that.

Moving to California from Louisiana made a huge difference in my life. Los Angeles High School was like a private school that public kids could go to, and my father made sure we got there. It was a whole new world to me. I would go home after school to some of these kids' homes and, for the first time, I really began to understand the gap—the very wide gap—between whites and blacks economically.

There was a kid with an archery range in his back yard. There were tennis courts, pools—all these things—and I wanted them. I wanted to use the law to try to change things, but I also knew that by being a lawyer you could get some of the better things in life. My vision of success shaped up to include the great values and character of my parents and the legal mastery and greatness of Thurgood Marshall, along with the lifestyle of some of the white families of my school friends.

I wasn't intimidated by being one of the only black students in high school because I could compete. When the teachers called on me in class, I knew the answers. When we had tests, I scored well. So, I knew I was smart, and I knew what I wanted to do with my life. Both were advantages. I didn't look like the other kids or have what they may have had materially, but I felt very comfortable about myself and what I did have. It was interesting, because then you were accepted. If you do well, and you're comfortable in your own skin, people will always respect you.

When I got to college, other kids kept changing their majors but I never wavered from law, and I saw that as an advantage. I also continued to do well. It was funny, because that led to a lot of comments like, "You know, you're a *different* black person—you're an exception." I never accepted that, but I realized that achieving made you more acceptable to whites and teachers. And I knew that achieving was what was going to get me in the game. More than anything, that's what I wanted: to get off the sidelines and be in the game.

In school, there's always that kid who knew the answer, who was smart but reluctant to raise his hand. You've got to get in the game in order to demonstrate what you can do. There's no way around it. It's not enough to stand on the side and let somebody else answer the calls, then think to yourself, "Well, I knew it all along." They'll never know you know it, and they'll never know the real you until you put yourself out there—and, really, neither will you. If you want success, it's never enough to know what you're capable of, you have to show what you're capable of.

At UCLA I really learned the difference between competition and being cutthroat. The first day of class the instructor said: "Look to your right, look to your left. Two of you will not graduate." That's how we started. We were there to get an education, but that set the tone.

These people wanted to succeed and they were aggressive. Being competitive is one thing, I learned that on the athletic field. But, in a word, they were cutthroat. But while they were doing all this stuff on the side to beat each other out and beat each other up, I learned what you really have to do is just work hard! To win, you have to be competitive and you have to be tough, but you don't have to be cutthroat.

Even when I dealt with [prosecutor] Christopher Darden in the [O.J.] Simpson case—even in that competitive environment, when I found out that Darden was going to [cross examine] Fuhrman himself, I said, "Don't do that. Don't let them do that to you. Let one of the others do it." I didn't even know at that point that we were going to get Fuhrman as we did. But I already knew he was a horrible, racist guy. That's the same reason I didn't take Fuhrman. Then, when we had the evidence of his statements, saying, "I hate blacks. I can't wait to retire because I hate them—they're lazy, they're sloppy . . ." it was terrible stuff, and it made Darden look bad to be the one to build him up.

I was trying to win the case, but I wanted to spare Darden that embarrassment. He was suspicious of my motives, so he retreated from my advice. If I was cutthroat, I wouldn't have cared. So, I think the defining element between being competitive and being cutthroat has to do with caring. It has to do with having character

By the time I was in my last year at UCLA, I was working full time at the post office. *It was hard*, mentally and physically. But I just did what I had to do, and I'm grateful for the experience, because it got me into the habit of working hard. People ask me now, how I manage to do all these things at once: practice law, host a TV show, do a lot of speaking engagements and all the traveling back and forth it requires. I do now what I did back then: I just accept it as my life.

Acceptance, in general, is an important concept and one that I strongly believe in. I have always accepted people for who they are. I have never let differences between us interfere with that. When I was in high school, most of the kids were Jewish, and several of us became very close. I learned a lot about Jewish culture, went to seders and other ceremonies. They accepted me, I accepted them. We both came out ahead as a result.

Even as a lawyer, whether I was a prosecutor or a defense attorney, my job has never been to judge people. It has been to pursue justice and to make a difference that, in the end, serves justice. In doing that, there are wins and losses, and you have to accept them both.

Even hot young lawyers understand that there are overwhelming odds against them. You are going to lose sometimes and you have to keep on going. My motto has always been prepare, prepare, prepare. Do your job to the very best of your ability, then deal with the results—accept them—whatever they are. If you do that, you'll be okay. I've only had one case where I wasn't able to do that.

Elmer Geronimo Pratt, a former Black Panther, was my client. In 1972, he was convicted and sentenced to 25 years to life for the murder of a Santa Monica [California] school teacher. The conviction hinged on the perjured testimony of a lying, conniving snake who was an FBI informant. In the overall scheme of justice, true justice, you can deal with the losses. But this was *in*justice. This man was innocent and I couldn't give up this battle.

This was just wrong, and I had this guilt! Year after year went by; motion after motion was denied. I could've quit. But, in that case, I couldn't have quit and lived with myself. So I was relentlessly persistent. Even when I became the assistant D.A. for L.A. County, I never wavered. I took flack for it, but when Pratt came up for parole, I wrote a letter on my own stationery saying, "This man is innocent." I was a district attorney. My job was to represent the interests of the county and the state. But my feeling was, I don't care where I am or what job I'm in. You didn't buy my soul. To get into these positions and then to let the position, or your title, prevent you from being who you really are, is something I have never done. I'm very proud of that.

We finally prevailed in 1998, and Pratt was freed. It was the end of a long journey for me—27 years—and it taught me a tremendous lesson. You cannot quit or stop or back up or blink. You have to move forward. You have to press the limits. You have to trust your gut. You have to pursue the possibility of success through failure after failure, if necessary. You've just got to believe. And you've got to accept that being right will not make you popular; it can in fact make you very unpopular. I accept that. What I will not accept, on any level, is *in*justice.

I like people who will stand up even when it's not popular. You have to do that to change things. I have done that a lot in my career, and some things have changed for the better as a result. I took on a string of cases in California where black men in police custody were being killed by the routine use of the choke hold. In one case, I represented a young guy named James Thomas Mincey who the police practically choked to death in front of his mother (he died a few days later) while she pled with them not to kill her boy.

We set records against the LAPD but, more importantly, the choke hold was outlawed as a result of our work. We made a difference.

My practice has been long and I've done a variety of things that I'm proud of. So, it would be great if, at the end of the day, I am known more for the practice overall—for the cumulative work—not just this case or that one. But the media will always shrink it down to a soundbite that will probably have to do with Simpson.

That was an important case. It was hard, and I wanted to win. Nobody ever wants to lose, whether it's a case, or anything else.

In this case there were so many things that happened, there had to be some spiritual aspect to it. I know a lot of people still question the outcome. There are people who question my involvement in the case. To them I just say, "Look, I accept. I believe."

I would do that one hundred times more. I don't like myself if I stand on the sidelines and watch things go on that I know I could impact if I got involved. I got a chance to be involved, and I would say, overall, that I have no regrets.

Although I will probably always be remembered as being part of the "Dream Team," I believe that there are other things in store for me. There's always something new and vital happening or about to happen in the future, so, I would be greatly surprised if, in the near future, something doesn't come along that has the potential to eclipse what I've been involved with so far.

The reason I say that is that the day we resolved the civil case against Michael Jackson [who had been accused of molesting a child], it was January 21, 1994, and [my partner] Carl Douglas and I were in front of the courthouse. I had never in my life seen so much press activity. There must have been 250 cameras on the lawn, and I turned to him and said, "Can you believe this? It will never get any bigger than this."

When I was a young lawyer, I won a case involving the Settles family, whose son was found hung in jail. The police had called it suicide, but we proved that they had killed him by using the choke hold. That was what started my work in that area. I remember all the press attention that verdict got, and thinking the same thing back then. "This is it. This will be my big moment."

I have had some high profile cases, but I didn't set out to be remembered in that way. I wanted to change the balance of justice. People see me on television, and they see the way I dress and express myself to a jury or to the press, and they make certain assumptions about me. They think I go after the attention, when, again, the truth is, I'm basically shy. As I said, most of us are really a bundle of contradictions. I happen to love bold ties and bright colors, and I love the excitement of my work, but I also love the quiet moments at the end of the day when I can just reflect on all of it.

I don't care about being famous. I care about changing things enough so that other lawyers will come along and do their part, and eventually the scales will be level. I may not live to see it happen, but I have to believe it will happen. The minister of my church has a saying: "Service is the price you pay for the space you occupy." I believe that, and whether you like my style or not, my work is my service. We all have to find our own best way of giving back.

In trying to find my best way, I have incorporated a lot of my father and Thurgood Marshall into my style – even in the courtroom. I'll start off kind of in a low key manner. Then I'll start to build. In the building I want to be like Thurgood Marshall. I understand where I want to go, and I take the [jury] there, bit by bit. But by the end, I want them up on their feet. That's the way I practice law. And that's kind of the way I live.

CHAPTER FOUR

Ann M. Fudge

Executive Vice President, Kraft Foods, Inc.
President, Maxwell House and Post Divisions

❖

For more than a decade, Ann Fudge has reigned as one of the highest ranking women in corporate America. It is a plum and highly visible position, one that she occupies with a mixture of pride and ambivalence. "So much is made of it," she says. "It's great, but it's also complicated."

A native of Washington, D.C., Fudge graduated from Simmons College and Harvard University Graduate School of Business. After receiving her MBA, she cut her teeth at General Mills, Inc., where she rose from marketing assistant to director in seven years. In 1986, she joined General Foods Corporation (which later merged into Kraft Foods) as associate director of strategic planning. She was named to her current Maxwell House position in 1994 and assumed her responsibilities for Post Cereal three years later.

In addition to overseeing several lines of familiar products (including Sanka coffee, Grape Nuts, and Shredded Wheat), she is a member of Kraft's operating committee and sits on several major corporate boards including General Electric Company, which was her first employer out of college.

Now 49, her next career move is expected to be a significant one, sure to make headlines. But then, what else is new? Fudge is married with two children.

❖

There's a lot of talk these days about mentors and sponsors. It's funny, when I was in school (I graduated in 1977), those words weren't flying around. To me, a mentor is somebody who is going to be a guide, somebody who has been in the organization, who knows the ropes. He or she tells you where the potholes are, [who] the people to know are, where you can learn, and what you should avoid.

A sponsor is a promotor; somebody who sees you and says, "I really want to advance this person." They don't have to be mutually exclusive, because there are people who mentor you who also can serve as a sponsor. That has been true in my case. There are a lot of capable people in an organization, so how do you manage to stand out from a group of capable and talented people? It takes a combination of people recognizing you and helping you along. So, both of these roles are important.

But, for me, what's far more essential is internal focus and what I can learn to advance. And it is very important that an individual understand his or her core beliefs, because those basic values come through in everything you say and do and, in the end, those are the things that can propel you or hold you back.

Leadership principles are pretty basic—and they're timeless. In fact, hundreds of years ago the ancient Chinese philosopher Sun Tzu defined leadership as encompassing these simple, basic principles: intelligence, credibility, humanity, courage, and discipline. I believe that definition holds true today and it is critical that our leaders reflect the total spectrum of those personal qualities.

Let's start with intelligence. Too many times this is the sole focus of assessing an individual's leadership potential. Are they smart enough? What was their GPA? What were their SAT scores? What was their class ranking? Numerous studies show that intelligence, while indeed a very key component in the leadership equation, must be developed in conjunction with less quantifiable traits, like credibility and integrity.

My core beliefs are honesty, integrity, and dealing with people as I want to be dealt with. I use that as a basis for the things I stand for, and for deciding when to make a compromise. Sometimes people have different ways of reaching an end goal. As long as I get there, I am willing to compromise on the approach. But I don't compromise on credibility and integrity or on treating people fairly.

Time and again my personal experience has shown that credibility is perhaps *the* key component in the leadership mix. You've heard the phrase, "I trust him enough to be in a foxhole with him." That pretty much sums it up. People want to believe that in a tight situation, they can trust their leader. They can't operate at peak performance if there is a question of support and commitment, or if there is a question of trust, of credibility.

We have to stop looking at what other people are doing and how other people are leading their lives, and decide on what is right for each of us as individuals. When we look at others and try to pace ourselves against them, that is when we get confused.

So, be real. Be you, not what you think you should be to fit into someone else's definition of what you should be. Once you start moving away from being who you are at your core, your ability to remain truly authentic, to have real credibility, will slowly and very insidiously diminish. And one day you'll wonder what has happened to you—the real you.

I truly believe that most successful people—and let me clearly state that I don't define success as monetary success or celebrity, but rather as full realization of life's potential—most truly successful people are authentic, they are credible.

You know a person of true character or integrity when you meet him or her. A true leader is not [solely] focused on themselves and their achievements, but, rather, is focused on others and their personal and professional growth. More than ever before, these are the people who are needed and who will be valued. Because the traditional model of deference to leadership, no matter what, is simply not going to fly in the future.

Compounding the challenge of building and sustaining credibility is the growth of today's "free-agent workplace," as I like to think of it. Today's free agent must depend on their own *skills* for job security, rather than on their company.

The traditional corporate ladder has been replaced by a worldwide web of options to advance—lateral moves, cross-functional moves, short-term international assignments. Today's employees are more actively involved in their career planning, and all the better, because I find people coming up with very interesting career options that lead to creative business ideas.

General George Patton said, "Never tell people how to do things.

Tell them what to do and they will surprise you with their ingenuity." And I am always amazed at what people can do when given the environment and the freedom to achieve business goals expressing their ingenuity.

This is where humanity, Sun Tzu's third fundamental principle of leadership, comes into play. As the first wave of women and African Americans began to enter corporations, the only success model they had was the traditional white male model of leadership. Many women and people of color in the first wave emulated those models. And in many instances, they were reluctant to show their humanity, because they felt it was important to model their behavior on what they had observed.

There are more women in the workplace, more people of color, than ever; I can visually see the difference. We still have a lot of progress to make in the senior ranks, but I definitely see it in the entry and mid-managerial levels. One of the many benefits diversity has brought to the workplace is the recognition that there is no one success model. We've brought with us different sets of experiences, culture and gender differences, even differences in leadership styles. After twenty-plus years in the corporate world, I am seeing evidence of change—change that enables both women and men to feel more comfortable revealing their humanity (and there's still room for more change).

I know there are studies asserting the claim that women and men manage differently—that women wait to master skills and then seek to lead others, while men seek to lead and then focus on mastery. I have seen many articles that have this qualitative perspective, but I have never seen any quantitative data.

From my personal experience, I have seen both men and women take different approaches depending on who they are as individuals. Managers are people first, and a manager's behavior is just reflective of who that person is. And that has more to do with their core values than with gender.

I am sometimes asked about my professional persona—do I feel as if I have to behave a certain way, to always be "on." I don't think I have a professional persona. I don't turn the switch on to be a certain way when I am at work versus when I am at home. There is not a big difference between Ann Fudge the person and Ann Fudge the businesswoman. That is why I enjoy being in business, because I am who I am.

I believe it is much easier for an organization to relate to you and to want to follow you when you show your humanity. It can go a long way towards inspiring trust because people will see you, not as someone on a pedestal issuing orders, but as a steward, a coach who wants to win and wants to elicit the best from all the team members.

It takes courage to show your humanity. I believe that courage is the quiet strength that truly helps separate the real leaders from the wanna-bes. They don't easily fold when encountering obstacles; yet they don't ignore their humanity. Real leaders are strong and courageous enough to be themselves, to express their full range of emotions and to be authentic.

I often think about these elements—particularly humanity and courage—because many times these qualities are overlooked in the drive for smart people who deliver superior performance and results. Now, don't get me wrong, I'm not in any way discounting the importance of intelligence and results, because we need smart leaders who deliver. But we also need smart leaders who care, who have heart, who value principles as much as they do performance, and who have the courage to champion changes and different points of view.

Women and people of color can bring a lot to the party from a decision-making standpoint. Despite that, advancing is not always easy, not in business or in any career. Each profession has its own challenges, and people will excel when they go into a field that they love—one where they feel that they have some unique skills to bring. Would I make the best lawyer or doctor? Probably not. But am I a damned good businesswoman? Absolutely.

The image of success and its realities are sometimes very different. People frequently ask me how it feels to be a pioneer. In reality, as I think about it, I probably am one. But I don't think about that as I go about doing what I need to do. I had a working mom, so it was never a question of whether I could do it. I never went through a trauma of "Can I have a career and have a family?" I just stay focused on the work to be done.

Nobody's life is perfect. And that's not what it's about. It's about making sure that you try to integrate things that are important to you and recognize that things shift back and forth. There are going to be times when you focus more on your family, and there are going to be times at work that are so intense, there is nothing else as important in your life. You have to understand when it is time to shift and you have to have what I call a "personal monitor."

You almost have to think of yourself as an Olympian. Olympians talk about achieving their personal best, and that's what we need to think about: What is your personal best, not, "Am I going to get promoted in this amount of time?" or "When am I going to get married?" or "When am I going to have children?" I counsel a lot of people to stop thinking about it so much. Instead, stay focused on giving life—in all of its facets—your personal best.

Postscript

In spring 2001, after 15 years with the company, Fudge resigned. At this printing, she has not yet taken her next professional step.

CHAPTER FIVE

Marcia Ann Gillespie

President, Liberty Media
Editor in Chief, *Ms.* Magazine

❖

In 1999, Marcia Ann Gillespie, the editor in chief who first gave *Essence* magazine its vibrant voice in the 1970s, made history again by piloting the relaunch of *Ms.* But the reemergence of the feminist magazine following a brief shutdown represented more than an editorial coup. It was a personal and business triumph as well.

Gillespie had teamed up with *Ms.* cofounder Gloria Steinem and a dozen other women to buy the 29-year-old magazine from businessman Jay MacDonald for more than $3 million. The gutsy move not only restored *Ms.*' ownership to women, it also made Gillespie the first black woman to have an ownership stake in a national magazine not specifically targeted to African Americans.

Brilliant, passionate, and outspoken, Gillespie's conversation is peppered with bursts of deep laughter, earthy asides, and the occasional bit of profanity. At 55, the native New Yorker, who is single, says she's proud of how she's mellowed with time. These days, she says, "I'm much more prone to keep my opinions to myself until my opinion is of some service and use."

The challenges *Ms.* faces on both the editorial and business fronts are significant, but if anyone is up to them, it's Gillespie.

❖

There's something to be said for ignorance because sometimes it frees you to do more than you would have if you knew more.

In 1970, I was interviewed to be the managing editor of *Essence* magazine. I got hired and seven or eight months later the editor in chief left. With all the arrogance you can have at 26, I just *knew* that I knew what to do with the magazine, and I got the job.

Sometimes things happen, and you feel like it was the hand of someone else acting for you. Was it you, your skill or talents, or was it something else altogether? Some destiny? I don't know. But I had this real vision of what I thought *Essence* needed. I wanted it to be a certain way and I convinced myself, and everybody else, that I knew what I was doing. And, thank God, it worked! But it was terrifying.

I mean, I didn't know how to be a boss. I'd never been a boss of anything before. My first job out of college had been at Time Inc. And, like all women that got hired at Time Inc. then, I got hired as a researcher. *Essence* was only my second job! I mean, one minute you're putting some captions on work as a researcher, and the next minute you're running a staff, trying to get the budgets right and all that stuff, working with people, being a manager! You can have all the bluff in the world, but in the end, you really have to do it.

I remember calling the woman who had been chief of research at Time Life Books the first time I had to fire somebody. I was a wreck. I went to church, I prayed on it. I asked her, "How do you do this?" She sat me down and said, "It should never be easy. You really need to know why you are doing this. You need to examine it, write it all down very logically." She was right, but when I actually had to do it, it was the worst moment of my life. I was almost in tears by the time I actually got the words out, but I had no choice but to do it. And I'm still learning about business—by doing it.

Running *Essence* was an extraordinary experience. Susan Taylor [the current publication director] started about six months after I did. We were all so young, in our 20s, trying to figure out who we were as women. And the thing that's so extraordinary was we could figure it out in the pages of the magazine.

Because I didn't have any experience per se, it meant also that I didn't know when I was breaking the rules. And that gives you a lot of freedom. It wasn't as if I could say, "What did we do five years ago?" It was, "Well, let's try this and see if it works."

When I made mistakes, I agonized, and sometimes didn't want to admit them. I remember a letter that I got from a reader. I had written this editorial and I was into this thing about black women and our travails and how we had suffered and *nobody* had ever suffered like we suffered. And this letter came back from a woman who was Native American.

She talked about how much she loved the magazine and how hurt she was when she read that. She kicked my butt—righteously. And I was so embarrassed, because I realized I was becoming the thing that I always wanted not to be—just myopic, like I had blinders on. I felt humiliated. But thank God there are people who will step up and tell you about your stuff. Good advice sometimes comes from the most surprising sources. There are a lot of people who have kind of appeared in my life at different moments with information and insights that I've really needed at the time. A lot of them I can't even call by name.

We often think of this mentor business as somebody who has achieved more on the work scale. For me, it's often been people like my grandmother or my Aunt Fannie, who never ran a business, but who just have wisdom on the life scale. And that can be far more valuable. I think of mentors as people who will tell you things you don't want to hear about yourself.

It's really clear to me that because I had taken that job so young, it was distancing me from a certain kind of a reality. You're suddenly queen in your own little world and you have to really work at not believing that your shit don't stink! Staying humble isn't easy and, believe me, I was not always humble! Sometimes I look back and I think it might have been much more interesting if I'd gotten that job when I was 35. It might have been a total disaster too, because maybe that's part of what made it possible. I was young; I didn't know any better. It's funny; all my life, that not knowing any better has led me to do a lot of things—worthwhile things—that I wouldn't necessarily have done had I known. I've learned a lot from that.

In my job at Time Inc., I did stuff called marginalia, the words in the margins by the pictures. Once, I was assigned an interesting photo of the U.S. Army surrounding Indians and children at Wounded Knee and shooting them, and I wrote it as "the massacre at Wounded Knee." It went through the process and a few days after I sent it, the editor came to me screaming, "I want you to change this." I said, "What are you talking about?"

"It's not a massacre, it's the *battle* at Wounded Knee."

And I said, "If we call Custer's last stand a massacre, and the other side had guns, you cannot say that killing unarmed women and children is a battle."

He kept yelling at me: "Change it, change it!"

And I said "Well, you're the editor. If you want it changed, change it your damned self."

I didn't know the rules. The fact was that the researchers were required to make the changes. Because researchers were also the people who got the blame if anything went wrong. I wouldn't change it, he was furious, and I got known as a troublemaker.

Would I have been so bold if I'd known the rules? Probably. I was always encouraged, even as a child, to stand up to people, to voice my own opinion. (I was kicked out of Sunday School for it when I was about eight—I asked the teacher, If God separated Adam and Eve, how did we all get here?—and when I refused to go back, my parents supported me.) So, I always felt empowered. But who knows? I just thought I was dealing with logic. And I also thought I was right. What was the worst they could do, fire me? Hey, if you're only going to be here for a minute, make that minute count.

That was a big lesson for me. It taught me a lot about power, the power of the media, and the power of the people who control it. I mean, who gets to say what a fact is? Who has the power to say something is this or something is that? In this case, the lowly researcher—me, without even knowing it—I had the power.

A few months later I decided I was going to leave Time Inc. I didn't know where *far* was, but it was really clear that I was not going to get there at Time, given the fact that women didn't. Ideally, I knew I wanted to be an editor. In walked *Essence* magazine.

Essence was very successful, and I could have had that job forever and ever, Amen, but I didn't think I was going to grow. And I had this horrible vision of being, you know, like [*Cosmopolitan* magazine founder] Helen Gurley Brown—70 years old, doddering down the hall, talking about "my girls at *Essence*"—and it scared the shit out of me. I also knew that it would be much more difficult if I waited. You know, the golden cord: The better the perks, the better the money, the harder to leave.

So, I kind of thought, let me just step out there and see what happens. And I think I had so much arrogance still, that I thought, if anybody's ever going to open other doors, it's going to be me. I know a lot of people, even to this day, would say that was a crazy thing to do. But, I think, especially for black people, it's as important how we leave a thing as how we come to it. Maybe because we've had so few opportunities for so long, it often seems to me that we're not good at stepping away. We tend to stay forever. We stay at the party too long.

I closed the tenth anniversary issue of the magazine and I left with no job and no real plan. I wanted to experience living in a predominantly black country so I packed my bags and off I went to Jamaica.

I remember filling out the immigration form once we landed, and it said "occupation." I broke down in tears. What was I? What did I do? Wow. . . . It hit me how much my identity had been caught up in that job. Now I had to figure out just who I was. I was 36.

I'd had a lot of success in my life. And I think that I just thought, well, once I figure out what I want to do next, it will continue. So I took a couple of years off and freelanced a bit, until I realized, look, you were not born with a silver spoon in your mouth. You need to make some green money; the purple and pink money down here is very nice, but either you're going to really get serious about a life in Jamaica, or you're going to go back to the States.

I didn't know what I wanted to do. I was lost. I had written for *Ms.*, and had decided to become a contributing editor to *Ms.* I didn't want to be like a ghost hanging over the editor of *Essence*, so I had really distanced myself from it. And then the Lena Horne opportunity came along. I was asked to write her second autobiography. Everybody said, "This is it!" They thought this was fabulous, and so did I.

So, I go on the road with Lena, and we're traveling and something's not quite clicking, but I can't figure it out. Sometimes we meet, sometimes we don't, and what was supposed to be this fast book was taking longer and longer. I'm getting all these signals; the publisher and the editor are on my case, and I'm having to call my lawyer to get my agent to fight with them. It was the most bizarre year of my life.

After about nine months, Lena just stopped talking to me and it forced me to examine myself: What had I done wrong? I finally figured out, it wasn't about me. She didn't want to do the book. She finally told me that, but meanwhile, I still had to write something so I could collect. And I was a basket case because it had so knocked my confidence.

I was about 39 or 40, and this was the first time I faced real failure. On many levels, I wish it had happened a whole lot sooner, because it really knocked the wind out of my sails.

By the time I finished the book, I no longer felt I could write. It took me several years to build my confidence again. This was happening at the same time my father was dying, so, God, it just really, really brought me to my knees!

But I *needed* to get knocked out like that. I needed to remember that not everything just falls into your hands. I certainly wouldn't recommend that everybody should have such a *public* failure. But it really forced me to do another level of taking stock. It made me think about what was really important—that I do good work, or that I get a lot of recognition? That I maintain some minor celebrity status, or that I go out there and just be a worker and, if so, like everybody else, *what did I want to do?*

Whenever I face these sort of "big" decisions, I talk to the people I can trust. I have an incredible circle of sister/friends and brother/friends who I know tell me the truth. I talk things over with my mom, who I think of as being so smart. I talk to my big sister. I talk to God. And I'm not sure what I'm listening for, to tell you the truth. It's just that some things resonate and others don't.

I decided I wanted to do magazines again. People kept telling me I was good at them, and I missed them. I'd been approached about being editor in chief of other things, but this is a very racist industry. I most certainly wasn't going to become the editor of another black woman's magazine and try to smother the baby that I grew. And it hit me, therefore, that if I was coming back into this industry, I might just have to take a mid-level job. And was I prepared to do that? Thanks to my humbling—the answer was, "Yeah." If you like the work, just do the work. Stop worrying about what it looks like.

So, I started doing consulting for *Ms.* Then it was sold, and the Australians who bought it asked me to come on as the number-two person, the executive editor. I said, sure. And I remember a friend saying to me, "You've been the editor in chief of a magazine. Why would you do this?" I said, "Because I like the work, and I like this magazine—so, why not?"

I do believe that the worst thing you can do in life is close doors. I consciously meditated on just opening myself to the possibilities. If you're already saying, "No, I can't do that" or "wouldn't do that" or "shouldn't do that," well, you're going to miss a lot. And you never know what's around the bend. Intellectually, I thought I'd always understood that. But emotionally, where your spirit lives, it took me a while to get there.

Yes, there was still this idea at the back of my mind that someplace, sometime, I'm going to be the editor in chief of a magazine again, because I'm good at this. And I did apply for a couple of jobs, and came close to a couple. But I had really reconciled myself to the fact that it might never happen. So, are you going to live in what-ifs or are you going to move forward and enjoy the moment? I came to enjoy the moment.

I was bowled over when I got asked to come and be the editor in chief of this magazine. I was completely surprised. I had left the magazine in 1990 to take a consultancy at *The New York Times*. Then Robin Morgan, my friend who was the editor in chief of *Ms.*, called me to have lunch. I thought she wanted to talk about something she wanted me to write. When she told me that she wanted to step down and she wanted me to be editor in chief — I nearly choked on my sandwich. And it wasn't one of those things I said yes to immediately. I said I had to think about it. And as I thought about it, the question that kept surfacing was, could I be of service?

This readership was not as known to me as *Essence*'s. I didn't have the gut feel for it. It's primarily a white readership. You know, to what could I relate? What did I think I could bring to it that would move it forward?

I thought about that for awhile, and finally decided I wanted to bring a sense of real diversity, and I wanted that to be not just about race, but diversity in terms of point of view. I wanted to bring more balance to it. So I thought, yes, I can be of service. But I had no idea what a roller coaster I was about to get on. None. That was probably best, because — again — if I knew, I wouldn't have done it. This has been a real rough ride.

I had no clue about how horrible the situation was for the magazine. It was like this little goose that lays golden eggs, but we, the staff, were always being disparaged. And the money we were making was never being put back into us. I was used to seeing a magazine whose circulation continued to go up; now I was seeing a magazine whose circulation was going down under my stewardship. I was prepared for a certain loss, because whenever you change editors there's going to be a dip, but I wasn't prepared for the fact that there was going to be absolutely no support.

After I closed the first issue of the magazine that I was the editor in chief of, I noticed the price when it was printed was $1 more than it had been the issue before. Nobody had told me. It went up a whole dollar! I'm like, "Excuse me! Is it that you really decided you want me to fail?" So there were lots of big challenges. And certainly, the idea that we would end up having to raise the money to *buy* the magazine and that I'd end up having to wear two hats—editor in chief *and* president of the company—was never part of the plan.

I remember when the owners came to me and said, "We're going to close the magazine, or you may want to buy it now." I was just about to go off on vacation (I had been one of the privileged group who was invited on that wonderful birthday cruise that Oprah Winfrey gave for Maya Angelou). So there I am, going on this cruise knowing that my magazine may be closed when I get back.

The ship left the Saturday before Easter; they were having a sunrise service Easter morning. And BeBe Winans sang this song that basically said, be grateful, be open, and let the spirit be. I sat there listening, and it was as if somebody just took [this burden] up. And I said to myself, "Okay, all I can do is my very best."

I remember coming back from that cruise, sitting down with Gloria [Steinem] and the two of us looking at each other and saying, "Are we up for this?" Gloria—God bless her—looked at me and said, "If you decide you want to go for this, I'm with you." So I said, "Yeah, let's do it."

There was no way I was going to see this magazine close. Is that personal ego? Yeah. But it was even more so the importance of what this magazine represents.

There are these points in my life where everything seems to happen at once. There we were, doing the magazine and my mother became ill, which immediately put everything into total perspective for me. Trying to save a magazine and trying to save my mother's life? I loved this magazine and, for me, it was a mission, but at the end of the day, *it was a job.* So, you just do what you can and then put it out there and let divine order take over. I put a business plan together and gave it to Gloria and said, "I got to go take care of my mother." Gloria stepped up to the plate and started raising money.

When we closed this deal, Gloria and I looked at each other, and we just laughed. That it would happen and that it would be *women* who would step up with the money was amazing. We had approached women and men. You know, money is green. That it would turn out this way was obviously a sign. Now it was time to rock and roll.

But I hadn't a clue what it meant to have to set up a business. Excuse me! I think if I had known, I might have said, "Well, maybe not." Again, I just think that there's something very important to be said for ignorance. Because I mean, it was more than a notion. And, thank God, my sister taught me a long time ago, it's really okay to say you don't know.

So many people are out there pretending to know stuff that they don't really know. It always intrigues me when I say, "Well, what does that mean?" And suddenly it gets quiet. So I don't pretend to know stuff. Thank God, there are actually people who do know, who will sit down with you and help you. If I need it, I don't hesitate to ask for help.

This business, Liberty Media, is in process, and while I do enjoy the business of this business, I really want us to find maybe a CEO or COO, to take some of the day-to-day stuff off my back. I'm often racing between two things, and I've come to a conclusion: I don't have to try to be everything. Let me do one thing *really* well, rather than two things, kinda.

So the question that I had to ask and answer was, Do you want to be the full time president or do you want to be the full time editor in chief? I want to be the editor in chief partly because this magazine is not nearly where I want it to be, and to get it there, I have to give it my full attention, and partly because I am challenged and excited by the editorial process. That is a real part of who I am.

There are a lot of people for whom the title is more important than the money. Well, honey, fine! You want to be "Queen of the World?" You can have it, because I know who I am. And that has nothing to do with the titles and the "stuff."

Let me be real, I'm still going to be a board member and a stockholder in this company. I also have a kind of historical memory that's very important. And I also have pure, good common sense about business. So, I'll always be involved in this business, but I don't feel I have to make that part of this train run, no. Let me get this [editorial] train, really, on the track.

You know, there's some young black woman out there who's as smart as can be and she's a great editor already, but she can't be just sitting there waiting for Susan Taylor to leave. She should have the opportunity to see herself heading up *any* magazine—not just *Essence*. But the only way that happens is if somebody starts to break down the barriers. My generation feels a sense of obligation to open a door that somebody else can also walk through; I have some of that driving me to do this, too.

I've grown up a lot since my *Essence* days. I'm a whole lot humbler now than I ever was then. And calmer. I used to have a *horrible* temper! I realize now how blessed I've been in my life. I accept the fact that, you know, I'm only here but a minute. When you're 22 you don't think about that.

What would I say to that young woman—or to anyone—who wants to know what I've learned along the way? I would say: Don't forget who you are. What I mean by that is, you know, we've been so busy rushing to become Americans in the last 40 years, we've picked up a lot of the worst traits and not the best ones. I'm sort of tired of everything being about white folks. It really is that we as black folks haven't decided what kind of black folks we want to be.

Some of us don't want to understand that the burden of history is real. We're black people. Our experience getting here was different, and it should be something that we take with pride and understand the truth that people gave their lives for it. And that's about community, and that's about service and that's about the fact that you gotta pass the same people going one way as you do going the other way in life.

I would say that, all the spirits of all our ancestors are with us at every moment—and they're watching us. And with us at every moment are all the spirits and hopes of all those who are yet to come—and they're watching us. So mind yourself. Mind yourself.

I grew up hearing people telling stories about hard times and hope. We don't tell enough stories these days about hope and hard times and the circles that bind us. We're getting very full of hubris these days. We have a lot of false pride. And we really need to take stock.

We have felt too often that success was being able to sometimes just look down our noses at others. I see how we get seduced that way. Well, I would say that if you think that your success is going to be about how many bucks you got in the bank, you're in trouble. It may be that the most successful person at the end of the day is the one with the smallest bank account but one who has made real dividends in growing people, in sharing some light, and making things happen for others. Yeah, part of true success is understanding that there's something bigger and more important than yourself. So, again, mind yourself.

CHAPTER SIX

Sylvester Green

Executive Vice President, Chubb & Sons

At the Green home, a farming home where money was always tight, the insurance salesman was not the most welcome visitor, although he was a frequent one. So a career in insurance was the farthest thing from Sylvester (better known as Sy) Green's mind. A track star in college, Green planned to become a teacher and coach. But when the opportunity to become the first black professional hire at one of the nation's largest insurance firms presented itself, even Green couldn't pass it up.

For 35 years, he rose through Chubb's hierarchy, leveling barriers and defying expectations with each new step. As executive vice president and managing director, Green has oversight of 56 branch offices representing approximately $4.6 billion in property and casualty insurance.

Success, he says, has clearly had its rewards—material and otherwise—but he still bemoans a gross lack of African American peers in his business. "My being here has made a difference," he says. "Black people here have told me that. But there are still just far too few of us in these positions. My career, my enjoyment of it, has surpassed my expectations. But the pace of corporate progress as regards diversity has not lived up to my expectations." Now 60, Green is married with three children.

During my senior year in college, Chubb came to recruit there for the first time. They sent a Pittsburgh branch manager. He and an alumnus of the college, who owned an insurance agency in town, met for lunch in our cafeteria, where, it just so happened, I was going through the line to get my lunch. The agency owner (who was white) was a very good friend of track and basketball players, and I was on both teams, so he knew me quite well.

On this particular day, I was on a break from my student teaching assignment, so I was dressed up, as required. My friend looked up and saw me, and said to the Chubb rep, "You see that guy going through the line? If you really want to recruit someone good, you should recruit him."

The Chubb guy looked up and said, "Uh, no . . . ," and it was pretty clear that he wasn't there to recruit African Americans.

So my friend said, "Well, if you want someone who's really good, he's good," and that was the end of it.

The Chubb guy went back to his branch office and found out that Mr. Chubb actually wanted to recruit some African Americans, so, before you knew, this guy was back on the phone to our college placement director trying to track me down. I had gone home for Easter break, so I got a phone call from the placement director saying, "Chubb would like to fly you out to New York and chat with you."

I didn't even have to think about it. I said, "I have no interest whatsoever in insurance." Growing up the way I did, my frame of reference for insurance was very negative. We lived on a farm in South Carolina for the first 10 years of my life, and I remember the door-to-door salesman coming to our house practically every week because we didn't have the money to pay less frequently than that. There was nothing positive about the image, so having a career in insurance was the farthest thing from my mind. I was going to be a teacher and coach.

The placement director said, "Now, cool down. This company is great. They are different. You have nothing to lose."

A day or so later, Chubb flew me to New York. I had flown only once before, to a track meet on the West Coast, but I had never been to New York. This was a big deal.

It was 1964 and, because of the Civil Rights Act, things had started to change. But a black person still didn't have a good frame of reference as to where he or she would fit in the business world. I did not personally know any black people who were in major businesses. For a long time, I'd get *Ebony* magazine, and the first section I'd go to was "Speaking of People." That was my only real window into the lives and achievements of successful African Americans in business.

There was a certain amount of intimidation about being in New York and interviewing with this company. I had done a little bit of research, and the company was very prestigious. Chubb was known as an "HYP Club": Harvard, Yale, Princeton. It had been an old family partnership that had just gone public. It was very conservative, very white, very Anglo Saxon. I was so impressed by the people. They were distinguished. Of course, they were also better educated than I was and had backgrounds more naturally suited to this business than mine.

My mom went through, maybe, the seventh grade; my dad had a third grade education at best. I was the fourth child out of five, we all had to work from about the age of five, and I was the only one to graduate from college. Mount Union was a small, Methodist college, but my going there had been a big, big deal to my parents. I had one business course in college: economics. That was the extent of it. My background and experience was as different from those at Chubb as my race was. That much was clear from the start.

The interview was an all-day proposition. I met with a good cross-section of senior managers, middle managers, down to trainee level. They got to know me, I got to know them. Because I was the first black person ever interviewed for a trainee position, I got to see some very top-level people, like the president. I didn't know how unique this was at the time, but I wasn't surprised when I found out.

I had a notion that there were not a lot of us anyplace in corporate America, particularly in financial services. So I was not surprised by the potential load that I would have to carry and, in the most important ways, I was prepared for it.

Throughout high school and college, I worked as a caddy at the local country club, so I got exposure to business people there. What that exposure did was really prepare me for survival in the business world. All the movers and shakers in our area were members. They were all white, of course, but they were quite supportive. Relationships I established there helped me to get jobs later on that I otherwise would not have gotten. I was able to get some college loans from the local banker, who had never granted that type of a loan to someone black. So it was a good experience—within very clear parameters.

One experience at the country club that stands out: Blacks obviously weren't members and weren't allowed to play at the club, but the caddies could play on Fridays and Mondays if there was room. One day, it had rained all morning, so there were very few members there. I had a pretty good relationship with some of the members' kids, and this one kid said he was going to go out and play. He took some of the white employees, and then he asked me if I wanted to play. I knew the head pro would be very upset by this, but I agreed anyway.

As it turned out, the pro was out on the course that day, and he saw me out there but didn't say anything. Later, he came up to me and said, "You know you can't do that, Sy. You should have at least come and asked me for permission." Yeah, I knew that. But I just had to test the system.

That was pretty typical of my experiences back then. On the one hand, whites could be supportive, even friendly, as long as you stayed in your place, and there were always little reminders of what that place was. My response in that situation was pretty typical for me as well: Controlled anger; assessing the situation; quietly doing it my way. That's always been my approach in life.

My childhood—starting out in the segregated south, moving north, to Ohio, when I was 10—really taught me how to live in three worlds. There was the black world: my own neighborhood, church, family, and friends. There was the white world: the whites-only golf club where I worked. And there was the integrated world of school, which was only about five percent black. That combination of experiences really helped me to prepare for dealing with issues in the business environment.

I learned how to assess a situation and then make the most of it. I learned that through a certain type of behavior, with a certain amount of knowledge, there are a lot of things you can overcome and there's a lot that you can accomplish that you may have never even thought of. I learned how to prove to people that I was a lot more capable than they might give me credit for.

There was also ample scar tissue there so that I was not really intimidated by the Chubb opportunity when it came. I can recall vividly, in my junior or senior year in high school, even though I had done well academically, I was told by someone who had come in to do some testing and chat with each student: "You don't expect to go to college, do you?"

Those kinds of things were always thrown in front of you. But those things, because of my very nature, created more drive. They generated a tremendous amount of directedness about what I wanted to do, what I wanted to prove.

I never questioned the fact that, if I chose to do something, I could do it well, so I never questioned my ability to deal with working in this type of environment. I knew it would be a challenge, but I knew that I would handle it. To me, it's all about dealing with situations, sizing them up, and figuring out what the obstacles as well as the opportunities are. It's about figuring out what you need to do to win.

One of the books I read back in those days was, *The Spook Who Sat by the Door.* That book helped me to deal with the issues. It was difficult. Many of the African Americans who are successful in business today weren't around yet, so I couldn't pick up the phone as I can now, and call a black friend going through a similar situation to commiserate, or to get advice. I used to walk around downtown Manhattan at lunchtime and there were very few of us dressed up, going to a [white collar] job. It was very lonely, and you were always misunderstood. People—white and black—didn't realize what it took to achieve what you were trying to achieve back then.

But whatever disadvantages I faced, I had some real advantages in being the first. I'm sure I got support from places in the organization that I never even knew about, because they wanted this to work as well as I did. I had a great relationship with the president who later became the chairman. He was really a mentor for me in the company. But, remember, he initiated this hire, so he had a lot vested in its being successful.

In many ways, it was easier in the 1960s than it was in subsequent years because there were so few of us—too few for us to be a threat. The backlash came later in the 1970s and 1980s, when affirmative action brought in bigger numbers of us and the political climate changed.

Each year subsequent to my coming in, we brought in a number of African Americans. None is here who came in those years. A lot of people, black, and white female, ask me, "How did you deal with all of that?" The "how" was, again, having learned early on to live in different worlds. You also pick up certain skills, the most important of which was learning what people couldn't take away from you.

I really believed that if I brought something to the party—if I could build a connection of customers, bring in revenue, improve the bottom line—I would succeed. If I have a good relationship with you as a customer, no one can take that away from me. If I have the knowledge about business between my ears, no one can take that away from me. So I figured out where the securities lay, and how to build them.

Our agents and brokers are compensated as a percentage of the business generated, so getting business was what mattered. I learned early to use the 80-20 rule: If I could clearly help people generate business, 80 percent of them would want me to help them make that buck, even those who maybe did not want to deal with me because of my color.

But other forces were less within my control. Early on, my color was definitely a factor in terms of where in the country the company was comfortable sending me. I started in New York, which was where trainees started, but, from there, the trainees would get relocated to other places. We were a fast-growing company. We moved people. In fact, if you didn't move every three or four years, you felt something was wrong.

Chubb was very committed to hiring and training me, but I don't think they had thought through what they would do with me if I were successful. Once it was clear that I was doing well, I think people were really surprised. I had moved up. I was running an underwriting region out of the home office and I remember a guy who was a senior officer at the time saying to me, "We don't know what we're going to do with you."

Around my tenth anniversary, I was running the Westchester [New York] branch, and my performance reviews and other feedback indicated that I was one of the best branch managers in the system. A few years later, a job came up in Pittsburgh. The feedback I got was that I would get that job, which meant a nice promotion. But the job was never actually offered to me. I later learned I didn't get the position because a [golf] club membership went with it and, because of my race, they couldn't get me into the club. The clubs were, of course, a prime feeding ground for business, so the offer never went through.

Instead, they made my job in Westchester bigger. I had a larger territory, but I ended up feeling that I stayed in that job too long. I learned later that it's all about positioning, making sure you're in the right job for the next job when the offer comes. Often that might mean taking a so-called demotion, or a lateral move.

For me, not moving into that job at that time was a real lost opportunity. By not being in some of the more senior-level meetings and one-on-one conferences with people at that next level, I missed out on some learning, some exposure, some critical experiences at a much earlier point in my career.

You can be in a comfortable job someplace and think you have a great learning curve, but if you're not learning how to deal with key strategic issues and political situations, you need to reposition yourself.

Being political is something you have to approach carefully. You can't be too political, because people perceive that as a negative. I've seen lots of very bright people spend a lot of time focused on the company politics rather than the company itself. As a result, they never figure out what the business is really about. That's a big mistake.

At the same time, you have to be savvy enough to understand the politics in your environment and to be able to deal with them in a constructive way. For me, it's easy because I'm fairly straightforward, direct, and honest. I have great credibility, and that minimizes the need to be actively political, but, at the same time, I fully understand the politics, and that is critical.

You've got to be very strategic. A lot of people don't know what that means. It's having two or three things that you really want to get accomplished better than anyone else. There's something quite powerful to the notion that you can always do things better. I've always focused on that. You can always raise the bar. Even if you're doing something better than anybody around you, you cannot be satisfied.

I subscribe to the theory of three. If I have ten things I have to get done, if I can pick out the three most important ones and do those exceptionally well, the other seven will fall in line behind them.

People can be tougher at times to deal with than issues. I know it sounds corny, but you get more with sugar than vinegar. That works whether I report to you or you report to me. I respect people. I always try to be fair. I try not to attack people; I attack issues. I would never intentionally hurt someone. I just don't believe in it. I get angry at people, because of disappointments, but, to me, it's fun working together, getting a concensus, leading people.

I go back to the 80-20 rule. I believe that, if you work for me, no matter what your beliefs or background are, if I treat you a certain way—train you, develop you, reward you, do right by you—you'll respond, at worst, in a neutral way, but by and large, you will respond in a positive way. People are basically good, but you have to deal with those who are not. You have to deal with nonperformance, you have to deal with people who get in your way, but you have to put your faith in the fact that, if you help people become winners, they will help you to win.

I say to my managers all the time, "When you're putting a team together, how many people are raising their hands saying, 'I want to work with you.'" That's the real test, because people know who the good managers are, they know who the poor managers are, and they know who's in between. I've never had trouble getting people to work for me. In fact, I've had them call me up, when they're off on another assignment, asking if there's anything they can do with me.

I grew up spending a lot of time in church, so I have a very strong Christian background, and I've always treated people the way I wanted to be treated. I'll say it again: It will work 80 percent of the time, no matter who you're dealing with, and no matter what your personal style may be.

I've never been the loud, gregarious type. I've always gone about things in a relatively quiet way. The things that I believe in, I have a real passion for, and you'd better believe I don't sit there quietly thinking about them. But if it's not important to me, I might not say anything. Just to talk for the sake of bringing attention to myself isn't me.

In the context of a long race, my style works well, partly because people will let their guard down. They'll even take you for granted. In my early days, as a regional underwriting person, I heard one of my brokers on the phone with a major client of ours. He said, "Now, let me tell you about Sy. Initially, you're going to think that you can just run right over him. But that will be your biggest mistake because he will listen carefully, take a lot of mental notes, and then come back at you, and you will surely lose the negotiation."

In the context of a short race, though, [my style] is a bit risky, particularly when you think about the fact that the first impression is so critical. I've learned that, in business, if you only have a few seconds to make an impression, you have to do that. In a large meeting, where everybody is grabbing to get their floor time, I am a lot more aggressive. We have a lot of meetings around here between very senior officers and senior-level customers, and you've got to be prepared to step up to the plate.

I can't sit here and tell you, "This is what it takes to be successful today: Add this, subtract that, and the result is what's required." Success is a moving target. Technology is constantly changing, the skill sets required are constantly changing, information is constantly moving, the balances are constantly shifting.

What you must do to succeed is be turned on by that reality. I think it's great. All that makes it enormously challenging, but it's also what makes it fun.

Second, you've got to want it. That sounds trite, but I've learned that not everybody does. One of my biggest disappointments involves a friend of mine who was doing very well here at Chubb and then just blew it.

We ran track together in college, but he was younger than I was and so he came to Chubb a few years after me. He was personable, people liked him, and he moved up pretty quickly. He ended up working for me in Westchester, and we spent a lot of time together. He became like a younger brother to me, and I was so proud of him when he was promoted to another branch.

He started out well, then he just lost it. He started to flounder. His manager offered support, but it wasn't helping. I kept after him, trying to find out what the problem was. He could never really give me an answer. Finally, I went up to his branch one day, and said, "You've already proven that you're capable. You're smart. You know what needs to be done, but you're not doing it. I think you are just afraid of the responsibility that goes with a bigger job."

He didn't really fess up to it, but he admitted that that had crossed his mind. I told him I'd work with him to handle it or to find another job, but he ended up leaving the company without one. Then he just disappeared. I've been trying to locate him ever since. So, it's not enough to want success. You have to want the responsibility that comes with it.

Third, you have to bring a lot to the party, and you've got to be ready to go with the beat. You know how it is when you go to a party? You get on the dance floor and you don't know what the beat is going to be. So you have to listen, and you have to respond, and when it changes, you have to adapt quickly.

In business that beat is going to differ daily. It's going to differ from job to job. It's going to differ when you're dealing with external versus internal issues and contacts. So, you have to learn to bring a lot of different steps to the party, and you've got to be ready to learn some new ones while you're there. But with all of that—and this is *the most important thing*—you have to be yourself.

I've learned from a lot of folks, but I am still me. You can learn new steps, but you're going to have your own unique way of doing them. And that uniqueness, handled properly, can be your most precious commodity.

I used to teach kids in Sunday school, and there was something I noticed about young African American males in particular and it really concerns me. When the choir walked in, the young females would walk in with their heads up high, singing. I don't know if it was a style thing, but the young males would walk in with their heads down, singing into their shoes. I'd say, "Get those heads up. You look good! Feel good!" That's so important. If you don't seem as if you're proud of yourself, how can anyone else have confidence in you?

At Chubb, I have been rewarded for doing things my way. My experience here was not always easy or pleasant or even fair. But, whatever the climate, the business, or the challenges were like, I have always been comfortable with who I am, and I have never wavered from it. I have kept my head up.

Looking back, knowing who I am has probably helped me more than anything, so I spend a lot of time appreciating that and trying to make me the best that I can be. It's a Christian value in terms of the soul: You are who you are. As I always urged those young men in the choir: Keep your head up. Be proud. It's important.

Postscript

On August 1, 2000, Sy Green retired from Chubb & Sons. Over the years he had grappled many times with the question, "Should I stay or should I go?" Ultimately, a combination of forces made him choose the latter.

For starters, his youngest child, Jessica, was clamoring for more time with her father, who was spending an inordinate amount of time on the road. Second, Green was becoming more and more aware of—

and increasingly excited by—the keen outside demand for someone with his level and breadth of experience. And, finally, he says, "I have held a paying job since I was about 10 years old. It was time to redirect some of that energy and commitment into some of the things I'm more passionate about."

That's exactly what Green has done. He is now chairman of the national board of Inroads Inc., a 30-year-old non-profit organization that connects black, Latino, and Native American college students with corporate internships. He is also involved in setting up an on-line property valuation company that would serve the insurance and mortgage brokerage communities.

Green was originally sought out by two of the company's founders (also former Chubb employees) to be a consultant. When they learned of his retirement, they asked him to be CEO. He happily accepted. Says Green, "One thing I've been blessed with is that I don't dwell on the past. My life can change and I just step into that next slot and I move on."

CHAPTER SEVEN

Bryant Gumbel

Anchor, *The Early Show*

Few people have experienced the highs and lows of fame like Bryant Gumbel. The Chicago native made a name for himself, first as a popular, award-winning sportscaster in the 1970s. He then transitioned successfully into news—no small feat—becoming the first African American to host a national morning show: NBC's *Today.* With Gumbel as anchor, the show rose to number one and began to increasingly dominate the time slot as its competitors dropped further and further behind.

While the show consistently won popularity contests, Gumbel did not. Some loved his tenacious interviewing style and serious, buttoned-up manner; others criticized him as arrogant, overbearing, and unpleasant to wake up to.

Love him or hate him, there was universal surprise when Gumbel opted to leave the show in 1997, after an unprecedented 15-year run. Even more surprising was his decision, two years later, to host *The Early Show,* CBS's version of *Today.*

Despite lagging ratings, Gumbel says he remains committed to excellence and to CBS until his contract expires in May 2002. Until then, Gumbel's HBO show, *Real Sports,* continues to do well, and he continues to live life on his own terms, popularity contests be damned. Gumbel, who is divorced, has two children.

*I*t was 1972 and I had decided to leave *Black Sports Magazine*, where I was editor in chief. I was interviewing with a lot of newspapers for writing jobs, and one of those papers, the *Baltimore Sun*, said, "We're going to call you on April 10 with our answer." This was a pretty big deal. On April 10, I got a phone call and I thought it was them. I picked the phone up and was told the devastating news that my father had passed away.

About 20 minutes and countless tears later the phone rang again and this time it was the *Baltimore Sun*. I quickly and politely told them, "I just found out my dad died. Let's put this on hold until I get back."

When I came back, my first day back, somebody called me and said, "Hey, look, there's a position in television opening up in Los Angeles. Would you like to do an audition?" And I said, "Well, sure." I did the audition in New York, and two days later they called and said, "We'd like to fly you out to L.A. to do another audition." Shortly thereafter the *Baltimore Sun* called and made me a job offer, but I kind of put them on hold.

I went to L.A., did another audition, came back and they called and made me a job offer: two-year contract. I remember the figures: $21,500 for the first year, $24,500 for the second. I accepted and I wrote in my little date book—I think it was in June of '72—"Success!" That's when I first thought, geeze, I actually made it. I'm going to be on television and I'm going to be talking about sports, which I love to do, and boy oh boy oh boy!

I was going to be doing something that I liked and thought I was *really* good at. I always thought that I could speak effectively, and so here was an opportunity to do something that I really loved in a new city, where they clearly wanted me for more money than I ever thought I'd make; and I thought—Whoa . . . this is something!

My introduction to the *Today* show was quite the opposite. I was the last guy to come to the party on that. I kind of thought, why should I do this? Why should I go from a life of leisure to somewhere where I'm going to work my ass off? Why should I go from a place where I'm celebrated and honored to something where everybody's going to second guess and nitpick me? Why should I go from being the guy in charge to being lower on the news totem pole with a bunch of people I don't even know? Why should I go from doing Super Bowls that are watched by 50 and 70 million people to a show that's watched by 5 or 7 million? Why should I go from waking up at noon to waking up at 4 A.M.?

It was like, excuse me . . . is there something wrong with you? Why are you doing this? Every guy in the world would want, would *die*, to have the job you've got! And you're walking away from it at the age of 32? Are you nuts? Are you *nuts*? Why would you go from a successful program to something that's struggling?

Why? To see if I could. And I was curious; I've always had a very curious mind. And that has served me well.

I grew up in Hyde Park on the south side, near the University of Chicago. It was a neighborhood where most people didn't watch television, they read. Even in the summer, we read. It wasn't like a punishment. It's just what we did. On any given day, I thought nothing of picking up an encyclopedia and just reading it. I read all of them. And you learn all kinds of stuff, which is probably why I have so much useless information stored in my head to this day.

In my neighborhood, and in my house, expectations were high. But I kind of caught on early that I had a pretty good memory and was a pretty good test taker. So, as a result, I used to be able to do very little, and do very well. I'm fond of saying that if my kids ever tried what I did in school I'd kill 'em. I'm not terribly proud of how I studied, but I got over.

I wouldn't necessarily characterize what I was doing in television prior to *Today* as "getting over," it's just that much of it came easily to me. I knew sports very well. I read about it like a demon and I watched it like a demon. I listened to it, I called it, I hung around it, I lived it and breathed it. It's my hobby; it's what I like. So talking about sports, articulating my thoughts about it on the air in a calm, knowledgeable, and competent fashion was something that, to me, didn't seem like real work.

That had an obvious upside. The downside was that I didn't envision myself saying, "Dodgers—3, Giants—2," for the rest of my life. I just didn't. It seemed to me there had to be something more in my life to do, something more fulfilling than what I did for kicks. I wasn't doing what I thought I was capable of doing. I wanted to see how much more I could do.

When I stepped into New York with the *Today* program there were a lot of obstacles to overcome: I was only 32 years old, I was African American, I'd been a sportscaster, all these weighty journalists had preceded me, and the *Today* program was this time-honored 30-year-old show. A lot of folks were like, "Oh my God, you've got to be kidding me . . . Not him." And so I really put my nose to the grindstone and became quite the opposite of what I was in school. I became the guy who worked relentlessly. As Gene Shalit used to joke, when I interviewed an author, I had actually read the book.

The executive producer of the *Today* show at the time was Steve Friedman, who had been my first producer in L.A.. The president of NBC was Bob Mulholland, who had been my first news director. They both knew me and knew what I was capable of.

At the time I was kind of known throughout the network, as this guy who was unflappable and could talk extemporaneously about anything for an exact amount of time. You need him to talk for eight seconds? He could talk for eight seconds. You need him to talk for 48? He'll talk for 48. And so, although at the time the *Today* show folks were looking at people like Chris Wallace, Phil Donahue, and Roger Mudd, they thought, hey, this Gumbel guy is a pretty good call.

But it was a risk. There was always a chance I could blow it. But my concerns were less about what I could or couldn't do, than what the perceptions would be. The *Today* show is such a huge ship. It's a little bit like a big ocean liner. You can get on and start to turn the wheel, but it ain't gonna turn for about 20 miles. I mean it's just going on its own momentum. I was aware that there were X number of factors involved in the success or failure of the *Today* show that I couldn't influence; it was just too big. And I was conscious of the fact that I was entering into an environment that resented outsiders, and would particularly resent some hotshot black sportscaster, who's a kid, coming on board and interested in telling them how they ought to do things.

It calls to mind what I said to reporters at the press conference announcing me as the host of the 1988 Olympics. After they introduced me, the first question somebody asked was: "Bryant, what's your biggest concern?" I said, "My biggest concern is the reality that I might do everything absolutely perfectly and half of you won't like it."

I realized growing up that, in certain environments, no matter what you do, there are going to be a lot of people who don't like it, plain and simple. They don't like you, or they don't like your color, they don't like your style, or they just prefer somebody else. I knew that going in. So that was a concern. My strategy was to simply try to out-work everybody, and try my best to ignore outside critics.

There were lots of bad moments, tons of them. They're not really specifics; they tend to be more general. They tend to be when you've done all you can and you think it's a pretty good program and you compare it to what you're up against, and think it's the best but the [ratings] don't reflect that, or the press doesn't reflect that. That's hard to take sometimes. Steve [Friedman] and I used to go out and drink ourselves under the table in misery about it sometimes. Steve says, he learned a long time ago that first you're the best, and *then* you're first. They don't come simultaneously. It's hard to accept when you truly think you're doing the best job, and you're still not winning.

That results in a lot of low moments, especially when you are the person in charge, the person responsible. When it doesn't work, you really beat yourself up. And I beat myself up more than anyone I know.

Contrary to what some have been led to believe, I'm not the hardest person to please on the planet. I don't ask for perfection, but I do want people to give me all they got. My own expectations of myself matter most to me and my self-criticisms are always the harshest.

Almost every *Today* show I ever did I walked away from it thinking, Boy oh boy, you're a stupid bastard. Very seldom would I pat myself on the back and say, "You nailed it." The best and the worst thing about doing the *Today* program was that the minute you said goodbye, you were just 22 hours from the next show.

So, I learned, leave it behind. Whatever happened, it's done. You can't change it. Focus on what's next. If you don't, I can guarantee that whatever happens next won't be very good.

I'm not a plotter or a strategist. I am somebody who tries to do everything he does as intensely as he can and as effectively as he can, and when opportunities present themselves, tries to take advantage of them. Some of what I do is good, some of what I do is bad, some pisses me off, some of it pleases me, some of it satisfies me. But when it's done, it's done.

The thing I took the most pride in at the *Today* program, was my role on those occasions when it was crisis time, and we were doing a live broadcast for three or four hours, and everybody was flying by the seat of their pants. I took satisfaction in thinking that everyone on the staff felt, Let's just get this stuff to him, do our part, and he'll do his best to make us all look good. I'd like to think that researchers, writers, technical guys, all of them felt that if something went awry, I'd pick them up and cover for them.

I took great pride in the idea that when these people went to war, they thought they had the best point man they could have. I'd like to think that I'm like my dad in that respect.

After 15 years as host of the *Today* program, I'd decided to retire. Shortly thereafter, I had some interesting conversations with people. African American people were telling me that I *couldn't* stop, that it was somehow important to our people that I stay on the air. That's like saying it's important for people like Michael Jordan to stay in basketball. In the grand scheme of things, *this is television*. I was amused, but flattered.

Fact is, I'm not nearly as driven as people would like to think. There are guys out there who, when they're off the air, they're planning a new show, new production, or this deal, or that deal. I'm not that guy. When I'm on the air I operate from a position of competence and knowledge and intelligence, and so I think outsiders view that and say, "Whoa—this guy really is focused," and I am. But when I'm off the air, I'm not thinking about how next to conquer the world or add another zero to my bankroll—I'm really not.

I used to tell people that I wanted to be retired when I was 35, and surely when I was 40. If you had told me when I was 35 that I'd still be working at 51, 52, I'd have said you were nuts. I enjoy my work. But would I rather be relaxing, playing golf? Sure. I stayed in it because CBS made me an offer too good to refuse, plain and simple, and I'm not talking about the money.

The money is not meaningless to me, but do I need to make X amount of dollars? I really don't. I was never afraid to walk away. I was always the guy who'd rather quit and do nothing than do [a job] for less than I thought I should be getting. I wasn't the easiest person to deal with in negotiations, not because I was a nasty person, but because I was always willing to say, "You know what guys? I'm outta here."

I've always felt that way. It doesn't bother me *not* to be on television. There are a lot of people I worked with whose whole being was caught up in being on television but mine is not, which has led some people to think I'm conceited. [The cartoonist] Garry Trudeau once said ours was the only country in which your *unwillingness* to promote yourself is viewed as arrogance. It's very true.

As I get older I'd like to think I'm smarter, although there's great evidence to suggest I'm not. For example, *Public Eye*, my first CBS show, was cancelled after a season. *Public Eye* was rushed into production. It was badly produced. And I take responsibility for that. I could've stopped that, and I didn't. Why? I guess, in part, because you're dealing with all this euphoria, and there's such a buzz, and you want to strike while the iron is hot and all that.

Would I have rather succeeded? Sure. But as I told somebody when they asked if I felt like a terrible failure about *Public Eye*, you could fill a hell of a hall of fame with people who've had a prime-time show get cancelled: Jackie Gleason, Lucille Ball, Mary Tyler Moore, Dick Van Dyke, Walter Cronkite. There've been a lot of them.

The Early Show is a whole different challenge. CBS's morning efforts represent the longest legacy of failure that exists in this business, and you just want to see whether you can break the string, whether you can start from scratch and take it out of last. I'll give it what I've got and hope that's enough.

I meet with [black] students every year at my UNCF [United Negro College Fund] tournament, and I always tell them that success, more than anything else, takes courage. It takes the courage to be who you really want to be, and sometimes that's not easy. Some of your buddies are going to make fun of you because you want to study, or because you speak effectively, or because you're courteous to people. They'll say it's not hip, not with it, that it's not manly, that it's not whatever.

Success takes the courage to know who you really are and be comfortable with that. There's a whole bunch of people who are going to tell you you're not worth a damn. And there will always be jealousies and envy, people who say they hope you succeed who really hope you fail — and not all of them are the opposite color. It's your own people sometimes who, for a lot of reasons, don't want to see you outstrip them.

It takes a lot of courage to be who you want to be. But it's worth it, at least, it always has been for me.

CHAPTER EIGHT

Elaine R. Jones

President and Director-Counsel,
NAACP Legal Defense and Educational Fund, Inc.

❖

In 1993, when Elaine Jones somewhat reluctantly took the helm of the Legal Defense Fund (LDF), she was stepping up to the challenge she unwittingly set for herself as a child in then-segregated Norfolk, Virginia. From the age of eight, Jones knew she wanted to be a lawyer committed to the pursuit of equal justice for all people.

After graduating with honors in political science from Howard University, and serving a two-year stint in the Peace Corps (in Turkey), Jones began a career marked by many firsts. She became the first black woman graduate of the University of Virginia School of Law. Then she joined the LDF staff, where she became the first black woman to defend death row inmates and was counsel of record in a landmark U.S. Supreme Court case that abolished the death penalty in 37 states. After briefly serving as special assistant to U.S. Secretary of Transportation William Coleman, Jr. in the mid-1970s, Jones returned "home" to LDF, where she has never paused in her passionate and steadfast pursuit of its mission. Brilliant and plainspoken, even steady attacks from the right wing never distract her laser-sharp focus from the cause.

"You have to believe that you *can* make a difference," says Jones, who is single. "Then you *will* make a difference." She already *has* made a difference, as was recognized last year when Jones' alma mater presented her with the Thomas Jefferson Memorial Foundation Award, UVA's highest award for outstanding achievement in law.

❖

I went to law school at the University of Virginia even though Howard University offered me a full scholarship. Some people find that hard to understand, but the reason was, I had gone to college at Howard. So I knew Howard, and I believe that when given the choice, you should do something you haven't done. Human nature is to do what is familiar and what is easier. But we have to fight against that. Taking on the challenges in life forces us to grow. So when Howard offered me that full scholarship to law school I said, "Uh oh, this is the easy way."

The University of Virginia, I knew, was going to be tough. They had never had a black female student. They hadn't had many women students of any color. I knew that racism was virulent down there in Charlottesville, but I wasn't going to fold and run from it. I don't know where that comes from, that motivation, that boldness. But knowing that it was going to be difficult, in itself, challenged me. I said, "I'm coming here, and I'm coming to graduate. I'm not going to be a statistic. I'm not going to pass through. I'm going to graduate from the University of Virginia."

I knew from the age of eight or so that I wanted to be a lawyer. There was so much wrong in the world. I mean, we were sitting in the back of the bus, going to segregated schools, living a life mapped out by signs that said "colored only." Little girl that I was, in my community I would see the policemen come down the street. They were all white, with big guns. And the community would quiver and shake: Cop on the block. Folks would go down to the precinct, and you'd never hear from them again. All of this you were taking in, and if you're not going to feel powerless in the face of it, you're going to say to yourself, "What can I do to change this?" My thought was, I can't do anything now. But I can prepare myself so I can be a player and make a difference later.

My father was a railroad man and he had a little landscape gardening business on the side and a lot of his clients were lawyers—all white. He wouldn't call their names, but he'd talk about "Lawyer this, lawyer that." I heard that, and I saw all the wrong in our world and I thought lawyers were supposed to right the wrong. So I had to be a lawyer.

I know my parents said to themselves, "Elaine will never be a lawyer." *But they never said it to me.* When people would say, "Well, what do you want to do when you grow up?" I'd say, "I want to be a lawyer." They'd pat me on the head, a little condescending pat, you know. My parents, standing there, would always say, "Well, be whatever you want to be."

They were patronizing me, that's clear. But they would always say, "Sister (because my older brother called me 'sister') you're going to be whatever you want to be." Only one time, my mother showed her hand by mistake. In my second year at Howard, I was taking all these political science and economics courses—now, she'd been hearing this lawyer thing for years—and she kept saying, "No education courses?"

Then she wrote me a letter in my junior year—I have it to this day. She said, "Sister, listen, it's fine, and I know you're going to be a wonderful lawyer. But it would be helpful if you would take some education courses. Just take some education courses. You may not need to use them, but I may even be able to get you on in Norfolk." Momma was teaching elementary school there and she knew the woman down at the school board, so she wrote, "I may be able to get you on with Mrs. so-and-so, but I can't do anything for you if you don't have the courses." That was her way of letting me know to get real.

My sister and I have compared notes. Momma did the same thing to her. To please her, my sister took three education courses; I took two. Today, my sister is a judge.

I was very different in college than I am now. I was really into the sorority—Delta Sigma Theta. I was dean of pledges. These are adult women now, but they remember me. I was not mean, but I was exacting. I'd do things like say, "Stand up and give me a three-minute oration on . . ." and I'd come up with a subject. Or I'd say, "Give me the Greek alphabet in one breath." I loved to make people think on their feet. I was not easy. But they learned, and it was great.

I've always had a strong sense of myself. I'm sure that comes from my parents. Both of them were full of fire—there were no wallflowers in our house—and they had a tremendous influence on me. One of the most invaluable lessons that I got from them was "Do not compare yourself to others, because when you do that, that can cause all kinds of problems."

If you let someone else set your standard, whether it's physical appearance, academic achievement, or economic success, then you will never be content with who you are. You have to maintain an edge, to keep pushing. But your purpose should be to set your own standard, not to catch up to or beat out somebody else. To always be thinking, "I wish I

had," or "I wish I was like so and so . . . " keeps us from looking at ourselves and appreciating who and what we are as individuals. You must
have your own inner compass.

Once you can really value your individuality, you have all you need.
That's self-worth and self-esteem, and I really believe that once you have
that, you can handle whatever comes. Particularly in your beginning teen
years, it's very hard to be an individual when you're in a group. But that's
where it's got to begin. You don't have to go where everybody else goes. You
don't have to do what everybody else does. That's the lesson of a lifetime.

I never heard my folks say, "Your brother's doing this," or "Your sister
is doing that." I was the middle child and they never did compare us. I
don't know whether that was by design, but the three of us were so different, and they dealt with us as individuals. It makes a difference. I believe
it helped a lot.

I don't know if it was youth, or what, but we were a bit judgmental in
our college days. I remember that very clearly. You have to be careful of
that. I don't judge people the way I used to, because I now realize that
I'm not walking in their shoes. These days I'm busy trying to understand
why people react the way they do, or behave, or think the way they think.
Rather than judging them based on my own perspective, I'm trying to
understand their perspective. Maybe it's because of the role I have to
play here at the Legal Defense Fund.

The fact is, I have learned that you can come from completely different perspectives and backgrounds and arrive at the same place. For instance, *Vogue* magazine did a story with John F. Kennedy, Jr. and me a
while back. He called me and asked if I would do it with him. He said it
would make them take him more seriously if I did. Contrary to the frequent portrayals of him as a mere hunk, John was a thoughtful guy. I
wasn't excited about doing this, but I really liked John. So I said, alright.

[The renowned photographer] Annie Liebovitz did the photo shoot
of the two of us. I'm thinking race all the time—somebody has to, so it's
me. So when I saw the proofs I said, "Look, John is white and he's in the
white shirt. I'm black, and I'm in the black blouse. Everybody knows I'm
black, and they know John is white. Why do you have to exaggerate it?"
She promptly tried to explain her vision and showed me other photos
and, finally, I understood her concept. What she was doing was illustrating how we both agreed on important issues of social justice even

though we came at them from completely different backgrounds. Once I saw it, I had to give the artist her due.

You can't be so quick to judge others based on surface effects, and making snap judgments can hinder the process. If you're trying to persuade someone (in our case, a court or a public official), you can't dismiss their position. You've got to absorb it, analyze it, and then really respond to it, or you can never be effective in changing it.

The greatest thing I took away from my college experience is that the way I got through college is not the way to get through life. Life is a course, but you cannot wait until the last minute, then cram all night, and expect to do your best. Over and over in college I was able to do that. I went to all of this sorority stuff, then I'd go to class and take good notes, and wait until two or three days before the exam to get with it.

Normally, being able to do that successfully will teach you to stay at it. But I got just the opposite lesson from it, because I knew that I was running a risk. Each time I did it, I got closer and closer to not being able to pull it off.

After I left Howard, I went into the Peace Corps and served in Turkey for a couple of years. I knew I wanted to be a lawyer, but I didn't want to go straight through. I needed a break. The Peace Corps helped me, because I surely couldn't cram for that. Whatever I learned one day, I had to build on to get through the next. So, that's where my better habits started.

Why the Peace Corps? I wanted to travel and I had no money, plain and simple. I also always like to do something with my time that lets me think I'm contributing somewhere. I took my nieces to Paris last May. It was great. The three of us spent a week there and, I mean, we *covered* Paris, but we were also *learning* something. I like to learn whatever I can as part of whatever I'm doing. It's fun for me—I enjoy that. Now, I had some tough lessons in the Peace Corps, but I loved the experience because it was all so new and there was so much to learn. I was exposed to a whole other way of life. That's something I have always hungered for: exposure to new things.

Law school was certainly new, but not in the best sense. That first semester at UVA, I *knew* this was serious business. No cramming would do this. You had to read every night, otherwise just forget it. As tough as I thought it would be, it was tougher.

I'll never forget the dean's secretary coming up to me during the first week of class, asking me to clean the ladies lounge. Here I was, the first black woman student, and one of only six women students in the entire law school. And there was only one place to congregate, which was in the ladies lounge down in the basement of the building. There was a refrigerator and a tattered sofa, and I was sitting there, having just gone to the bookstore, looking at my books, trying to figure out a plan to get through this crazy workload.

She comes through and sees me sitting there, and she was just so polite as she said, "I know you're takin' your break now. But when you're finished, would you mind cleaning out the refrigerator?"

She didn't see books, or proper clothes, or anything. She saw a black woman sitting there on the sofa, and that could only mean one thing: cleaning woman.

Now, whenever I tell this story, people say, "Elaine, you're fire. What did you say?" To be frank, I said nothing. Because by the time I realized she was talking to me she had gone out the door. Even as I watched the words coming out of her mouth, it never dawned on me that she could be talking to me. Later, I learned it was the dean's secretary, and she never apologized. But I know something else: In three years of law school, there was nothing I ever wanted from the dean's office that I didn't get.

Later that same year—April 1968—Martin Luther King, Jr. was assassinated. Nobody said a word. Here I am at law school, and Jimmy Benton was there (the only other black student in my class) and nobody said a word about it. The rest of the country was going up in smoke. But at UVA, no classes were cancelled, no professor acknowledged it. There was *nothing*. It was as if it hadn't happened. Finally, I saw Jimmy at around 4 o'clock that day, and I said, "Jimmy, *do you think they know?*"

I can understand that a lot of those people thought King was a rabble-rouser, and they really didn't like him. But I couldn't understand the silence, the acting as if nothing had happened. That's that genteelness, though. That's that Southern way. There was just a complete denial of our experience. Even in the curriculum.

The civil rights laws had been enacted, but they never taught me anything about civil rights law. I got none of it. I got one discussion as part of a lecture about how *Brown vs. Board of Education*, for social reasons, *may* have been correctly decided, but when weighed against the constitution, was *wrongly* decided. That's what I got.

What made me stick with it was the same thing that made me go there. I viewed the University of Virginia as just a necessary tool, a necessary cross I had to bear, to get where I had to go. It's just like when you buy yourself a new suit, and it's sharp. Then you look down, and you've picked up six pounds, and your big presentation is two weeks from now: You have to lose that weight. The goal is to get your act together to put on your suit. And you know that what you're going through is temporary because, after this one big presentation, you don't ever have to wear that suit again. So, you don't focus on what it takes to get there, you focus on the goal.

Despite a history of strict segregation, the University of Virginia took a chance on me, and I took a chance on it. Ours wasn't a perfect union, but it was a beginning. I did have some positive experiences there, and I did make some lifelong friends, but it was not easy.

I knew I wanted to be a trial lawyer. I knew I wanted to litigate civil rights cases and make a difference through the court system. And that kept me on course. At UVA, I could let the institution hinder me from reaching my goal, or I could use it to get where I wanted to go. I was just determined to do the best I could. The job of "the first" is to make sure other folks come through the door. So, if you're a first and things aren't any better when you leave, then you haven't done what you're supposed to. I like to think I made a difference.

In my last year of law school, I got a job offer from [former President Richard] Nixon's law firm, Mudge, Rose, Guthrie & Alexander. It was for big money. I'd never made any money. This was $18 thousand a year; that's about $100 thousand today. So I took it. But after I said yes, I could not look myself in the mirror. I would have been the first black associate there, but I felt so guilty. I said to myself, This is not why you went to law school. What are you doing, fool?

It's not that I don't want young lawyers to make it in the big firms. No. I encourage it. I just say, go, but have your eye on the prize: Know why you're going. If you get in there, and you make it, fine. But if you get in there and get disappointed, use it for your own ends. Just be purposeful, that's all I'm saying. My view then was that I wasn't being purposeful. I was going for money only.

Now, I often quote Joe Louis, who is reported to have said, "I don't like money, really, but it quiets my nerves." You know, there are worse things. But the problems come when you do something *solely* for money. Doing something where money is a factor is fine. Money can even be a big factor; that's fine. But when the only reason you're doing it is for the bucks, well then you have to step back and look at it. That's another one of my routines: Step back and look at it.

Once I realized it wasn't worth it—because money or no money, I would be unhappy there—I went to the dean and told him I needed a job. He told me to go see his friend, Jack Greenberg at LDF. Right away, I knew it was the right thing for me. It was exactly what I always wanted to do—and it was going to be *hard*.

I wanted to be the best litigator I could be, and I knew I was in an environment in which I could learn to do that. I wanted to try cases. I wanted to learn how to select a jury and do investigations. I learned all that, and I got thrown into some of the toughest cases we had around here.

I started in death-penalty work. We were assigned states, and Alabama was my state—one of the worst ever. Nothing but black people on death row, almost all convicted by all-white juries. Many, many, many were wrongly convicted! And with nobody doing a thing about it, but LDF and our small group of cooperating attorneys.

Those of us who live in big cities forget, but there are huge pockets of this country that are so provincial and so unexposed. When I would walk into court the bailiffs would come up to me and say, "You have to move to the back. This is for the lawyers." And, here again, this mind—it just helps me out—it said, "Alright, they're underestimating me, and *that is a plus for me.*"

I never had anybody convicted and given the death penalty when I tried their case. Never. Not one, because of a combination of luck and hard work. I didn't care how long it took to pick a jury. Give me one black person, and I was in trouble. I had to have at least two or three. But I would spend my entire closing argument talking to those two or three people. I didn't address my argument to anyone else. Others could listen in if they wanted. I always told them the same thing. I said: Everybody's vote here counts. *Every single vote.*

There was one case in which I had just one black juror and he was a Vietnam vet. In my closing argument, I looked right at him and I said, "Some people believe you have to go along to get along. If you don't believe my client is guilty, just refuse to go along." He hung that jury.

There has been no singular thrilling win for me. We've had some big victories. But the law changes, and we will make a mistake as a people in thinking that because you have a victory today you're going to have it tomorrow. *Brown vs. Board of Education* is a good example. Thurgood [Marshall, who argued the landmark case before the Supreme Court] didn't want desegregation for the sake of desegregation. He wanted to get those resources to African American children. He also wanted white children to learn the value of diversity. The case did that. But look at our [public] schools now. They are essentially re-segregated and the resources have gone away with the white child. So, a win today is great, but I know that it is not necessarily going to stand the test of time.

The same is true for the losses. The losses hurt, but the losses aren't going to be static. It's a pendulum: Things swing. What I have to do is stay optimistic, work hard, get the resources and *learn from the losses.*

We deal with so much adversity in this business, and sometimes, you look back on things and you say, "My God, how did I make it?" You make it by just shutting out part of it. If you give in to the adversity and unfairness, you aren't able to function. You can't do your job. I can blot out certain things, just compartmentalize them and not deal with them, so that I can focus on what I need to do.

It does take a toll though, and I have had to remind myself repeatedly that there's supposed to be joy in life. I mean, you really are supposed to smell the roses; to have some fun. Life is not just about work and making a difference; life is also about laughter and whimsy and taking time for self. I have had to teach myself that, and it took a while, but I'm there now. I used to take great pride in the fact that I'd not had a vacation. At the beginning, "Vacation?" I'd say. "Oh, no, no, no. I can't take time away." At one point, I think I went almost ten years without a real vacation: Stupid. You've got to refresh yourself, or, eventually, you'll break down.

I've never been a long-term [career] planner. My philosophy was, do your best in what you're doing, and what's for you will come to you. Except for two years, when I left to be special assistant to Bill Coleman, when he was secretary of transportation, I've been [at LDF] for my entire career, but I have had so many different jobs that it hasn't really seemed that way. I was working in the D.C. office handling a lot of public policy issues in addition to the litigation when this job as head of LDF came along.

I didn't know if I wanted this job. I was considering saying no, because I had the best of all worlds. Here I was, enjoying my work, I could do what I wanted and somebody else had the responsibility of running the place. The same things I'm doing now with public policy and litigation, I could do then, except I didn't have the headache of all the administration, which is a huge issue in the nonprofit world.

I remember what Nathaniel Jones told me (he's on the Sixth Circuit Court of Appeals and used to be general counsel to the NAACP) when I was thinking about it. He said, "Elaine, it's not a job. It's a calling. There's not anything for you to decide. You have to do this." And then I had a practical consideration: If I said no, I would have had to leave.

You can't stay at a place where you're unwilling to take on the burdens of helping the organization do what it must do—at least that's what I believe. You can't be selfish enough to be in a place that you enjoy, taking from it what you like and not giving back to it some of the things it needs. And Nate was right. It is a mission. It never was a job. And, as I think about it, in my whole life, I never wanted just a job.

I think that is one of the reasons I never married. Women have choices, and I applaud that. My sister is married and she came through law school right after I did. But I know what I'm like. I know how I move about and travel and where I put my work on my [priorities] list, and I'm old fashioned, I guess. I know you've got to believe in a marriage, and you've got to work at it. I didn't think I would give a marriage what it was due. But, like the law, life evolves, and you never know what the future holds.

By the time I agreed to [become director-counsel], I had litigated for nearly 20 years, so a part of my decision was just like going to UVA instead of Howard. It was time to do something else, something even more difficult. And I discovered that I'm meant to do this! What I do is a part of my being.

But, also like UVA, it's been tougher than I ever imagined. You've got an institution that makes a difference and lawyers who are committed and bright that you've got to train and nurture and provide with an environment in which they can continue to grow. You've got to raise money, you've got to have a substantive agenda, you've got to have a structure and a board that's committed to the organization, and you've got to build on that. We've got to have people who care about us, especially because we're being attacked from everywhere—by the right wing with all of its money. They don't train us in law school to do all this.

But I worked under [former director-counsel] Jack [Greenberg], and I worked under [former director-counsel] Julius [Chambers], and I learned a lot from them. So, when I came into this job, I started doing a lot of reading—not just about legal issues, as always, but about business—and I learned how to reach out to others who have the expertise I don't. I now know how to go to consultants and say, "Please help us out." I am not ever afraid to ask for help when I know we need it. To hesitate would be foolish; we have too much to do.

My role here at this moment reminds me of a speech my sister gave at a Woman's Day luncheon once. She mentioned that in the Bible, Queen Esther, when she hesitates to take on a daunting task, is asked, "Who knows but that you come into the kingdom for such a time as this?" Well, here I am at such a time as this.

This is a critically important time. All that we have gained is on the line, and all of our people don't see it in the same way. We buy into this whole notion that all that civil rights stuff is history; that it's behind us and we can just move forward. Desegregation has separated us from each other, even isolated us in some cases. But it shouldn't take physical proximity for us to have spiritual and emotional proximity in the millennium. It's still about what each of us can do for all of us. Our sense of ourselves as a people is still there, but it's not as strong as it once was.

But I'm hopeful. I believe that we can solve some of these problems, and, really, what is the choice? My job is to get the message out, and to hold the line as long as I can.

Martin Luther King, Jr. had a lot of great sayings, but my favorite is, "The arc of the moral universe is long, but it bends toward justice." You can't necessarily see where it begins or where it ends, but *it bends toward justice*. I believe that. I love that saying, and I love what I do.

Whatever role you play in bending that arc, you should do your best and celebrate the struggle. Love what you do.

CHAPTER NINE

Tom Jones

Chairman and CEO, Global Investment Management and
Private Banking Group, Citigroup Inc.

❖

The job title is a mouthful, but then, so is the job. Tom Jones, 52, oversees three primary asset management business platforms: Salomon Brothers Asset Management, Smith Barney Asset Management, and Citibank Global Asset Management. SSB Citi Asset Management has hundreds of billions of dollars in aggregate assets under management.

It may seem an odd sphere of power for a man who studies the Bible in his spare time and has contemplated attending divinity school, but then Jones has never been ordinary or predictable.

The Cornell University alumnus joined Travelers Group as vice chairman and director in 1997 after serving two years as vice chairman and director of TIAA-CREF. Regardless of the venue, Jones' leadership style has been marked by his unerring sense of conviction, deep integrity, and good old-fashioned hard work.

His primary advice for success in life: "Learn how to give everything you have to give." Jones expects no less from those on his team, but he demands it, most of all, of himself. Jones is married with three children.

❖

I started my career in 1971 at one of the big-eight accounting firms after leading what was considered to be a student revolution at Cornell. It was a highly publicized event, and a picture of me, brandishing a gun on the steps of the student union, became quite famous at the time.

I remember it as if it was yesterday. The standoff was the culminating event of what started as a civil demand. The black students wanted a black-studies program, but conservative elements of the faculty resisted. It was 1965. The Civil Rights Laws in the United States were enacted that year but America still was ambivalent about where African Americans fit in. Did the Constitution really apply to us, or were we still three-fifths of a person, so to speak? This question was still hanging in the balance.

My family had been successful in the context of black success in that era. My mom was a schoolteacher and my dad was both a nuclear physicist—he did a master's in physics at Indiana University—and an ordained Presbyterian minister. I grew up in New York, and had never personally faced harsh, ugly discrimination other than on visits to the South to see my parents' relatives. So my life wasn't one of hard racial feelings.

But I became much more knowledgeable about African American history at Cornell. And I came to understand the student demands for black studies in the context of that civil rights era. We were saying, "The way you're defining history leaves out my story."

The final confrontation developed one day when black students had taken over the student union building and a white fraternity busted in with the purpose of throwing us out. I had not been in the leadership of the group that decided to take over the building, but I was there and I supported it.

When I heard an argument break out, I remember thinking that if, somewhere along the line, my ancestors, in the company of many, many others, had been willing to draw the line, our entire history would have been different in the sense that you can't be enslaved unless you cooperate to a significant extent. You can't be oppressed unless you cooperate, because your choice is always to fight and die.

That day at Cornell, I was prepared to do that. Dying isn't the worst thing that can happen to you, if you die the right way. I knew that was a moment in history that I had to be a part of creating. The choices I made that day make sense to me now, as they did then, but they were not without consequences.

You know the John Grisham book *The Chamber*, about the guys on death row, and when they go by they say, "Dead man walking"? I entered the business world as somebody who had shown that I could potentially lead an armed revolution. So, I figured I was a marked man professionally and that I just wouldn't get a break at whatever I tried to do. Because of that, I worked very, very hard at Arthur Young & Co.—just so there would be as little excuse as possible for me to not make it.

Most people—if they're really good—operate at a 90 to 95 percent level of effectiveness. That's the way people are trained. If you get a 95 you get an A. If you get 100, for most people, that's the same; you got an A, I got an A. What difference does it make? Doesn't seem like much—it's just five points. But if every day you're putting out five points more than the other person—after awhile the people that you're competing with have fallen so far behind you, they suddenly look and you're around the curve. It becomes almost impossible for them to catch up if you can sustain the 100 percent over time.

It doesn't show up that much in your first year at work. But after a few years it begins to. It began to show up for me, without my even realizing it, in things like the bosses who chose to be my mentors.

I began to be picked up fairly early in my career by very senior people. Without my realizing it, one of Arthur Young's senior managing partners from New York began to come to Boston and to pay attention to me. Not everybody liked the fact that I was there, and they talked about it, so I guess he decided to check me out personally. To many people's surprise, including mine, he liked what he saw. He just happened to be around on days when I was in the office, and would just happen to invite me out to lunch. I didn't realize it, but he was taking me under his wing.

I ended up with two primary mentors at Arthur Young: That fellow—he was the regional managing partner—and the Boston office's managing partner. They were two of the most powerful people in the eastern region managerial structure of Arthur Young (now Ernst & Young).

I know now that this was not unselfish on their parts. A company is like a big sports team in many respects. Most successful people are looking around to pick people for their teams. Top executives are always thinking, What great athletes can I get on my team; who are the players that will work for me?

Today, when I look for people to put on my team, the first thing I notice is how hard you work. Second, I notice if you're somebody who is a continual self-improver, not somebody who hits a plateau and seems to start coasting. And then, third, I really do care about your character. I look for people with that package, and two out of three isn't good enough.

Usually the teams that win are the teams that have the combination of best talent and best effort. So, I found early in my career that my ability to give 100 percent and sustain it made me stick out.

A few years after I started working, I formed the habit of making a short list at the beginning of every year of ways to improve myself. Sometimes those are technical things. Other times it's something like, "You're getting to be too narrow; you need to read a higher percentage of the best-seller list" or "You haven't taken enough vacation time."

I focus on three things each year that I can do that would make a significant improvement. There's no point having a list of 10 or 15 things if you don't get to them. But if you can get three big things done, and sustain that, over time it accumulates in a pretty incredible fashion, just like the difference between 100 percent effort versus 95 percent. You need to be able to be your own best critic in terms of understanding where you've gotten out of balance.

I had done both a bachelor's and a master's at Cornell, but after being at Arthur Young for awhile, seeing how good these guys were at what they did, I realized I didn't really have the full skills set I needed to compete long-term. So, drawing on one of my annual self-appraisals, I decided to get an MBA in finance and accounting.

I knew exactly what I wanted and why I wanted it, but I had a family, and I couldn't afford to go to school full time. So I went to Boston University night school.

I worked at it intensely; went year-round, even to summer school, because I knew I needed to get this stuff and get it fairly quickly. I got the best grades that I ever got in school. There were almost no classes where I got less than an A minus because I really knew why I was there. At Cornell I didn't strive to be a straight-A student. I had decent grades, but mainly because I was smart enough that I could cram the night before.

You find in business—I think this is also true in sports—that, at the highest levels, everybody is pretty good, otherwise they would have been weeded out a long time ago. There may be an aberration, but that's rare.

(Again, it's like pro sports: By the time you get to the pros they're all pretty good players.) So once you reach the top levels of business, it's foolish to think that there's going to be a big gap between you and the next person. We're talking about shades of gray, fine differences of distinction. So, if you can give 100 percent and the other person is at 95, 96, or 97, that's enough. Frankly, very few people have the discipline to do that. People settle for much less than they're capable of doing because that's the way they're aculturated.

I got lucky in a way. I would have settled for much less, also, except I happened to be in a circumstance in which, because of what had happened at Cornell, I didn't think I could survive doing less. It's not unusual in life that what you think is your biggest problem can also be your biggest blessing. Your strength can be your weakness.

In this case, what I thought was my biggest obstacle led me to behave in a way that made it an advantage. If I had just been a regular guy, figuring everything's okay, I would have probably gone along at 90 percent.

It's important to understand the fine distinctions that, in the end, put one person in the winner's circle and another person who appears to have all of exactly the same capabilities, credentials, and potential, on the sidelines.

Take my brother and me. He was finishing Harvard Business School when I was starting the Boston University night school, and he kind of sneered at me. "Boston University night school? What are you going to do with that?"

I had checked out the curriculum, checked out the cases, and I said, "Well, it appears to me that it's the same material. The only difference is that your professors are more famous than my professors."

He had a great situation. His employer, the New York Telephone Company, paid his tuition and fees and continued his salary. He performed well in school and came out as a Baker scholar, but he didn't come out with the subtleties.

When his career faltered and he began to get bitter, I said, "You know, the piece you're missing is that you don't recognize that you're competing for something that one-twenty fifth of 1 percent of all the people who are in the business world are going to get. Everybody who's left [at that level] is smart, sharp, ambitious, a superstar. Your credentials may look better, but that doesn't mean that you're more effective than they are. You're focused on how good you are as an individual. I think the way the game really gets played is, can you be good but have that reflected in how good others are."

As a manager of a big entity, it's not like you alone carry a company or beat the competition. It really comes down to whether you are somehow able to get *other* people to do more, rise to a higher level, accomplish more than they would have without you there.

My brother was so captured by his credentials and by his own excellence that I think he tended to try to dominate people. I think he tried to always be the smartest person, to always have the right answer. A lot of people do that, and that's not what I'm talking about when I'm talking about how you excel. It's not about having to be right in that narrow sense. It's a broader definition. It's more collective.

So, as you go up the line and operate in that context of continual self-improvement, there would be a number of situations in which your strategies ought to be focused on how to learn to work better with other people, how to better interact with other people, how to share with other people.

I ended up lucky in a couple of dimensions that I didn't realize at the time. The B.U. thing was luck in disguise. I worked so hard, I was focused, and I had to really want it, because when you go to night school, you basically have no other time. You're working all day, you're in school at night, and you've got to study all weekend. I ended up feeling, when I finished in 1978, that I had really found out what giving 100 percent was all about. And that gave me an advantage against anybody who's never really had to dig deep and sustain it.

If you're in a crisis, it's important to have a good sense of what your capacity is, how much you have inside of you, how long you can sustain a given level of effort. You have to be able to pace yourself; you can't hold back so much that you don't do your best, but you also have to know how to not go so hard that you burn out.

I first learned that at Cornell, where crisis was the last thing I expected to have to manage. When I started at Cornell I was just 16. I thought I had died and gone to heaven. This was the most beautiful campus I had ever seen. I felt like I belonged there. I became the freshman class president, then was one of the handful of students who ran the student judicial system.

As I met other black students who were more politically conscious than I was and began to be educated about a broader reach of black history, I understood that we were asking Cornell to have black-studies programs so that we could learn more about ourselves. To understand what had happened to us historically, to understand the sociology of our communities, to understand the economics of slavery, to understand all of those things, was a form of self-empowerment. Because if you understand what's happened to your people historically, you're much better prepared to not let that happen again, and to succeed in shaping your own destiny.

I remember feeling that if my ancestors had fought instead of allowing themselves to be taken as slaves, they could have changed the destiny of our people. In many respects, I came to feel that this random wheel of history had come around to where I happened to be. All of America was in this civil rights uproar, and there was a question: Is there going to be a revolution in America? I felt that I happened to have been born in a time and a place where it was my generation that was going to draw the line and say, "Enough."

We were saying, "If the constitution doesn't really apply to us, we're going to fight about it. If we don't have full respect and equal treatment under the law, we're going to fight about it."

The potential outcome of fighting, which was quite obvious at the time, really didn't frighten me, because the way I looked at it, if I had been born in 1845 and had been 18 years old, I would have been willing to march across the field at Gettysburg. If I had been born in 1925, I would have had the courage to hit the beach at Guadalcanal. If I had been born when I was, 1949, and my circumstances had been slightly different, I would have been in Vietnam. So it's not unusual for teenagers and people in their young 20s to be put into life and death situations. In fact, it's fairly common throughout history. You don't think you're going to be the one who's killed. I just thought this was my destiny.

When this frat broke into the building—big, tough football players—and I heard an argument going on, I went to see what it was. It just flashed in my mind, "This isn't the way it's going to be. We didn't come this far to have guys like this decide that they're going to be the vigilantes." So I went and just popped the first guy in his face. It became a group fight, we threw him out, and then we decided to go get guns. We just decided, we're not going to walk out of here having achieved nothing; we're going to fight.

I knew this was going into other territory. To be honest, a lot of the students were scared. What a leader must do in those situations is try to help others to be strong. Because if you show fear, things deteriorate pretty quickly. You have to have an instinct for crises.

My oldest son is a good guy. He finished Harvard in 1987 and joined the Marines. A lot of people couldn't believe it, but he wanted to do something where it didn't matter whether you had money or whether you knew certain people. He wanted to find out how he would perform in a situation in which it was just about how good you are. He wanted to know if he was tough enough to be a Marine.

He talked about it, and asked me how I really felt about it. I said, "You're going to be an officer. It's okay as long as, before you get in, you think about whether you really have the ability to help your guys to die well if you're in that situation." It was shortly after one of these stupid banana-republic things, like the Reagan invasion of Grenada, and I said, "You know, war isn't always made up of noble events like D-Day. It's just as likely that you and your guys will end up trapped in some place that isn't worth a damn, and a year later, nobody's even going to remember why we were there or what your names were.

"You could get caught in one of these situations in which the only valor you can give your guys is a sense that there's meaning in how you die together, that you're true to what you're supposed to be." I told him, "If you have the courage to do that, if you're not the guy who's scared, but the guy who can rally your men to be what they're supposed to be, then do it. But if you don't have that kind of courage, stay out."

I didn't know that I had it until I was already in that critical moment at Cornell. If somebody had said to me two days before, "You are going to do this," I would have thought they were crazy. But sometimes it's almost like God is speaking to you. You just know there are certain things you have to do and you see the way to do them. You have to be willing to just meet your destiny.

I knew that either way, there was going to be a victory, because if we did it the right way and they ended up sending the National Guard in, and they killed us, the shame of that would reverberate around the country. To kill a hundred black students at Cornell over an argument about whether they can *learn about themselves*? I knew that the shame of that would change America.

Alternatively, if we got out of it without bloodshed, I knew that being that close to the precipice would so frighten people, that the powers that be would say, "This is crazy. We have to change this dynamic." In fact, shortly thereafter there began to be a lot of energy put into affirmative action and opening society up. So I think that was a turning point.

If anybody had said that this country would change as rapidly as it has in a 30-year span, most people back then would have said, "Not possible." I'm often told I've changed a lot since the 1960s, and my response is, "America has changed more than I have." I'm just operating in a different mode right now, and it's a different mode that's possible because it's a different country.

I was much more gregarious and outgoing at Cornell. To be freshman class president, I had to be a pretty popular guy. That changed dramatically once I left, and not just because of the working environment I entered. Our victory at Cornell was followed by a very ugly confrontation with some of the black student leaders who felt that I wasn't militant enough.

The university had granted us the money to get an African American studies program going, and a lot of the people who had been the most militant in pushing the issues immediately said, "Cornell is institutionally incapable of being responsive to the educational needs of African Americans. We're going to start an alternative university." So they went down to Greensboro, North Carolina where there was an effort to start something called Malcolm X University.

I had been quite sincere in wanting Cornell to do certain things for the education of black students, but I felt that if we could just get this piece, then Cornell would provide a wonderful educational experience for African Americans. So I wasn't about rejecting the university; I was more about reforming the university.

This tension between reform and revolution was reflected in the broader black society. That was the tension that existed between the Black Panthers, as an example, feeling that Martin Luther King and the Southern Christian Leadership Conference were too conservative.

So, there was this split, and the people I knew were playing for keeps. I had straight razors at my throat. I had loaded guns at my temple. In the end, I almost got killed by the guys who were once my allies.

The takeover happened in my senior year and I had not planned to stay. But I thought, to have gone through all of this and not accomplished anything just made no sense. There can be a pot of money there, but nothing ever happens unless somebody makes it happen. So, I stayed to make sure that something tangible came out of this.

I ended up doing my master's at Cornell, and when it was done I drove away from there thinking, "I'm walking away from this stuff and I'm never walking back." I figured I was a dead man walking as far as much of white society would be concerned, particularly the business world. And I knew that to some in my own community, I was considered an Uncle Tom—one of those people who needs to be eliminated for holding back the revolution. That was the rhetoric. So I knew I was *persona non grata*, or dead man walking, with the [black] guys also.

A number of years later—in 1980 or 1981—one of my self-improvement projects was to read the Bible cover to cover and really understand it. There are many wonderful stories in the Bible, but one really struck me. I don't know why, after all these years of going to church, I had never realized that the very same people who, on Palm Sunday, are throwing the palms in front of Jesus saying, "Hosanna to the Highest," not even seven days later—it's within *four days*—these are the very same people who are saying, "Crucify him!"

The more I thought about that, the more I realized that's the way human society is. They're with you one day, they're not with you the next. And so, to a certain extent, I just withdrew. I moved to Boston and, in a lot of respects, I never joined anything ever again. I never again became part of a crowd. I wanted my family and my close relationships. But I lost my appetite for being a popular guy, or thinking that that mattered. I try to do the right thing. I try to be generous to good causes. So, as far as my core beliefs, there hasn't been much change. But I never again tried to get deeply involved in movements or to care so much what people thought about me.

This issue of spiritual depth and character absolutely makes a difference. It's all about who you are, how you live, the ability to develop deep relationships with your spouse, your children, and people who depend on you. You've got to get centered in terms of what you stand for. That's tremendously important, because it's not just a matter of what you accomplish in terms of position or wealth, it's very important how you get there and what you stand for once you get there—or what you stand for if you never get there. And you need to get centered fairly early on, otherwise, it's hard to maintain your equilibrium later.

It's not uncommon with athletes or people who suddenly get lots of wealth or fame, that they're not centered enough to manage it. So they end up running around with all the wrong people or getting into all kinds of bad situations, and it's not too long before it's all gone. An important ingredient of being successful—and of sustaining success—is that you have to have your own scorecard that is measured in terms of the things you stand for as a person. That's what character is all about.

It's important to have that also because you need to be able to walk away if the price becomes too high. If you're offered a zillion dollars, but it means working for somebody you don't respect or being asked to do things that you know are wrong, you need to be able to walk away. And if you're keeping score just by money or position, you may not be able to walk away.

I have walked away from situations in which I felt that the respect I was due was not afforded to me. I've done that twice. My scorecard is based on doing—and doing things the right way.

I've got a stack of notes, cards, and letters that I've received over the years from women and minorities thanking me for my presence. What that usually reflects is that they feel they got a fair shot, maybe even a promotion or a raise—or they just didn't get hammered—because somebody else was watching and that made it more of a level playing field.

Most African Americans who are senior executives in major corporations have probably had a similar experience: You drop the stone into the pond and concentric rings go out there. There are a lot of people who get treated differently because there are folks who think if they don't do the right thing somebody may notice and do something about it. It'll come through in subtle ways like which people get sent to executive-development or tuition-support programs. I don't say that that's superior to those who are doing more visible or overt things, but neither do I think it's inferior, because it's still real people affecting real lives.

What I find is becoming more and more ingrained in me over time is that there are only 24 hours in a day. By the time you work 10 hours (if it's only 10), and sleep six hours, and spend a couple of hours getting back and forth to work, you're down to where—if you're lucky—you've got about six hours a day that you've actually got some choices over. And often that's not even available, because you might have a dinner meeting, or some other obligation. So then you're down to maybe four hours, and if you try to spend a couple of those with your family, talking with your kids, you're now down to just one or two hours a day that you can say are *your* time.

I really enjoy taking that time to reflect, to just think. It can be about an issue that's confronting me. It can be a problem. Toward the end of the year, I think about my short list of improvements. You just need quiet time to figure some of that out.

I often look at people who seem to be constantly engaged in this activity or that activity and I say to myself, "When do they ever have any quiet time? When do they ever just think about stuff? When do they sort it out?" I think the answer most of the time is that they don't. They just keep going in a constant buzz of activity. It's easy to live that way. It can seem almost carefree. But it's not the way that I choose to live. Time is precious, and you ought to be thoughtful about what you do with it.

I know a guy who's had such a long commute from his family for work that he spends most of the week away from home. Now one of his kids is leaving home to go off to school, another one is leaving in a couple of years, and he's saying, "How have I spent my time? I haven't spent any time with my wife or with my kids. What am I doing?" The millennium makes you think about stuff like that. It makes me very conscious that I'm into what almost certainly is the last third of my life.

In my head, I keep a mental clock. Citigroup is one of the most fascinating big-business stories to come along. I signed up to make a run with Sandy Weill to create one of the premier global financial services companies. When Sandy's run is over—probably in three or four years—that's my time to say, "Do I want to spend my time like this? Flying around the world, always in Europe or Japan or Australia or Latin America? Always on the telephone?" I know that there's a juncture out there where I'm going to say, "I've done this. I've either done a good job of it or I haven't. But what do I want to do with the next five years of my life?"

Maybe the answer will be "more of this." Maybe it will be something different. But I deeply believe you need to give thought to things like that and not just be on auto-pilot.

In some respects, what I'm doing here is playing out the string of destiny. I started my career as a kind of test, after the things happened at Cornell. America put a lot of energy into opening its society and I wanted—even though I knew the odds were against me—to test the limits of what could be accomplished. I've gone much farther than I predicted and, at each step of the way, I've made a conscious decision to play this out, and see where it goes.

If it turns out that my destiny is to be the CEO of [our parent company], I'll probably play that string out. If it turns out that that's not my destiny, the odds are better than 50-50 that I'll walk away. There are such subtle shades of difference and luck that end up determining who gets what that I'm not going to feel like I've been denied something that I uniquely deserved. I think that's unhealthy.

I've often been fond of the model that at the latter stages of one's career you try to give back to society. We need more people who go into government because of what they can give, not because they're trying to set up what they can get. So that might be an option. I've toyed with the idea of going to divinity school, but more for the purpose of education and intellectual curiosity than vocation. I'm too selfish to pursue that as a vocation.

I don't know where the end is but I'm at peace, and have been for a long time. And I'm glad, because from what happened at Cornell to what's happening now, is a uniquely American story. And I think it's as poignant a story of America as any. It's a story of hope and optimism.

I've always tried to be a positive person. One of the reasons that split occurred between me and the black students who considered themselves more revolutionary in the 1960s, was because I've always been of a mind that you have to forgive. You have to accommodate. You have to move on. Otherwise you become what I call a prisoner of history. And if there's one thing I was determined I would not be, it was that.

CHAPTER TEN

Debra L. Lee

President and Chief Operating Officer, BET Holdings Inc.

The minute Debbie Lee stopped doing what had always been expected of her was also when she launched a new career in which she would exceed everybody's expectations—most importantly, her own.

Her 1986 decision to leave the Washington, D.C. law firm Steptoe & Johnson and join Black Entertainment Television—then a fledgling enterprise—was the biggest risk she had ever taken. Nonetheless, taking it "felt really good," Lee says. That feeling got even better when the risk very quickly—and literally—paid off.

Having run the company's legal affairs department as well as its publishing division, taken the company public and then private again, Lee, 46, knows BET to its core. In March 1996, she took charge of operations for the entire company. She's helped it grow from a toddling cable TV company into a multimedia powerhouse. In the process Lee realized a power all her own.

A recognized leader in the telecommunications industry, she is a recipient of the Silver Star Award from American Women in Radio and Television, among many others. Lee has two children.

My father saw no limits for me. I don't know if that's because I was the third child—the baby—and he said, "Okay, this is my last chance," but he really believed I could do absolutely anything.

He always told me not to burn bridges. That's one lesson I always hung on to. But I think, above all, the idea was that you just do your best at whatever you do. He always wanted to be a lawyer himself, but he always instilled in me, and I think in my sister, also, that we could do *anything*—that we shouldn't be hindered by sexual conventions. I think that's unusual for a lot of black men, and I think it made a huge difference in how I approach my life and my career.

My father was an officer in the Army, so we moved around a lot. I was born in Columbia, South Carolina. Six months later we moved to Germany, and then we moved to L.A. and lived in Compton through the Watts riots. After the riots were over, we moved to Greensboro, North Carolina. That was one of the biggest influences of my life.

Greensboro was still very segregated, separated by downtown. The whites lived on one side of town and the black folks lived on the other. Because of that, the black community had to support itself. So we had black doctors, black lawyers, black bankers. Everything we needed was right there. It was a small community, so everyone knew each other. And even though we were new to the town, all of a sudden you're part of this, and you're expected to do well. I had never been in a community like that before, that was so tight-knit and so proud and so independent. It forced me to become more of a leader. I just started to try harder.

In Greensboro, if you were smart, you went to A&T. If you were *really* smart, you went to Chapel Hill. And if you were *brilliant*, you went to Duke. I was, sort of, in the middle but I wanted to go to an Ivy League school. That was part of my father's success formula. So I applied to Brown because some black students came down and talked to us in a session called, "Blacks at Brown." I thought they had the biggest, most perfect afros I'd ever seen. I said, "These people really know what they're doing."

Once we decided on something, my father would find out as much about it as he could. So once I decided I was going to go to Brown, that was it. That was the world for him. He got hold of a Brown course catalogue, and he plotted out four years of study for me.

One in geology, because there were no black Ph.D.'s in geology then. And then Chinese language, because he thought China was going to open up at any moment.

I always wanted to be a journalist, but after I got to Brown journalism went out the window. Freshman week it was made very clear that you went to law school or you went to medical school. At that time, business school hardly existed as an alternative. So I became a political science major and prepared for law school.

It was a very militant time and, even though black students were in Ivy League schools, we still were very segregated. We found ways to survive. Getting away, to me, was the way to survive. I went to Asia when I was a junior to study Chinese ideology. I went to Thailand, Indonesia, Malaysia, Singapore. I wanted to go to China, but China was closed at the time.

When I went to Indonesia, my father was working in a community re-development center in Washington, D.C., and a guy who worked with him knew someone in Indonesia. He was a military attaché. Anyway, he hooked up some studies for me with Pretemina, which is a national oil company in Indonesia. So while my classmates were going to rice villages and studying family life, I was being flown around by this oil company, and they were showing me their community development projects. My father was always really good at finding contacts and doing whatever you needed to make the most of a situation.

In my senior year at Brown, I had already applied to law school when I decided I really didn't want to go. I think I just saw the rest of my life passing before my face, and it was kind of boring. I was thinking, "Why am I doing this? Because someone told me freshman week, this is what you do to be successful?"

I really wanted to be a fashion designer. I decided that, instead of Brown, I should have gone to the Rhode Island School of Design and gotten the right education. I remember calling home and saying, "Dad, I think I'm going to take some time off, and I'm going to apply to design schools. You know, I don't think law school's really for me." He went ballistic. He said, "You do that, and when you go to law school you'll pay for it. Or you'll go next year, and I'll pay for it."

I had a boyfriend who went to UCLA Law School, so I decided that if I had to go to law school, I wanted to go to law school in California. But I had a dean who, at the last minute, said to me, "Your grades are good, you really need to apply to Harvard or Yale." Yale had rejected me as an undergrad, so I rejected the idea of applying there. I applied to Harvard, but I remember crying because I knew if I got in, I was going to have to go because it was the best school—and because of my dad. In fact, I never even told my dad that I applied, because I assumed I'd get added pressure. Once I got in and made the decision myself, I called him and said, "I'm going to Harvard." He was surprised and he was thrilled.

He and my mom had divorced by that time. She was the type to say, "Whatever you do is okay. I just love you." She was always with you no matter what. She always supported you, but she didn't really push. The first time I took the bar exam I didn't pass. I remember telling my mother, and she said, "Oh, you know, Baby, that's okay." I remember telling my father and he was not so understanding. In fact, he wouldn't accept it. He really just thought, no, this is not possible. So I appealed it, and I passed on appeal.

I hated law school. All I wanted to talk about was saving the world. Everybody else wanted to talk about making money. And people who talked about making money made me very uncomfortable. In fact, after my first year, I applied to the Kennedy School [of Government] and then went there and did a joint degree. That's really the only reason I made it through. It sort of got me out of my classes, where we were all going to be corporate lawyers.

Did I ever consider walking away from it? No. It just wasn't done. The way I was raised, you don't give up. You just get through it, and then try to figure out what you want to do. One of the things that kept me going through the dark times at school—and those were dark times—was knowing I had enough credentials that I would always have something to fall back on. I decided I was going to go to the Securities and Exchange Commission where I could do government and do good. But then one of my instructors, who was a judge, told me at the last minute about a clerkship opportunity with another judge. So I put the SEC on hold. It was another one of those things that I just believed you should do.

In 1980, while I was clerking, Ronald Reagan won the presidency, and my dream of a government career went out the window. He put a freeze on hiring—and I didn't want to serve in the Reagan administration anyway—so, at that point I thought, "I need a big firm where I can go hide out until the Democrats come back." Little did I know that it would be 12 years before they would be back.

The law firm of Steptoe & Johnson sort of reminded me of Brown. It had a good reputation, the people were nice. So I went there and started doing regulatory law. I did some oil and gas, some transportation. And then all of a sudden I found communications and found I really liked that industry although my feelings about law firm life were more mixed. So here I was, this corporate lawyer that I never wanted to be. The question was, how long are you going to stay?

There were female issues. There were black issues. You had to dress a certain way. You had to act a certain way. I never really found a mentor. I never felt I had any insight into the real workings of the firm. But I made good friends there. And, there were 12 of us [African Americans] so we had a support system.

My father got a kick out of coming to visit me at this 200-person law firm. I had some clients I really enjoyed working with, like BET, and I learned a lot. But I saw the black partners struggling even after they had supposedly made it. At your fifth year you really have to make up your mind: Are you going to stay and go for partnership, or are you moving on? If so, to what?

I got good reviews all the way up to my fifth year, and then, all of a sudden I was not getting the right signals for the partnership track. I was a little bit angry, but I was more disappointed. You know, rejection of any sort is tough. I remember talking to the partner I worked for, saying, "How did this happen?" I had been sort of going with the flow. But finding myself in that position just confirmed what I knew about firms all along: That it was a tough battle and if you wanted to be a partner there were sacrifices that you had to make that I wasn't willing to make in terms of life style.

I think that if I had said, "This is what I really want to do. I'm going to kill myself for the next two years to get it . . . " I probably would have had a shot at it. But there were so many other things I was interested in. I just wasn't ready to have tunnel vision.

For someone who's as goal oriented as I am, it was somewhat of a failure. But I don't think I considered it a failure on my part. It was a failure of what I wanted and what the firm wanted not coming together. So I recovered quickly, and it was probably the best thing that happened to me. I needed to get out of the holding pattern. Right about this time I had lunch with Bob Johnson.

I was working on the [BET] cable franchises deal for Bob and we were at a hearing one day, and he said let's go have lunch. In the middle of lunch, he said, "Would you consider coming over as general counsel?" All of a sudden it was the perfect job. It was an entertainment company. It was cable. It was an easy decision. But I said, "I'll think about it. Let me know when you're ready." This was December, and then I didn't hear from him.

Months went by and I was getting anxious. I remember talking to my husband about it and he said, "You should call him." So, after agonizing about it, I did, and we set up a meeting. I remember climbing the steps to the three-story townhouse where all the offices were. I knew a lot of people who worked there because I had been doing legal work for them. I thought, I know they're all wondering what I'm doing here: I'm here looking for a job.

I went in to Bob and said, "You know, a couple of months ago you mentioned a job. I'm very interested, and I'm ready to leave Steptoe. What's the status?"

He said, "Well, we've had some personnel changes here. But I have an office right downstairs for you, and if you're ready, just give me a date."

At the time, Bob had just started making money. He had 80 employees, one office, one cable network, and people were saying that cable wouldn't last. There was a lot of risk. But after talking to him, it clearly seemed like a risk worth taking. So we worked it out. In April I started.

I was real hesitant about telling my dad. When I said I was going to work at a cable programming network, he said, "*What?*" They didn't even have cable in D.C. I remember people at Steptoe saying, "You're going *where?*" But, you know what I said to myself through this time? I've done everything the establishment has told me to do and everything that was expected of me. I've done the Harvard thing. I did the clerkship. I did the big law firm. Now it's time to take a risk for myself, which is something I am really excited about, and see what happens. It was scary, but it felt so good.

The fact that it was a black company, was a huge "Yes" button for me. When I grew up, Motown and *Ebony* and *Soul Train* were just it! To think there was something else called BET, which was similar, was very exciting.

The first thing you always look at is whether it's well run. And it was. It was also profitable, and it had the potential for great success. Mind you, I never defined success as what we are today.

It was the first job I accepted that I really didn't look at as a stepping stone. I just assumed I'd be here forever. Not only did I have an opportunity, but I thought I could contribute to the management team. They were all my age, and they'd never had a lawyer [inhouse]. So I thought I'd have something to add to the mix. Beyond that, I didn't really think about it. I just took it one year at a time.

But we started growing at such an incredible pace that it's been more than I could ever imagine in terms of opportunity and growth. After a few years in the legal department, I began doing more business deals. Then I was given the assignment of building our first studio. I left to have a baby, and I came back and, in 1991, Bob decided to go public. So, all of a sudden we were the first African American company to go public on the New York Stock Exchange. And four years ago I became president.

That was a whole new challenge. There were six of us [in senior management], most were men. We all reported to Bob. He liked that. A lot of them I considered friends. They were no longer friends when they had to report to me. So, on a personal level it was tough. But it made me stronger. I learned a lot about management, and all of a sudden that was my career path. All of a sudden I *was* management.

I finally got rid of the lawyer thing—I had been trying to do that for years. But the transition from lawyer to business person/entrepreneur was tough. I don't think I had a lot of expectations for what it would be like. It took me awhile to set my own agenda and set my own style, and really start running the company.

When you're a lawyer you're trained to listen to both sides. At first,

I found myself in staff meetings saying, "Okay, what do you think? Now, what do *you* think? Okay, I'm going to think about it and I'll get back to you guys." I found out very early that didn't work. If there are two sides, listen, but you have to make decisions, and keep moving. Sometimes Bob would even say to me, "Think like a business person; make a decision."

I was reading management books and management theory and thinking a lot about women in management, because I really think women manage differently. I had to learn how to be direct and forceful and not leave wiggle room.

When people ask me about being one of the most powerful women in corporate America, I don't feel that way from day to day. I'm running a company, and the goals and the report card are very clear. I can look at market valuations, I can look at earnings per share, I have a hundred ways to measure how I'm doing. So I'm focused on that, and on motivating people. I realize there is some power associated with what I do. But I just do on a day-to-day basis what I think is best for the company. That's my job. The power doesn't depress me, and it's not what motivates me. What motivates me is the future of the company. This is a company I've always cared about, and I like taking it to the next phase. It was already a very successful company, but we're now a two-billion-dollar company. I was intent on proving that I could do that.

I always wanted to be successful, but to be wealthy was never a goal I had. I mean, my dad lived paycheck to paycheck. He wasn't concerned about leaving wealth to his children. He gave us the best education possible, and then said, "You guys go do it yourself." I think that was the way a lot of black parents thought. My mother's the same way. So I wasn't really raised to consider wealth.

When I started making six figures, I thought that was the end-all. I remember when I told Judge Parker—the judge I clerked for—that I was going to Steptoe. He said, "Well, how much will you make?" I said, "I'm making $42,000 a year." Another judge was coming into the office and Judge Parker looked up and said, "Judge Bryant, she's going to make $42,000 a year. She's just a little girl. That's too much money for her." They really got a kick out of it, but I remember thinking, *That is a lot of money!*

Around the time Bob offered me the job at BET, he asked me, "How much money do you think you ever want to make?"

I said, "A million dollars would be good."

He said, "Only a million?"

Now, having gotten to a point where I don't have to worry about money, and thinking about passing on wealth to my children and my grandchildren, wealth is something that I think more black families should think about. But it has to be in a realistic way. It has to be as part of building something. You know, it's nice that NBA players and entertainers make a lot of money, but if that's what kids are talking about when they want to be a millionaire, that is just not realistic. There are so few people who get there. And there are just so many other opportunities in the business world. That's one thing I've always respected *Black Enterprise* for, is being a mirror to that world of who's doing it and how you get there.

I gave a speech to black students at Harvard recently, and I told them, "Every one of you should have a dot-com proposal in your briefcase." We're living in a crazy world today. White kids are out there becoming millionaires—billionaires—with these things every other day. That's what we need to be doing.

That's the kind of wealth generation that black kids really should acquire. They should want to be owners. They should want to work at companies where they get stock options. They should demand that they're paid a decent salary, and that there's some equity involved. I think we've just been shut out of that process for so long, it's not something we're used to going after.

When BET went public in 1991, I remember we went out to dinner with all of the senior staff members, and we had two or three of them saying, "Oh, we shouldn't go public. People are going to tell us what to do." It just never dawned on them that this is the American way. This is how you make money. Some of them just didn't realize that with their stock options and the value of the company, they—and others in the company—would make more money than they ever imagined. Even among those who did realize, that wasn't the issue. They were afraid that we would lose this black-owned business that we had built.

I knew it was a new era for the company, and it was going to take a lot of work. The two years after that, we killed ourselves just getting used to quarterly reports and other public obligations. It was the pits. But it was worth it.

The hardest time was when we went private. That was a very difficult process that put me between Bob and Liberty, who were buying the company, and the shareholders, investment bankers, and lawyers on the sell side. I had to run a company every day without thought of this deal in the background. Bob and Liberty were trying to buy the company at what they considered a reasonable price. The shareholders and bankers wanted the highest price. I had to leave my lawyer training behind. It was easy to worry about the legal implications of everything we did, because either side could argue that the other side was trying to impact the price or do something questionable. There was such a tug of war going on and I was in the middle, trying to be the mediator and trying to keep the company going. Finally, I had to just stop worrying and leave it to the general counsel and the slew of lawyers or I wouldn't have made it through. It was the worst year I ever spent at BET.

It was finally over on July 30, 1998. We had a shareholders meeting and they voted to approve the price we had agreed on. Instead of celebrating, I had to go up to New York to be with the lawyers because they needed a business person there to finish negotiating with the bank to get the $600 million that we needed to pay off the shareholders. I planned to come back that night, but I missed the 10 o'clock flight, so I ended up staying in New York another day.

This was a time when I should have been happy. This horrible year was over. The deal was finally done. All of a sudden I was very wealthy. The price was 50 percent higher than we thought it was going to be and the company was going to give me a huge check the next day for more money than I thought I'd ever have.

I got back to the office the next day, and learned that my father had died. It sort of just took the air out of everything. He'd been sick for a long time. He had Altzheimer's, but it was still a shock. At a time when the worst was over, and there should have been celebration, to have something like that happen just put it all in perspective. I experienced one of my greatest successes in business that week, but I always think back on it as a low point. I had surpassed my wildest dreams profession-ally, but my father—who would just have loved this—was gone.

There have been other times when the good going on in my per-sonal life has helped to balance the difficulties of business. That balance is important. Keeping that sense of perspective is important. BET has be-come so much a part of me that my job and my life are all tied up to-gether now. But I do have both. Some people don't. And sometimes it's hard to juggle. But having both, for me, is important.

CHAPTER ELEVEN

Spike Lee

CEO, Forty Acres and a Mule Filmworks

He burst on the scene with his first hit film, *She's Gotta Have It*, and was immediately labeled as a maverick and a marvel, among other things. Since then, Spike Lee has picqued critics' interests and pricked their sensibilities with virtually all the 15 films he's made to date. He has also grown firmer in his resolve to stay true to his own style, his own vision, his own talent, his own self, which has led to his being solidly established in a business that's built on veritable quicksand. At the same time, he remains distinctly un-Establishment.

In recent years, Lee has added credits as an author, producer, husband, and father (of two) to his resume, the latter role inspiring him to star in his own Sesame Street spoof, entitled, *Summer of Snuffy* (a takeoff on his controversial 1999 film, *Summer of Sam*). He has also made a name for himself as the New York Knicks most faithful (and visible) fan.

At 43, Lee remains as passionate about his work—past, present, and future—as ever, but he is less inclined than he used to be to defend it. "I'm not going to write my own epitaph," he says, smiling, when asked about his legacy. "Whatever they come up with will be derived from the work. Of course, they haven't done the greatest job of that so far, but it's always different when you're dead."

*F*rom the very beginning, I wanted to be about building a body of work. I didn't want to be one of these one-hit wonders, a flash-in-the-pan. I wanted to build a considerable body of work. So from the very beginning I was looking at the overall picture, at the long view. And I wanted to be here down the line.

In film school, I noticed that a lot of the generation of black independent filmmakers ahead of me—people like Charles Burnett, Larry Clark, Julie Dash—who all did very good, monumental work, it took them sometimes three, four, five years between films. And the majority of those films never got theatrical distribution. They were played in black film festivals and screenings at discos around New York and libraries and places like that. I admired them and the work, but I said I just have to take it up to another level. I don't want to make a film and have one print, and travel all over the world with one print under my arm. I have to try to get it out there more so people can see it.

I always visualized myself being successful at making films. If I couldn't have done this, I don't know what I would have done. I never even thought about it. I never thought, what if this doesn't happen, what else could I do? I didn't want to be a filmmaker until my sophomore year in college. But once I knew that's what I wanted to do, I was going to make it happen. There was no other choice.

I believe in destiny. But I also believe that you can't just sit back and let destiny happen. [The former major-league baseball manager] Branch Rickey had a famous saying: Luck is the residue of design. A lot of times, an opportunity might fall into your lap, but you have to be ready for that opportunity. You can't sit there waiting on it. A lot of times you have to get out there and make it happen.

I have always been driven in that way, but there wasn't a lot of evidence of that early on. My mother, Jacqueline Lee, was the one who pushed me and my sister and brothers. My father had expectations for us, but his way was the hands off, natural way. His philosophy was, let them do whatever they want and somehow they'll do the right thing. So my mother had to be the bad cop, the enforcer.

All of us were expected to excel. I remember, if I came home with a B, she'd say, "Well, I bet a lot of those Jewish kids are bringing home A's."

Like a lot of kids who grew up in New York whose grandparents lived down South, my parents shipped us down South to get rid of us for the summer. I would write them letters, and my mother would send my letters back corrected in red. The papers looked so red that you would think there was blood on them. She always used to call me functionally illiterate.

So very early on it was instilled that we couldn't just be as good as our fellow white classmates. We had to be three, four, five times better if we really wanted to get ahead and make a way. And she did a great job of explaining that it is not fair, it's not right, but that's the way it is.

My father went to Morehouse, my grandfather went to Morehouse, and my mother and grandmother went to Spelman. Since I was the first born, it was expected that I go to Morehouse, and I had no problem with that. It was just a great feeling being in an environment in which all your classmates and all your teachers were African Americans. And it wasn't just Morehouse. It was being part of the whole Atlanta University Center—Spelman and Clark and Morris Brown. It was just a great time and it definitely changed me.

That's where I got a lot of my nurturing and that's where I decided what I wanted to do with the rest of my life.

My family was 100 percent supportive of my wanting to be a filmmaker because we were raised in a very artistic household. My father was a jazz musician and composer. We grew up going to see him play at the Newport Jazz Festival, and the Bitter End in New York. His attitude was, if that's what you want to do, go ahead and do it. My mother taught art and black literature, so she was taking me and my siblings to museums and Broadway shows and stuff like that at an early age. So we were very lucky. We were just brought up in a family where art was always pushed.

I'm also lucky that not just my parents, but my grandparents, had the same attitude. Because I have a lot of friends who graduated with me from Morehouse in the class of 1979, and today, a lot of these guys are old, fat, and bald, and they're miserable because they're doing something that they don't like.

It was my experience in school that a whole lot of people were taking majors in things that they didn't want, but they were told to take [them] because they were expected to make money. Even [my wife] Tonya, from a very early age, she knew from her parents that she had to go to law school or med school. So she went to law school. For a lot of people art is just really discouraged. Especially in schools like Morehouse, which is a very strong business-oriented school.

But at Morehouse a lot of these kids were either the first or second ones in their family to ever go to college and at great sacrifice. So it's like, "Look, your mother and I did not work two jobs and spend all this money to send your black ass through college so that you could be a singer or a poet or a painter. Your ass needs to get a job where you're going to be getting a check every two weeks."

I understand that. I really do. But I still think that it makes for a lot of miserable people, especially people who have creativity. And I'm just happy my parents weren't like that.

There are people who are doing whatever they're doing for money. And you have people doing what they're doing for love. For me, it's always been the latter. I never equated my being successful with money, because that's not why I became a filmmaker.

I became a filmmaker because I wanted to tell stories and, when you break it down, that's what directors do—the good ones, at least—they tell stories. That's what I wanted to do, and I wanted to be in control of my work. So that meant that I would produce it, I would write it, and I would direct it. That was success to me.

That's not to say that I don't like to make an income from some of my stuff. But that was never the sole purpose, to be famous or be so-called wealthy. All that stuff is a byproduct.

I think those [motives] matter when you do become successful because it has to do with being grounded. If you're well grounded before you become successful, for the most part—unless you lose your mind, like all those people on VH-1 *Behind the Music*—you're going to continue to be like that. And then, also, I think this is where your partner in life—your girlfriend, your wife, or your siblings, or close friends, the people you surround yourself with—that's what they're there for, to kind of give you some levity.

I was not self-guided. Anytime I came to two forks in the road, people or events or spirits or forces pointed me in the right direction. Whenever I could have gone this way or that way, I always managed somehow to get pushed, prodded, or pulled the right way.

So you have to have people you respect and listen to. But it's important *who* you listen to. I don't listen to the Academy [of Motion Picture Arts and Sciences]. I listen to people I trust and work with, and Tonya. She's very smart and very sensitive. Those are the qualities I admire in people, but I put a premium on intelligence. She's the first one who reads, as soon as I finish a script. Whenever I'm thinking about doing something, she's the first one I tell. Everybody has peers and people they respect. You have to listen to *those* people, not to the hype and not to the people who just don't know.

There's no school you can go to to help you know how to handle success or fame. And some of it is definitely hard to deal with. The media just concocted this Spike Lee persona of who I am: angry black man, anti-Semitic, racist. People are very susceptible to that. I've had people come up to me in the street, and say, "You know, I was going to see your film, but you're a racist." These are people who don't know me and have probably never seen my films. But because of something they've read, they feel they know me, they feel that's who I am.

But it's something, with experience, that you just have to get used to. You get tired of explaining stuff. And I'm beyond the point where I use anger as a motivation. I just say [to myself], "They don't know," and let my work speak for itself.

If I wasn't who I am I wouldn't be sitting courtside at Knicks games. They don't give those tickets to anybody. You gotta pay for them and, even if you got the money, they want [people with] visibility. So, [fame] has more upside than downside. But so many people mess up, because they just get overwhelmed by this side of it. You just gotta be ready for it and you gotta be real.

The only thing that's kept me straight so far is my upbringing, my relatives, just common sense, hard work, and luck. Luck is a big part of it. A big thing, also, is that I don't get high. I've never, ever smoked a joint in my life. The idea that getting high will enhance your creativity, your art, that's bogus. It almost destroyed my father.

Success changes everybody—it made me more cynical—but it's not world altering. You are who you are. You need to be who you are, whatever happens. And you need to stay focused on what you're doing and why you're doing it. That might mean putting off some things that you want. I always wanted a family, but I wanted to be established first. Because I knew that in order to make it in films I had to be totally focused and committed to that.

I knew I had made it when *She's Gotta Have It* was a success. It just exploded! When the film opened it was only playing in one theater in

America for like a three-week period. The theater got torn down, but it was on 66th and Broadway. In August, after we came back from Cannes, I mean that was the hottest spot in New York.

My friends and I would go out there and just watch the lines wrap around the block. People were having a good time just waiting in line. And we were handing out buttons, selling "Please Baby Baby Please" T-shirts and stuff like that. It was a lot of fun.

I always envisioned that film being successful. I knew the script was good and that we would be filling a void. We were completely confident about the material. The struggle was, where were we going to get the money to make the film?

There were many times when I thought *She's Gotta Have It* wouldn't get made. That's a film that got willed to life. We pushed an elephant up a mountain and down the other side to get that film made.

The biggest misconception about success is, I think, mostly in the minds of young people. Young people expect everything now to be instant gratification, like popcorn in the microwave. Just put it in, press the button: Boom! You're a success. No. It doesn't work like that. I've always believed, and always will believe, there's no substitute for good old elbow grease. You got to roll your sleeves up, get out there, and do the work. And you got to want to win.

I hate to lose. I mean, *I hate to lose.* I think that's good and it's bad, because you can't win all the time.

Before *She's Gotta Have It*, I tried to get this film made called *The Messenger*. It was a total fiasco. The money never came through and my name was mud. People had been working on the film in preproduction for weeks, and nobody got paid. It was terrible. It was probably the biggest screw-up of my career.

It wasn't a good script, but that wasn't the reason why it wasn't made. It was too ambitious. I had helicopter chases and car chases, people jumping off roofs, and I did not have the money for stunts like that. And even if I did have the money, you have to know how to shoot that stuff. I didn't have the technical capability to do the stuff that was required on that film, and I didn't have the experience working with actors.

But I didn't see any of that. I just kept hoping against hope, and wishing on a star, as Rose Royce sang, that somehow this money was going to come through. And it was obvious that this thing was not going to work out. So, I failed because the film didn't get done. But it was heaven sent that that film never got made. That was the best thing that could've happened, because I learned not to overextend myself. In fact, if that film had been made, it could have destroyed my film career, period.

That has happened to me a lot—I'm working on something and for some reason it doesn't happen. I'm upset about it. But then I remember what happened to *The Messenger*, and say, "Well, it wasn't meant to be." And more often than not, it works out that I'm glad I didn't do it. That's not to say that it should be easy. In filmmaking, it's *never* easy. Unless you're [Steven] Spielberg, [George] Lucas, or a couple of other people, it's very hard to get a film made, no matter what color you are.

The second misconception about success is that the work gets easier. It's really just the opposite: It gets harder.

This last film we just finished, *Bamboozled*, is starring Damon Wayans, Savion Glover, Tommy Davis, Jada Pinkett, and Michael Rappaport. Everybody in Hollywood turned this film down except New Line [Cinema]. People thought it was too expensive, and they were scared of the subject matter. It's a satire concerning modern-day television. There were many times we thought, "Oh, man, there's no way we're gettin' this film done." But we just kept pushin' and pushin' and pushin'.

Even at New Line, at first, they weren't feeling it. They wanted to make it, but they only wanted to make it at a certain price. So to do this film, everybody took a cut: I did, the actors did. Nobody was building a wing or putting up a tennis court or a swimming pool on this film. But what's great is everybody had to sacrifice, but it didn't affect the product. We were very fortunate. Everybody was working in concert on the film, so it was a great feeling.

I'm 42. I expect to be doing this until I die. I'm not going to be making a film a year when I'm 80. But so far, I've done 14 films in 15 years. It's not just about quantity, it's about creating a body of work that will stand the test of time.

Most filmmakers don't gauge whether their films are a success or not solely on box office. When you're writing a script or reading one, you have a picture of that film in your mind so you can tell when it's done how successful you were by the transfer of that picture that you had in your mind to the screen. That is very hard to do.

I go back periodically and look at my films (everything except *She's Gotta Have It*. I don't like the look of it. I'm not embarrassed by it, but I see all the flaws and mistakes). When I do look, I look for growth, and I look just to remember what it took to get the different pieces of it done.

What drives me is the quest to get better, to be a better storyteller, to find different ways to tell stories. The drive is just to grow, and to learn. I teach at NYU film school now and I get nothing but positive out of that, especially with people who really want to learn. The thing about learning is that you have to be open to it. You can't just think that because a person is younger than you or less experienced than you, that you have nothing to learn from them. You can learn from anything. I'm learning all the time.

So, if you want to be successful at anything, I think you have to be learning all the time. And growing. And putting in the work and the time. And, no matter what you want to do, you gotta be able to write. Jacqueline Lee taught me that a long time ago.

CHAPTER TWELVE

George R. Lewis

President and CEO, Philip Morris Capital Corporation

Like every sharp finance expert, George Lewis is a person of exacting standards who always looks for growth, not just in assets or capital, but in himself.

A true pioneer, Lewis was on the front lines of African Americans entering corporations. The Virginia native snagged a job as a product analyst with General Foods Corporation in 1963, and he hasn't stopped defying the odds since. Early on, he boldly set his sights on a senior management position in finance.

For a black man to have such ambitions in the early 1970s seemed like more than a pipe dream, but Lewis made it happen at Philip Morris, the company he joined in 1967. Under his leadership since 1997, Philip Morris Capital Corporation, the $7 billion financial services arm of the world's largest consumer packaged goods company, has shown impressive growth.

In recognition of Lewis' leadership and outstanding performance, he was named a member of Philip Morris' Corporate Management Committee in 1999. As uncompromising in his ambition as ever, Lewis, 59, says, "I never viewed failure as an option. I always had a plan." Lewis is married, and has two grown daughters and two grandchildren.

I have always believed, even in my days at Hampton University, that the one who has economic power has the advantage.

As long as I can remember, I have had a passion for numbers, especially numbers relating to money. Therefore, it was no surprise to my parents when I announced that I was not going to be a doctor, or a lawyer, or a teacher. I was going to major in accounting and pursue a career in finance. Recognizing that, at the time, there were very few African Americans who had succeeded in that area because the field had not yet opened up to us, their only concern was about my ability to earn a decent living doing this kind of work.

I thought I would start out in government and get some experience and then hang out my own shingle. But just about this time, Fortune 500 companies began recruiting at Hampton.

Sun Oil Company was one of the first corporations to recruit and hire a Hampton finance and accounting major. This was in 1962. The following year, my senior year, Sun was joined by General Foods, Mobil, DuPont and several other companies that were actively recruiting on campus. I interviewed with them all and received follow-up interviews at the headquarters of three corporations.

The old adage that luck is preparation meeting opportunity proved true for me. Had I been in the Class of 1960, or even 1961 instead of 1963, my story might have been a very different one. It seemed, as I went off to these interviews, full of optimism and ambition, that I was in the right place at the right time.

On the day that I received the offer from General Foods, I had spent hours interviewing for a cost accountant position in their Jell-O division. The day dragged on and, with it, some of the fire and optimism I had walked in the door with that morning, had started to wane. I was sitting outside the personnel office, wondering what the outcome would be when this black woman who was walking by stopped and asked me who I was and why I was there.

I told her and she said, "Wait here a moment." She was back in a minute, armed with a finance test, which was a normal part of the process for positions in accounting. After I took the test, she introduced me to the vice president of personnel, who then introduced me to the controller and the accounting manager.

By the end of the day I had an offer from the Kool-Aid division. The position was sales accountant, and it paid $100 a week, $5,200 a year. When I told my parents they said, "Well, we don't blame you for not wanting to go to medical school." I felt great. I will always be indebted to this lady; her name is Eileen Johnson. She took the time to help me. Because of her, I got a break.

My first day of work at General Foods was exciting and scary at the same time. You just didn't know what to expect. My co-workers were not exactly the welcome wagon. I was among the first African Americans working at a professional level in an operating division of the company (by the end of that summer there were others), so, it was very lonely.

I decided that I would just buckle down. I would be the first in, and the last out. I would just do my very best. Eventually, people started to notice that I was a hard worker. They started to notice that when I gave them something, they didn't have to check or double-check it, it was thorough.

My efforts were rewarded. Over the next two years, I got a series of promotions from accountant to profit planning analyst to senior planning analyst. I started to look around and evaluate who were the winners and who were the losers. By this time, African Americans had started to come into the rest of the company, but we weren't represented in Maxwell House, and Maxwell House was the place that groomed senior executives.

I have always been a planner, so, I developed a short-term plan and a long-term plan. The short-term plan was to get an MBA. My long-term plan was to become a senior corporate executive.

I started pursuing my MBA at New York University at night. The classes met in downtown Manhattan near Wall Street. My office was in White Plains, an hour away. My workday consisted of long hours, my wife and I had just had our first baby, the trek to lower Manhattan became harder and harder. Then I heard that Iona College, 10 minutes away, was starting an MBA program. The decision to transfer was an easy one.

I was on my way. I knew I had to continue to be creative. I had to do things that made me stand out from the crowd, things that would make people stand up and take notice.

I was hoping to move into the Maxwell House division. I tried to get a mentor, but things did not work out. I kept asking people about

Maxwell House and they kept saying that it just wasn't the thing for me. I always believed, because of what I learned from my mother and father, that the harder you worked, the more you would succeed. Well, it does take hard work to succeed, but that is not enough. It also takes knowing the corporate culture, having great communication skills, and having at least a little luck.

When I realized that things were not going to go my way, I was disappointed but still confident. After all, I was only 25 years old, and I knew I had the ability to make it to the top echelon of corporate America. If I didn't believe that, I wouldn't have been able to do it. Every time I would run into a wall I would come at it again from a different angle.

Why did I even want it? My own competitiveness; I love winning. I also wanted to prove to my parents, my wife, and friends who had faith in me that their faith was well placed. Of course, I also felt, and still feel, an obligation as an African American to pave the way for others.

I decided to look for opportunities at other corporations. By this time corporate America had opened its doors much wider to African Americans. Black-owned search firms were even beginning to spring up. We were in demand, so to speak.

Charlie Fields had a search firm at that time. His was one of the few African American firms that recruited for positions beyond entry level. I had a talk with him, told him what I was interested in. He called me back about two months later and said, "You have to go to W.R. Grace. Peter Grace, the Chairman and CEO, is looking for some people for his financial staff." I took the job earning $10,500—big time—while still working on my MBA. This job dealt with strategic business issues, as well as analytical work.

It was a close-knit group. Since we were all dealing with Peter Grace, CEO, there was genuine respect and appreciation among us. We were all in the same boat. We worked together on projects, we went out to lunch and dinner. It was my real first exposure to being with whites on a social basis and feeling like part of a real team.

Call it paranoia, but I never allowed myself to believe that my white co-workers accepted me as one of them. My paranoia is not completely unfounded. By this time I had had experiences that shaped my feelings. Nevertheless, being at Grace gave me the opportunity, at a very early age, to see how [white] people thought and behaved in business circles.

We had some good times together, and I worked on some very interesting projects.

My experience at Grace reinforced my view that success depends largely on being in the right spot at the right time. The closer you get to the top, the better your chances are for getting a sponsor to look out for you.

Although my experience at Grace was valuable, I soon realized it was not going to get me to my goals. In leaving, I looked around for corporations that had a good track record for hiring minorities. I learned that Philip Morris was one of the first companies to integrate the manufacturing facilities in the South and, being from Virginia, I was very much aware of the name Philip Morris.

So, I wrote a letter to the vice president of personnel and got an interview. When I went in to see him, he said, "We can give you a job in accounts receivable." I said, "Let me tell you what I want."

"I know Philip Morris is diversified already"—because at that time they had a chewing gum company, a razor blade company and, of course, cigarettes—"but at some point in time, you're going to have to diversify even more. Planning mergers and acquisitions is an exciting area of your business. That's what I'd like to do."

He said, "Let me see what I can do." Within a week, he called and had me back for another interview. I was hired as a planning analyst in the planning department, a high-level think-tank group. Our mission was to come up with the types of businesses that would mesh well with Philip Morris, identify existing companies in that sector, and, ultimately, buy those that made sense.

By working on these projects, I was constantly in and out of the offices of the president, the CEO, and all of the senior managers. I developed some very good relationships there.

I got to know the CEO at the time, the president, and the executive vice president. And after three years, we began discussions about my career aspirations. I told them I was interested in achieving a senior financial position. A plan was implemented. Shortly [thereafter] I moved into the position of Manager of Investor Relations. I was 28 years old.

I thought the work was interesting. Investor relations gives you a view of how Wall Street looks at a company and what kind of information you give Wall Street to value a company.

Now, I'm on my plan. I'm a manager. After 18 months, I moved to the treasury area. I was named manager of financial services. Then I was elected assistant treasurer. I was on the fast track. Then I was offered a position in an operating company, Philip Morris Industrial.

Industrial was a flexible packaging company in Milwaukee. It was about a $400 million division. I was vice president of finance and planning. At 33 years old, I was one of the youngest vice presidents Philip Morris had ever appointed.

My wife, Lillian, and I did not want to move to Milwaukee, but we agreed that this was a great opportunity—too good to pass up. During my time there, the division grew and things were going well. But an assignment that I expected to last three or four years was becoming five, then six.

During that time, a close friend and I became partners in an automobile parts manufacturing company. I had always thought about starting my own business, and had tried once before with a cosmetics company when we lived in New Jersey. In truth, I was beginning to wonder when, or if, I would get back to Philip Morris in New York. I was feeling a career stall. However, just as it had in the past, the right opportunity came along just in time.

After seven years in Milwaukee, I was asked to go to 7-Up in St. Louis, which we owned at the time, as vice president of finance and a member of the management team working directly with the CEO. The carrot was too tempting to walk away from.

Eighteen months later, I was elected vice president and treasurer of Philip Morris Companies Inc. At the time (1984) the press reported that I was the first African American elected treasurer of a Fortune 100 company. I had responsibility for our worldwide treasury activities. We moved back to New York.

It is true that I have a good relationship with the chairman and CEO, as well as good relationships with our past CEOs. But, I never really looked at them as mentors. I saw them as people who were available to me and, when I really needed to talk with them, the door was always open. They got to know me because the deals I worked on brought us together. From that, they recognized that I did a good job. My doing a good job wasn't an accident. I have spent many long evenings making sure my i's were dotted and my t's were crossed.

There are many smart people in this world, and most of them don't get the shot. You can only get to this level by being creative, a bit bold, and somewhat political.

I was always active in trying to open doors for African Americans at Philip Morris, even when I was in Milwaukee. I would get on a plane and come into New York and talk to the CEO about the lack of minority retention and opportunity. We would propose programs and plans. They were not always popular, but I have been able to say what I believe.

There have been times during my career when co-workers have tried to undermine me. I have been fortunate; because of the support from higher management, I have prevailed. I come to the corporation to do a job; making friends is not my primary objective.

Nonetheless, slights from co-workers do affect you, they even hurt sometimes and, at times, I have gotten very angry. But you learn that you must let go or else the resentment and anger will immobilize you. When people do not want to deal with you because you're African American, you might tell them off, but then you move on. You move around them or you move through them. Just make sure that you keep moving.

If it hadn't been for my wife, Lillian, I would not have been able to make it. She was always very, very supportive. The road I was on was so lonely. I did not feel I could confide in my co-workers. She was the one who listened and understood my objectives. She was behind me no matter what. When times at work were tough, I'd go home, talk about it, cry, smile, and then come back in and resume the fight to move ahead.

She always felt that I should hang in, but she took the approach that if at any point I thought I had to walk away, I should. I had some touchy moments, but I stuck with it, and I'm glad I did.

My children were never interested in corporate America. I am not sorry about this. It's a tough environment, and it is exponentially more difficult if you are African American. Having said that, would I do it all over again? You bet I would.

More of our children are graduating from competitive schools. They have extensive opportunities for various work experiences. They are coming into the workplace a lot better prepared than my generation. But their high level of achievement and success sometimes makes reality more difficult for them to deal with. They are not accustomed to setbacks as we were. Therefore, some find it more of a challenge to cope with failure. To be successful in the long run, they must learn from failure and adversity, using all of their experiences—good and bad—to their benefit. They should not give up too quickly on the possibilities because there are wonderful opportunities our here for them.

I tell all of them to get some international experience. The world is coming closer together, and you've got to be able to understand the different cultures, different languages, different currencies, and the only way you can do it is to work in that environment. In the long run, people who get to the top are going to have to have some international exposure.

Another reason the international path is worth pursuing is that, in talking to people who have worked overseas, they don't seem to have as much difficulty dealing with the people there as they do here. I am in the midst of building a global financial service company for Philip Morris, and I have not had any problem in Europe or the rest of the world trying to set businesses up. It's been a much more level playing field. I am having a great time. I continue to work hard and they have pretty much left me alone to run this business the way I want to run it.

One day, I'm sitting at the desk and I get this phone call from the CEO of Philip Morris, and he said, "We're very pleased with what you're doing. I like your style. I like the way you're running the business. And as a result of that, I want you to come onto the corporate management committee of Philip Morris."

I was surprised. I felt good about it because it was recognition of the hard work of my organization. My contribution to Philip Morris has been reflected in the bottom line and also in the diversity of faces throughout the ranks today and, to me, that's been equally as important. I see the committee appointment as recognition of that too.

It's still lonely in many ways. As you move up in an organization it becomes lonely anyway, because the buck stops with you. Couple that with being African American, and it's going to always be a little bit isolated. But at least you have the financial resources to help you with your loneliness. You can go out with some friends to a golf course and just hit that little ball and forget everything else for a while.

Postscript
In 2001, George Lewis retired.

CHAPTER THIRTEEN

William M. Lewis, Jr.

Managing Director, Morgan Stanley Dean Witter & Co.

❖

If there is one trait that Bill Lewis possesses in abundance, it is loyalty. He remains a passionate supporter of both Andover, the prep school that shaped his teen years, and A Better Chance, the organization that enabled him to go there. He holds Harvard—where he received his bachelor's and MBA degrees—in the highest regard. But his enduring admiration for his employer, one of Wall Street's premier investment banking firms, is most palpable of all.

Rising through the ranks there during the high-flying 1980s, Lewis loved the do-or-die daily commitment required. It paid off. He was promoted to managing director in 1989, blazing a trail for African Americans in his firm and on Wall Street in general, where, even today, there are far too few black partners. Lewis is co-head of the firm's worldwide corporate finance department as well as a member of its Investment Banking Division Operating Committee.

Married, with four children, Lewis has a reputation for being impatient, hard driving, and no nonsense. But in response to the notion that he has the capacity to invoke fear in others, he smiles broadly. "My kids would fall out of their seats laughing at that one."

❖

My first real job was raking leaves at the convent in front of the house I grew up in. I started when I was in third or fourth grade, and did it for about four or five years. Every Saturday I would get up and sweep an area that was probably the equivalent of four city blocks. Everybody would be out playing, and I would be there, brushing leaves for probably an hour, hour and a half. I think I used to get 50 or 75 cents. But that to me was a *real* job.

I always liked that routine and the knowledge that I was going to get paid every Saturday morning. I was always a saver and, to me, that was just money in the bank. Even back then, I knew that I wanted a future very different from what I saw in inner city Richmond, Virginia. I was already hungry at [age] seven.

I was the oldest of three, and whatever we got involved in, whether it was school work or chores, the focus was on excellence. My father was a very, very demanding guy, and that worked well with me. He was not very communicative; he showed things through his actions. He would take our report cards to work, and he'd show people. We just knew that he was proud, and that we had to have great report cards for him to show off.

I was very self-guided and mature early on. I truly enjoyed academic work. I had a real thirst for knowledge. My mother said that when I was two or three years old, we'd be on the bus, and I'd start pointing out the alphabet on signs and yelling (I've always been very loud) at the top of my lungs. She would try and quiet me down, but somebody said to her once, "You're going to be real proud of him one day, don't try to quiet him." And she said from that point on she never, ever tried to muzzle me.

I made the decision that I wanted to go away to prep school when I was 13. A Better Chance in those days was a national program that sent kids to prep schools, and the guidance counselors in the junior high schools, particularly in the south, spent a lot of time trying to find kids that they thought would do well in prep school. At my junior high school a number of people had gone away to prep school, and our guidance counselor used to bring them back to parade them and tell us about prep school. It sounded great to me, just awesome.

First of all, it was a total immersion into learning and that was very appealing to me because I was getting to a point where I was going to try to have to balance all the different demands that would be put on a 14- or 15-year-old in the inner city. I had friends who are now dead, in jail, or strung out on drugs. My friends covered the full social spectrum and I had no problem moving back and forth. But I could see that as I got older, it was going to be more and more difficult to do that. Andover, to me, was going to be a great way to not have to think about balancing those pressures.

My parents never talked about an end game per se. They just talked about a process, a path, and I knew that if I just stayed on that path—if I did well academically—that would open up all kinds of opportunities for me.

In Richmond, the black people who had been successful were by and large school teachers, nurses, and some governmental bureaucrats in the city government. I raked their leaves and did errands for them. They had nice houses in beautiful neighborhoods, and they had well-spoken and well-dressed children. So, any of those people would have been perfectly acceptable in terms of whom I wanted to emulate.

At one point I thought I wanted to be a doctor; at one point I wanted to be an engineer. I never really knew what the end game was. But growing up in the ghetto of Richmond, it didn't really matter. Anything was going to be such a welcome change.

I had no reservations about going away to Andover. I've always been extremely confident. I've never felt uncomfortable in any setting. I had spent 14 years in the inner city and my view was I was going away to some cushy prep school in New England. I mean, what possibly could you have trepidations about?

It was great to be on this 500-acre campus without any responsibility except to do your work. I loved the whole experience. All the kids were different in a lot of ways and they all thought that their unique differences were really cool. There was this black kid from Cleveland who used to wear a hat about *that* big, which I'm sure was the style in Cleveland. And he used to wear these sneakers that came up to his *knees*. I had seen this look on Soul Train, but I'd never seen it in real life. And this guy is strutting around campus. I *know* that he thought *he was* cool.

I used to braid my hair, and I thought that was pretty cool. White guys used to wear jeans with holes in them. Everybody did things that they felt comfortable doing; and they thought that they were cool and everybody else was sort of *not* cool. I'm sure there was a lot less diversity than I'm making it sound like, but tolerance was an incredible part of the culture there.

The most obvious difference between me and the majority of the kids was material. All the white kids had expensive stereo systems. That was always the class symbol, if you will: stereo system, speakers, huge record collections, and money enough to go home for vacations. I didn't have any of that stuff, and I couldn't go home until Christmas. There'd be long weekends, Thanksgiving breaks, and I was always stuck on campus. So, there I was different. But it was okay. I just didn't dwell on what I didn't have.

I focused on what I had. I mean, as a child I wanted more than to be poor in Richmond, but it wasn't because I wasn't happy, or because I felt lesser than anyone else. I simply knew there was a lot more to be had, and so I was a striver. But I was always essentially comfortable with myself. I don't know where I got that quality from but I'm glad I've got it, because there's no end to that game of measuring yourself against others. You can right now have the best apartment in New York City, a nice country home, and golf memberships and there's always somebody who has more. I mean you can drive yourself crazy thinking about that. I've always focused on what I have, and I've always been happy with what I've had, even when it was next to nothing. So I never felt uncomfortable in the Andover environment or in any other environment.

Whatever differences existed among us at Andover, the common threads had to be confidence and intellect. I was academically talented. But I never ducked my shortcomings and I never minded hard work. When I got to Andover I aced my French classes, I aced my math classes, I aced my science and physics classes. But I didn't do well in the literature courses—that was the one thing in which we did not get good training in Richmond. I remember in a ninth grade midterm exam having to analyze Jack London's *Call of the Wild*. I just retold the story, and the teacher just ripped me apart. But I thought that was great, because I realized what I had to work on.

It wasn't until well into my junior year that I was acing papers on Shakespeare and the like. It took a lot of hard work. But I never ever doubted that I would get there.

To this day I get tickled because there were classmates of mine in that ninth grade English class who were so impressive. I can clearly remember them talking about things like metaphors and imagery, and I had no idea what they were talking about. Given my performance in that class, I'm sure some of them would be surprised at my success. So, nobody can predict what it's going to take to be successful or who's going to make it.

I would characterize my level of competitiveness as healthy. I want to win and I don't like losing, but my philosophy is what I've taught my kids from day one: I want to do my best. Once you've done your best—and only you know when you've done your best—that's it. If somebody's better than me, then good for him or her. You have to keep it in perspective.

When it was time to apply to college, I was going to go to [University of] Penn because I played lacrosse and the lacrosse coach recruited me. I also wanted to be a civil engineer and Penn had a school of civil engineering. And then two things happened. I saw a graph that showed lifetime earnings of an engineer versus lifetime earnings of a liberal arts major. And what you saw—and I imagine it's still true today—is that an engineer started out at a much higher salary, say $25,000, but the slope of that line was pretty flat, so that over the course of a career, you weren't making a lot more than $25,000. Liberal arts majors on the other hand started out a lot lower than $25,000, but for any number of reasons, they made a lot more money over the course of a lifetime.

The second thing was that my football coach made a comment to somebody else, which got back to me. It was a very simple comment and, quite frankly, it's the kind of simple thinking that I typically use to guide myself and most of the decisions I have to make. The guy said, "Bill Lewis has a full scholarship to go to Harvard. What's there to contemplate? Harvard is Harvard."

When that comment got back to me I realized that at age 17 or 18, I didn't really know what I was going to be. But what was critical at that point was taking the right path; and how could you go wrong, going to Harvard? That was the bottom line.

I'm pretty conservative when it comes to making big decisions. I'm not a gambler. I'm risk averse in lots of ways. I subscribe to a notion of maximizing option value. What will create the most options for you? That sort of guides me in every way I think about things, whether

I'm looking at what college I'm going to go to, what area I'm going to work in, or what kind of home I'm going to buy. Create options; don't limit them.

Bachelor's degree from Harvard: I could see endless options being created by going there. U. Penn: I saw the engineering option. MBA from Harvard: endless options. Ph.D. in Economics (which was my major): few options.

I got into Harvard Business School right out of college. But I hadn't really thought it through, so I asked them if I could take a year off. They said sure (they actually prefer that you do), and that's when I really started to sort out what I was going to do.

It was late in the process, so I asked Harvard to suggest some names of some places where I might still get a job. They suggested Morgan Stanley and three or four other companies.

My first trip ever to New York was when I was interviewing for Morgan Stanley. I interviewed in *navy blue shoes*. I had one pair of shoes—don't laugh—and my logic was that navy blue went with more things (remember, *option value*). Remember I talked about the guy with sneakers that came up to his knees? Well, I thought I was *cool*.

I never really compared Morgan Stanley to Andover, but it's a good comparison. The people were friendly and approachable; they weren't condescending. They were all over themselves to make me feel like a part of Morgan Stanley. And when I got here, I realized that it wasn't just a recruiting gimmick. By and large the people that I have known at this place over the past 21 years are good, sincere people who are focused on excellence. They are just high quality people.

Now, I'm no sort of naive knucklehead. I realize that we have all types at Morgan Stanley Dean Witter. But the culture is characterized by a very tolerant environment, very much like Andover.

When I joined Morgan Stanley, my Procter & Gamble offer was for $15,500, in Cincinnati; my Morgan Stanley offer was for $13,500 and it was in New York City. So, clearly, the Morgan Stanley offer was less attractive financially. But once again, just like I had done the long-term analysis of an engineering career, people had convinced me that investment banking could be very lucrative in a relatively short period of time.

What especially excited me, though, was the work that people were doing. I remember reading an article about Bob Greenhill who used to be here. He came across like a real maverick, and at age 22 I found that really exciting. I don't think I ever consciously said, "I'm going to do investment banking, I'm going to Morgan Stanley, I'm going to do [mergers and acquisitions], because there is an opportunity to make a lot of money." I just sort of knew, again, that I was creating options.

The investment banking business is unlike any other industry, with the possible exception of what we're currently seeing with the Internet startups. This business is not corporate at all. It's very much a day-to-day business. We don't work on five-year plans. This is very much an entrepreneurial business; every day you have to perform. People come and people go, strategies change. It's also a young person's business.

Most people realize that this business can create a fair amount of wealth in a short period of time. So, the end game very quickly becomes something other than money or wealth creation, because you can retire from this business pretty early on. When I rejoined Morgan Stanley out of business school in 1982 I wrote down on the back of an envelope, which I still have on file in my office, a set of goals that I wanted to attain over a period of time. That plan had me retiring from Morgan Stanley when I was 44. I was 26 years old when I wrote those goals down.

I wanted to make partner in eight years. And I wanted to be a partner for another 10 years, so I wanted to be at Morgan Stanley for 18 years. I then wanted to spend another 10 years doing something either very senior in a corporation or doing something entrepreneurial. So that was going to take me from 44 to 54. From 54 to 64 I really wanted to cut back on the corporate side and, if I had pursued path A (i.e., working in a corporation) when I was 44, then I definitely wanted to pursue the entrepreneurial route at 54. But in any event, I was going to be calling my own shots. And I wanted to make a meaningful commitment to the not-for-profit sector. I also wanted to carve out time for a significant contribution to philanthropy from 54 to 64, and travel.

I'm one year ahead of that schedule because I made partner in seven years instead of eight, so I'm sorting through what I want to do.

But here I am, 22 years later, still having a really good time.

I've been able to be a leader here, and that's a good thing because I'm not a good follower. Whenever you get the opportunity to lead, you should do it.

I'm very opinionated when it comes to choosing people for whatever endeavor. I look for people who have great judgment, and are very decisive. I like people who can say yes or no. If I ask, "What's the answer," and get, "Well, on the one hand . . . " it drives me crazy. Everybody has to process a lot of information, but we should be able to do that pretty quickly. Just make a decision and do not be afraid of being wrong. Everybody is going to be wrong. Our traders are wrong—hopefully less than 50 percent of the time—but they're wrong sometimes.

Many of the things that I have to make a call on aren't black or white. By the time they get to me, it's a judgment call, meaning there is no clear right or wrong. I make the call and if I'm wrong, hey, what can I say? I was wrong. Does it keep me awake at night? No. There probably are situations where I'd say, "God, if I had it to do all over again, I'd try to do things differently," but rarely in the execution of my business responsibilities.

I like clear thinkers, people who aren't afraid to articulate what's on their mind. I like people to get engaged and to have a point of view. I want to know where you're coming from. I let people know where I'm coming from. My job is to be very clear in my vision, where I want to take the department, where I want to take the area that I'm responsible for. And I want to know if you agree with that or disagree with that. If you disagree with that, that can be very helpful to me. But you've got to be very clear in terms of why you disagree with that.

I like people who bring solutions to the table; I've got no time for people who come in complaining, for people who are great at identifying problems. Any [business] school student can identify a problem in any business setting. What I really care about are people who are very thoughtful in coming up with solutions.

I like getting your perspective, I like getting advice, but I like being able to say, "Yeah, that's interesting, but no thanks." And that's the way I like to give advice. I'll say, "Here's what I'd do," but I don't force it because I've never liked people telling me what to do. Unless I think you are going to walk into a truck, you can choose not to take my advice. I'm not controlling in that regard.

People, at the end of the day, are going to make bad choices, they're going to make bad decisions, but they are not going to result in the world coming to an end. You can learn from them; that's my philosophy.

The thrills I've gotten have mostly been outside the workplace but it was very thrilling to get promoted early to partner. Every person here truly thinks that he or she is the best at what they do, so getting promoted to partner in seven years — five, maybe six, other people have ever done that here — is just confirmation of the fact that you're pretty good.

The other really big thrill of the job occurred during the 1980s, working on most of the high-profile hostile takeovers. That was where all the action was back then. I was young, so it wasn't like I was calling the shots, but I was out there working on just about all of them, and I enjoyed the ride. You worked around the clock, you never took vacations, you felt like you were in the Marines, and I loved it.

Do I think what I do is meaningful? What we do is very meaningful to our clients and we bend over backwards to give them the best advice and service. But look, this is a job; we're not out there trying to figure out a cure for AIDS or poverty.

I feel as if I'm doing a lot of meaningful things away from the workplace, and this job enables me to do that. I'm contributing in a major way to my family and to my extended family. Lately, I've been spending more time working with a lot of nonprofit organizations: A Better Chance, the National Urban League, the NAACP Legal Defense Fund, the Central Park Conservancy, the Studio Museum of Harlem, and others — and I really enjoy it. One theme that runs through a lot of my work is getting black people who can to give more back. We don't have a history of giving. We did not grow up just giving it away. We often didn't have it to give. But I know what some black people are making today, and when I solicit for a really worthwhile cause and get a $500 check from somebody who's making more than a million dollars, that is really disappointing.

I will not stop trying to get black people — those who can afford it — to write big checks and make meaningful contributions to worthwhile causes. It's important because, until we start doing it, we are very much perpetuating the whole notion that we're victims and that others need to take care of us.

In terms of what else is meaningful for me, I feel as if I'm really trailblazing for any number of African Americans who want to build a career in investment banking. And what I'm doing here may be meaningful for them.

Notwithstanding all the positive things I said and believe about Morgan Stanley and Andover, I still believe that our society at large looks at most things through a prism that doesn't reflect a lot of different colors, but sees everything as basically black and white, and I think it's getting worse and more intense.

[White] men often have lower expectations for people of color and, to a certain extent, for women. In this sort of environment, and maybe other environments, there's often the perception when a black kid walks through this door that somehow they're there because of some special program or some nod toward diversity; that somehow they haven't earned a seat at the table.

Having done years and years of recruiting, the people of color that I talk to are by and large *overqualified* for the business. You know, this is not rocket science. I think that what is incredibly important for people of color is to establish a great first impression. Somebody said you don't get a second chance to make a first impression, and I really like that saying, because in corporate America—I don't care what people say—I truly believe that there is a suspicion that somehow a [black] person doesn't deserve to be there. You need to spend your first two or three years in this job—not proving that you deserve to be here—but confirming your *right* to be here. You do that by having a single-minded focus on your job.

In my first two or three years here, I *lived* at Morgan Stanley. My roommate and I would get together at this club called The Cellar on Friday nights and blow off steam. But invariably, I'd be back in the office on Saturday and back in the office on Sunday.

I remember meeting [my wife] Carol, on a blind date. It was a Friday night in November of 1985 and we went over to the 21 Club, two blocks from the office. She had champagne and I had a glass of water, and I went back to the office.

I liked her immediately; I knew that there was something there. But I didn't call her until March of 1986. I was just too focused on my job (and she on hers). But it was that sort of single-minded focus that got me here, and that's what I tell people to this day. If you want to be successful at Morgan Stanley—and I'm sure the advice would hold for any other enterprise—then you decide on the first day you walk in here that this is the only thing that matters.

You know, there's a lot of talk about generation X, and unequal balance. I tell the kids of color to let the other kids think about balance. You don't want balance; you want to be focused. And while they're working on balance, you're going to lap them. You can get the balance later on.

Now the downside is that you get married a lot later, you have kids a lot later, but you've got to make trade-offs. And I'm happy with the trade-offs I've made. Family life is incredibly important to my overall sense of success, but what I'm learning is that it's a *sense* of family and a *sense* of community as opposed to getting home at 6 o'clock in time for dinner that's important to me. I don't do that. And I don't feel guilty about that.

The fact that that may be unreasonable for women is absolutely the one thing that women here talk about all the time: How can a woman who wants to get married and have children apply herself the same way that some of these guys apply themselves? Now, some are doing it. But I realize women are in a somewhat different predicament than men, and we [in corporate management] have to work harder on this issue. My wife makes that point to me all the time.

We all think about the trajectory we're on: Where do I go next? Do I have a chance to be the president of this firm? Those kinds of things I think about. Remember, one of the things that drives me is creating option value, and I'm at a point now where I've got a lot of options that are available to me. Again, at Morgan Stanley, we're not very corporate, so I have no idea what I may be asked to do next. There are a lot of things that could appeal to me. So, I can conceive of staying here a bit longer.

I love this environment. I'm at my desk at 6:45 every morning. I like getting up and coming to work. There's so much to be thankful for and satisfied with.

At the end of the day, life is simple. In many ways, the elements that I believe are critical to success, are also simple. Trust in God at all times. Teach your kids about God, honesty, and sharing at a very early age. Tell them to always do the right thing. Work hard. Save your money. Lead, don't follow. Don't be afraid to go it alone. Don't be afraid to lose. Don't be afraid to ask questions. Don't be afraid.

Everything else falls into place.

CHAPTER FOURTEEN

Joseph A. Moniz

Partner, Day, Berry & Howard

When Joe Moniz attended the twenty-fifth reunion of his New York University Law School class in May 2000, he received a booklet that contained the responses to a survey that had been done of the group. It stunned him to note that he was the only member of his class who was still working at the same job he accepted out of school.

At 53, the distinction of "only" is all too familiar to Moniz, a native of Rhode Island. In 1981, he became the first African American to be elected partner at Day, Berry & Howard, Connecticut's largest law firm. Twenty years later, he remained its only black partner, even though the firm doubled in size during that same period.

"[Black] people have told me that it's been important that I've been here," Moniz says of his long tenure at the firm. "They say my presence made a difference. But I grapple with that. Has it really?"

Moniz, who also holds a degree from Iowa Wesleyan College, specializes in commercial defense litigation, product liability, employment law, and criminal law. He presently serves on the board of directors of Saint Francis Hospital and Medical Center and is a past president of the George W. Crawford Law Association. Married, Moniz has three daughters.

I hadn't planned on being a lawyer. In fact, it was ironic that I became one. When I was in the eighth grade, in the college [bound] division, my teacher came around to ask us what we wanted to do after college. I was petrified, because the only people I knew who had gone to college were teachers. And I knew *no* black people who had gone to college. My father and mother left school in the tenth or eleventh grade. He was a self-taught mechanic and drove trucks. I knew you didn't need college for that, but I literally did not know why you would go to college. So I watched and listened.

The guy in front of me—an Italian guy—said he wanted to be a lawyer, and the teacher started explaining what you have to do to become a lawyer. I thought, okay, that's safe. So when it was my turn, I said I wanted to be a lawyer. She stopped and said, "Well, you know it's very difficult, and only one out of 500 make it, and you ought to really think about whether that's what you really want to do. Give it some thought, and I will come back around and ask you again." So, I gave it some thought, listened to a few more kids, and then said teacher, or engineer, or something, and she said, "Fine," and here is what you have to do.

I did teach for a while after college, until a friend of mine from high school steered me toward opportunities in graduate school. In sort of a snap decision, I took the LSAT, and ended up at NYU. I loved it. It suited me. I knew it right away. Law turned out to be something that I probably could do as well as I could do anything. But I found that out almost by accident, and in spite of that teacher who considered it beyond my reach.

I came to the firm in 1975, directly out of law school. I was the first black lawyer to ever work here. I walked in with this big afro and high heeled shoes. God knows what they thought when they saw me. But they were under pressure from a major client—Aetna—to get a black lawyer. So there was a search made to pick one, and I fit the bill for whatever reasons, probably because they felt I could talk with and get along with different people. And I came along at the right time.

My first week here, they were still preparing my office, so they had me sitting in the office of a partner who was away. The head of the hiring committee made it his business to come around to all the new associates to talk to them about acclimating themselves to the environment. So, he came in to see me, and I'm sitting at this partner's big desk, and he's sitting on the other side, as a client would. He starts talking, and he's turning red. He's obviously very nervous, and I couldn't figure out why or exactly what he was trying to say.

He's saying, "Well, if there are questions you have, you being . . . you being . . . " and he's stumbling along when it dawned on me, and I said, "Oh, you are talking about the fact that I'm the first black lawyer here."

He said, "Yes, yes." He was so relieved that I brought it out. Then he started talking about how if there was anything they could do to make me feel more comfortable here, me being the first and only, to please let him know.

I said, "Okay, but if there is anything *I* can do to help *you* all deal with *me*, I've been through this before. Obviously, you haven't been." It was clear to me that I was more comfortable in that situation than he was.

His nervousness in dealing with me gave me confidence. He was a nice man, and a good lawyer, but it occurred to me for the first time that there are disadvantages to not being able to deal with us. Here was this successful partner appearing so uncomfortable, so insecure. It was a weakness in him that he didn't know how to deal with people unlike himself. It's a weakness as a person and as a lawyer, but it goes unrecognized as such, because it is still so common.

What *we* need to recognize is that the converse reality in ourselves is a great strength. We have a natural advantage, because we *have* to deal with all different worlds. We are able to walk anywhere and survive.

I once worked with a black associate here who had a sort of litmus test for folks. He called it the surviving-in-the-middle-of-Newark test. He'd say, "Take any of your partners and drop them in the middle of Newark, New Jersey. Would they be able to survive?" The answer, almost universally, would be no. Then he said to me, "If, on the other hand, you were dropped in the middle of Iowa," which I was in college, "could you survive?" Well, of course. I did. We all have. And I have here.

I never thought about becoming a partner. I had no idea of what it took. I had no idea about mentors or office politics. All I wanted to do was learn to try cases, learn to be a good lawyer, and Day, Berry seemed to be the place to do that. I chose it because it was somewhere between Rhode Island and New York and because they said that I would try a case in my first year.

They kept that promise, although, early on, I began a habit of taking on cases that were not typical of the firm at all. Generally the cases that came to me involved black people. They didn't pay as much [as corporate matters], but they got me in the courtroom. I forced myself to get in there and just learn by my mistakes. I had no fear of making mistakes. I learned that lesson early on from my father, who always held that if you are going to be good at something, you got to deal with being knocked down first.

Those cases did more than shape my trial skills. They made me visible and involved in the community, and, ultimately, they kept me sane, kept me rooted. I also believe, absolutely, that it was those cases that set me apart from the pack and helped make me a partner.

Someone said to me in one of my performance evaluations early on, "We understand that you like doing these community activities, but we really think that you ought to focus on some other things." I said, "You don't understand. This is something that I decided I was going to do when I went to law school. Whether I do it here or elsewhere, that's what I'm going to continue to do."

I made partner in 1981. I remember the day exactly. I was on trial in New York, the Southern District, in a discrimination case. I was representing a black woman suing NBC because she had gotten passed over for a promotion. She came to me through a friend from law school, Marianne Spraggins. So, I took the case, but it was clearly not a Day, Berry type of case. Here we were *suing* the corporation. Usually we represented them. I was out on a limb—again.

The day the partners voted, we happened to have a break in the case because someone was sick. At that time, you had to have a unanimous vote. It's now changed, but back then it would just take one person to say no and you'd be out. Four of us were up for partner, and we all ended up sitting in my little office, nervous, waiting for this phone call to come on whether or not we had made it.

In those days, the senior partner was Ralph Dickson, who was a wonderful, wonderful man. He would call you into his office and tell you, "Congratulations! Welcome aboard," that kind of thing. It was like a rite of passage, and he was such a personable guy, he made it an extra pleasure. I believe it was his mission to make sure that a black partner was made before he retired. If ever there was a godfather that I had here, it was him. He sincerely wanted to see it happen, for the right reasons.

When it did, I remember thinking about those early evaluations, the comments that were passed about some of my cases. I felt so validated, but, more important, I realized then that if you do what you feel is right, and continue to do it, rather than worrying about how it is going to affect your chances for partnership, you'll do okay. And, even if you don't [make partner], you won't have to regret not having done what you wanted to do.

So, when the news came, it felt good. I felt proud, and the people around me—in my community at home and other black associates in the firm—felt proud. They had been very supportive of me, I think because we all had the sense that if I made it, it would be a little bit easier for them to make it. We were fooled by that. I was fooled in many ways.

Knowing what I know now, I would not want to be "the first" anywhere. I have no regrets, but I would not want to go through that again. I was able to do it because I was sort of naïve. I never thought about becoming a partner, and then it happened, and I assumed that once you became a partner, that was it. You were blessed by your colleagues, you had proven yourself.

But it's clearly different for people of color. Whatever you do, whatever your title is, whatever successes you have, you are going to be questioned. I've had people make comments to me over the years, "Oh, you won that case because . . . " or "You had a black person on the jury and that made the difference." In other words, your successes aren't given the same credence, and your mistakes are going to be counted twice.

Most kids today are much more savvy than I was. A while back, some of us went to talk to a bunch of high school kids about careers and were encouraging them to try law. I had a kid look me right in the eye and say, "Why should I?" I just looked at him. "Mr. Moniz," he said, "I have a better chance at making it in the NBA than I do at making it in a major law firm and actually becoming a partner like you."

That was bad enough, but then, he really got to me when he said, "But even if I don't make it in the NBA, at least I'll know it's because I'm not good enough, and not because of the color of my skin.

"I can accept that," he said. "I can live with not making it because I'm not good enough. But I can't accept not making it in the law profession, or in your firm, and not knowing why."

He was right. What could I say to him, except, those are the realities that we have to live and work with? There are countless ugly truths like that one, and we come up against them every day.

A perfect example was that case I was on during the partnership vote. I have never forgotten what nailed that case for me. I had the senior vice president of all of NBC on the stand, and I was cross-examining him about some comments he had made. As I began my questions, I started to approach him. He got scared. He actually started to panic as I got near him, questioning him. You could see it on his face, and he literally said—and I've kept the transcript to this day—"Get away from me. You're intimidating me."

The judge practically jumped out of her chair. She said, "How dare you, sir, ever say that to a lawyer in my courtroom." She had realized, as I had, that this man could not deal with a black, especially a black man, coming close to him, challenging him. It was the most effective cross-examination I've ever had and it had nothing to do with the questions I was asking.

I'll never forget that case or the lesson that came out of it for me. You can be the best educated, the best dressed, a partner, whatever, it doesn't matter. To him, I was just another black man, and he was afraid, even in a courtroom with a judge sitting right there.

But there was another lesson, and it was more important. When the judge made her decision, she gave damages for some back pay. But she would not grant future damages and she was very clear why. After her NBC experience, my client had just become obsessed with this case. For years, she hadn't worked, she hadn't done anything but focus on this thing.

The judge, a black woman, said to my client, "You've been around long enough to know that racism is in this country. It's been here forever, and it's no surprise. Don't you think I face it every day? But I have to go on, to move on. You needed to move on. You didn't, and I'm not going to reward you for that." We can't get stuck in the negative experiences we have, or in the anger or bitterness we feel. She said it best: You need to move on. Otherwise it will just eat you up.

If you were to ask me, would I encourage someone else to go where I have gone, I would say, if you do, do it with your eyes open. My situation as "the first" black partner at Day, Berry, quickly became one of "the only." When I became partner, I went into it with the notion that I was going to help, that I was leaving an open door for others like me. I believed it would be easier for them.

Now, in 25 years at the firm, 19 as a partner, if I've been able to get some summer jobs for people working as messengers, and maybe make the difference in somebody [black] being hired as an associate, that's not making the difference that I thought I would. That's not changing the landscape any.

People have said to me, "But it's still better that you're there. It still means something." Maybe. But I have seen bright, talented black lawyers here get so angry, or so disheartened, they are nearly destroyed. There are great benefits to being in a position like mine or at a firm like this, but there is a high price to be paid, and if you're not up to it, it's not worth it.

You have to have thick skin and a good sense of humor. You have to be prepared to deal with the anger and loneliness. And, most of all, you have to be yourself. If you can't do something as yourself, don't do it. If you lose who you are, you lose everything. If you assimilate fully, the institution won't change. Then what have you gained?

Several years ago, I won one of Connecticut's most notorious and controversial cases. After being approached by representatives from the Hartford branch of the NAACP, I agreed to defend Joe Lomax, a black teenager accused of the brutal murder of a young white woman, Tara Laczynski. It was the toughest case I've ever had and, once again, it was as far from a Day, Berry sort of case as you can get.

I took it on because I fully believed in Lomax's innocence, and because it offered an opportunity for me to do something right, something good. I also took it on to prove to my partners and to myself that I could do as well or better than they could. Even after a decade as partner, I couldn't shake the feeling that they discounted my abilities. No matter how many successes you have, that makes you question your own abilities, and I was doing that.

The case turned into this very public, very difficult three-year battle. But I rode it out, through two mistrials and significant personal and professional trials until, finally, Joe Lomax was acquitted.

When it was all over, I walked into a partnership meeting and got a standing ovation from my partners. I couldn't believe it. That was probably the warmest moment I've ever felt at my firm. And it represented a turning point for me.

A few years back, someone went through the firm's trial records and put together some data on wins and losses. My record stacks right up there with the best in the group, and people started saying, "My God, we never realized . . . " and so on. I know they didn't, but that's okay, because years before, I was able to look at myself and say that I've done the right things, with the General Motors of the world, with the Goodyears and with other major corporate clients, and with clients like Joe Lomax. And that hasn't just led to my personal benefit, it's benefited my firm.

I believe they know that, and that small acknowledgment can be the beginning of real change.

Postscript

On August 31, 2000, many months after this interview, Joe Moniz resigned from his partnership at Day, Berry & Howard to launch a new law firm: Moniz, Cooper & McCann.

Several days before, some Day, Berry clients and partners gathered to wish him well. In toasting Moniz's new venture, one of his colleagues said, "You may no longer be with the firm, but you'll always be my partner." The statement "made me feel great," says Moniz, "and I absolutely feel the same way about him and some other individuals although I can't say that's my feeling about the institution."

At a separate event, several former black associates from Day, Berry gathered to surprise Moniz and to thank him. They gave him a beautiful print of a black hand reaching down with another reaching up toward it. They also presented him with a brand new door-stopper and a note that read, "Thanks for keeping your door open." Whatever questions Moniz has grappled with over the years regarding his impact and the value of his presence at Day, Berry, he says, "That single gesture was the answer. That made it all worthwhile."

Having his own firm is a dream deferred no longer. Says Moniz, who is 50: "The other day, my sister told me, 'The first part of your life, you live for others. The second part of your life, you live for yourself.' Now is my time!" Meanwhile, Day, Berry & Howard, still Connecticut's largest law firm, currently has no black partners.

CHAPTER FIFTEEN

Joan Parrot-Fonseca

President, JPF & Associates

One only need scan the list of Joan Parrot-Fonseca's credentials to get a sense of her wide-ranging interests and winding career path. She holds degrees in public administration, law, human resource management, music history, and education. Perhaps even more impressive, she's put them all to good use.

Parrot-Fonseca rose to the fore as the first woman to serve as director of the U.S. Department of Commerce's Minority Business Development Agency (MBDA) in its 30-year history. During her tenure there, in addition to successfully retooling the embattled agency, she spearheaded a minority matchmaking program in partnership with the International Trade Administration that resulted in $480 million in business for U.S.-based minority businesses. Soon after the plane crash that killed Secretary Ronald H. Brown and much of his staff, Parrot-Fonseca resigned.

Now 50, this spirited networker extraordinaire has reinvented herself. A consultant to emerging businesses and a highly effective speaker/lecturer, Parrot-Fonseca, who is divorced, exclaims, "I'm on the move again!"

My mother was probably my greatest role model. It wasn't so much that I wanted to be like her, but she taught me how to be.

She was a schoolteacher, and she was brilliant. If she had been born when I was, she could have become anything she wanted. We were so different in what we were good at. She was tone deaf; I have perfect pitch. My mother was a mathematical genius; I'm dysgraphic, which means, I can't add two and two. Like dyslexia with reading, dysgraphia involves the reversing of numbers and graphs. But what I lack in numerical thinking, I've compensated for with words and language. So I think, to some degree, I was a wonder to her, but she was a wonder to me.

Ernestine Parrot was this very petite, southern woman who had these big, Bette Davis eyes, and she would look at me all the time and say, "You're so beautiful." Now, I don't think I'm bad looking, but I'm nowhere *near* as good-looking as my mother. She was gorgeous, but she could not see it. Instead, she always focused on me. She would wear the same old polyester dresses over and over again, but she was very strict about how I looked and she spent a lot of money on my clothes. Even in my baddest teenage, sneak-out, do-whatever days (and I was a terror!), I still had on pearls. She made me love good things.

I could come home dirty from playing, with my hair sticking straight up, looking crazy, and she would look into my face and say, "You're beautiful." It's so funny. I'm not sure whether she really thought that, but sometimes you can be loved so much that you become beautiful.

She had grown up feeling trapped in a segregated town, knowing that she could only go so far there. By the time she had married my father and moved to St. Albans, New York, I think she felt as if the time for her to take chances had come and gone. But she wanted to make sure that I had every experience that she missed out on. At the same time, she was fiercely protective. She was afraid of me being hurt, being rejected. I really wish I could talk to her now about the feelings of rejection that she must have had, because she spent her entire life trying to keep me from having those feelings.

My mother raised me to be not so much rich, but famous. She talked about me like I was a famous person. She made me think that everybody knew who I was. For example, [England's] Princess Anne is about my age and Prince Charles is my brother's age. My mother had us thinking that we were somehow connected with them. She'd say, "You know, Anne went to her first dance and she wore stockings, and you can wear stockings, too."

It was so odd. She didn't talk about them like they were from this royal family someplace far away. She just knew that we were the same age, so we should do what they did. At the same time, she and my father never compared us to others. We were taught to only compare ourselves with ourselves. They would say, "What could *you* have done better?" No one ever said to me, "Look at Jane. She's got better grades than you, why can't you be more like her?" I think that was important. It taught me to be responsible for myself. We were in charge of our lives, no one else. I think the Princess Anne thing was her way of saying, the whole world is your oyster. It was funny and strange, but, in a way, it was powerful.

She was very conscious of race and of the limitations it could create in your life, of the hurt that could be caused by racism. Her way of dealing with it was to say, "Well, if I can't change these rules, I'm going to create another set of rules." So she did things like encouraging me to study opera in high school and putting me into international settings, where color wouldn't be an issue. When I was five, she sent me to sleepover camp for a month. It was so far north, I thought it was in Canada. My older brother, Monroe, was there too, so I wasn't by myself, but I was *five years old*! My father said she cried the entire drive home but, he said she did it because she wanted me to be exposed to broader things than our neighborhood.

Our house was the constant meeting place. On Saturday mornings my mother would cook fish and grits and do the whole southern thing, and all the neighbors would come over. This is where my father would debate. He loved that. He would say things like, "I'm going to join the Ku Klux Klan," just so the whole neighborhood would debate it. I learned generosity from those gatherings. My parents would share with anybody. I learned to hear diverse ideas coming from different people, and I learned to have an opinion, and to express it well—and fight for it if necessary.

I was always allowed to say what I thought in my own house. As a child, I didn't realize that other children weren't allowed to do that or that grownups didn't always say what they thought. My family put the "func" in dysfunctional, but we were very healthy in that way. We didn't keep a lid on things. We didn't censor ourselves. That led to some wild battles, but then it would all be fine, because everybody got to have their say.

My mother encouraged lots of exotic activities, but she also had her feet on the ground. Degrees and credentials were important to her. She always said, "You gotta have something to fall back on." She wanted me to be a full-bodied person, and she wanted me to be independent.

My mother never encouraged marriage. Even though she was a very good helpmate—my father still reveres her—she didn't want me to look for that only. She never said, don't [get married]. Instead it was, "Do everything you want to do first, and it won't matter because the longer you wait, the better you'll do." She would not let me be in a cotillion because she said it was like a fake wedding and all the girls that had been in cotillions ended up getting married early. I think what she was trying to say was, you'll know yourself better and you'll make better choices as you have more experiences. I think that is true.

One day when I was in law school, I just got up one morning and said, "I'm tired. I'm cutting class. I'm driving home." I knocked on the door and there was Mom. She had just retired from teaching and she came to the door wearing her spectacles and pearls (she loved those pearls). We went to all our old haunts. We went shopping, we had a ball, and she asked me to do two things that day. She asked me to save my money and start wearing a bra. That was the last day we spent together.

She died of smoke inhalation in a fire in our house. She had gotten out, but she went back in to save her dog. She knew better. She had taught me and my brother that you never go back into a fire for anything. But she did it anyway. I was 27.

That was the first of two horrible, tragic losses I've experienced. The second was the loss of [Commerce Secretary] Ron Brown, and so many of my colleagues and friends when their plane crashed in Bosnia. Losing so many people so suddenly and at one time was almost more than I could handle. I think I'm still handling it to some degree. It comes back on you at times, like a wave, when you least expect it.

I learned a lot from Ron. He was very supportive of women. His Cabinet looked like America, and I was one of two black woman on it. He was brilliant. He recruited top talent and, once he chose you, he demonstrated his faith in you. I remember just three weeks after he met and hired me, he sent me to South Africa for six weeks to represent him. That's how he was. Once he chose you, he said, "You are the one." That's what he said when he hired me to be the head of the Minority Business Development Agency. I thought my staff was kidding when they said, "It's Ron Brown calling from Turkey." I got on the phone, and he said, "You're the one." I can remember it like it was yesterday.

That was my best job by far, but it was probably my hardest. I had to create public/private partnerships, raise money, organize conferences. Successfully bringing various, and often distinctive, parties together to do business was a huge part of the job so my ability to network was critical.

Throughout my life, people have commented on how great my networking skills are. I believe I developed these skills as a result of being put in so many new and different situations at such a young age. It has sort of been a survival technique. Others believe it is a natural facet of my outgoing personality. The truth probably lies in some combination of the two. I do know that I wouldn't understand the power and the value of networking until I worked as a consultant with A. M. Herman and Associates several years ago. Among other things, Alexis Herman (who would go on to become Secretary Herman in the Clinton Administration) taught me what a powerful professional tool networking could be. She was my first professional role model and one of my greatest mentors. Ron Brown was, of course, another.

By the time I went to MBDA, I'd had a lot of jobs and I'd use one skill here, another one there, a different one in another job. MBDA was the closest I've ever come to using all my skills on one job, and I was grateful to Ron for giving me that opportunity.

I ended up doing a lot in that job that I'm proud of. I created new programs which still exist and are very successful. Ron took notice of that; he always expressed appreciation, and that meant a lot to me. Working for him, I didn't have to fight for everything. He was the first boss I had who validated me.

From Ron I learned how valuable public service is. His Minority Trade Mission program was so important and through it I learned so much. When I took the job, I told Ron I thought we needed to focus more on minority business opportunities right here. He said, "*There is no more here*. We are in a global society." His vision expanded my vision, it expanded the reach of our program, and it changed my whole perspective on the world.

Traveling the world on those missions changed my life. None of the places were what I expected based on what others had told me. For example, people in South Africa are never late. It's the ultimate insult to waste somebody's time. They waited so long for Apartheid to end that I guess waiting on anyone or anything else is unacceptable. In China, people were much warmer than I thought they would be. In Haiti, I discovered such incredible art, which taught me that beautiful things can still come out of dire poverty and disarray. Outside of South Africa, it is my favorite place.

I learned a lot of practical lessons on those trips, too. They lost my luggage once in Trinidad and I had a press conference just after my flight landed. I learned then that the show must go on, and that I can give a speech in dirty clothes. Substance over form always wins.

I was probably one of the few who didn't know Ron well on a personal level. I was part of the gang; I wasn't part of the inner circle. I was just getting to know him when they died. In a way, I mourned the relationship I didn't get to have.

I will never forget the day of the crash. I was out of the country on a trade mission when it happened. Ron had encouraged me to go with the Chinese American Business Association from New York. I got a whole different view of China, because their relatives came to the airport and they had a party in my honor. We had flown down from Beijing to Chin-Dao where we had gone to visit a Pepsi plant and a beer plant. It was such a wonderful day. We had done all this touring, and sealed a couple of deals between Chinese Americans and Chinese citizens, so we were very festive. I remember standing there thinking, "I'm in China. I'm looking at the China Sea. This is fabulous!"

The mayor of Chin-Dao celebrated with us in this private room and we had a ball. After dinner, when my staff and some of our party went to hang out, I went back to the hotel. There are certain things that, as women, we can't do, especially when we travel. We can say that we're equal, but we're really not in the way in which we are viewed and treated socially. So, I do not drink and hang out when I'm on a trade mission or a business trip. I don't wear shorts, and I never lay around in a bathing suit. I know it's old fashioned, but I believe the people I work with or am trying to do business with will view me differently if they see me behave or dress a certain way. It's a rule that has served me well.

So that night, I get back to my room and it was beautiful. The trip was going so incredibly well from a professional standpoint that I felt giddy. And, at the same time, we were having a ball! Then the phone rang. "Miss Fonseca, you've got to come back to the States. The White House has called you back."

I said, "Why?"

"Because the secretary's missing."

I said, "I get called back because [Warren] Christopher's plane is missing? What has that got to do with me?"

"No. Ron's plane is missing."

It was a long trip home and we were still in shock when we got here. It was so painful, and it would be that way for a long time. We were going from one funeral to the other; it felt like it went on for a year. And a lot of people exploited it, and were insincere in their testimonials. I hated that part of it. It made me bitter and resentful on top of everything else lousy I was already feeling. It took a while to let go of all of that, but you have to. If you hold on to things like that, it starts to destroy you.

I only worked with Ron for two years, but it colored my life in many ways. It validated for me that there were, and there are, good people doing good work in the world. I also remember what Jesse Jackson, and [Ron's widow] Alma [Brown] said. They said, "Don't get caught up in how he died and conspiracy theories. Get caught up in the work that he taught you to do, and make sure you continue to do that work."

I wanted to, but I couldn't do it there. So, I packed up and went to Harvard. I have a girlfriend who says she loses sleep over me leaving jobs. When I left MBDA, she said, "How could you leave a six-figure job in which you traveled all over the world?" I said, "Because Ron was dead and the way in which I could operate was over." I've always been that way. Even in high school, if I got into class and saw that the teacher was not that bright, forget it, it was downhill for me. Ron was a good and smart teacher. Once he was gone, I was done there.

I went to Harvard depressed. I felt that all my government service was a waste. Most of my friends were rich. They had gone for the money, and I had gone for the experience. So, I knew a lot, and they had a lot of money. I felt like I'd made the wrong choices. I felt like a fool. I had done a lot, but what was it all for? Growing up, thanks to my mother, I just knew I was going to be somebody, but I didn't know what that meant. I've been trying to figure it out ever since.

I was at my all time low. And it wasn't just over all the people lost in the plane crash and how they died, I realized I had never really dealt with my mother's death completely. I had a lot of stuff to resolve.

Those two experiences changed my life. They changed my priorities. They changed the way I thought about myself and my goals. At least, I thought they did at the time. But, I didn't really come to a full stop until one day when I was, literally, forced to.

I had graduated Harvard and was back in Washington, D.C. I had just gotten back from a business trip. I had bought my first house and I loved it but I don't think I had spent more than three nights in it because I was always on the road for work. Then I had a car accident. I was okay, except that I fractured a number of small bones in my foot. So, after racing around my entire life, I was literally stuck in place, forced off my feet for months.

At first, I thought I would lose my mind. But then, I had an epiphany. I had taken a job in investment banking to prove that I could make money and I was sitting here with my leg up thinking, "I hate investment banking." I was making more money than I ever had, but I felt no real sense of purpose and I had no time to enjoy anyone or anything. My life was total chaos and I was always on the move. I hadn't even been able to unpack my new house. It was only when I actually stopped and thought about it that I realized I wasn't the least bit happy. That's when I decided to go into business for myself.

When I made that decision, I felt my mother's approval, like a window opening, letting the light back in. My mother believed I could conquer anything. She was proud of everything I did. She always knew that whatever roadblocks I hit, it would be temporary for me. She said the difference between me and her was I was not afraid to move.

She was right. I never thought about going anyplace and staying long. This friend of mine once said to me, "You go after things like a dog. You sniff. You want the information, you figure it out, and then you say, 'Is that all there is,' and you go on to the next thing. One day, you're going to come to something and say, 'Ah, this is where I'm supposed to be,' and all those things that you gathered, all those skills, are going to come into play." I've been waiting for that my entire life.

After college, I got a master's because I got a full scholarship. I went to law school because I was curious about it. I wanted to see what the big deal was, and it was another credential. Harvard was the other nut I wanted to crack. Each time, I was able to get some new skills, to open myself up to another community of folk, to add another layer of credibility. When I was 40 I thought, by 50, that I would stop this kind of thinking because it's ridiculous. But I'm now 50 and I'm still trying to discover my true purpose in life. The difference between then and now is that I know I'm closer now than I've ever been, and I'm not trying to rush it or force it anymore.

If my maternal grandmother's life is any indication, I figure I've got time. She was a teacher for 43 years, but at that time, only a two-year teaching certificate was required and she'd always wanted a four-year degree. So, at age 70, after she retired, she went back to college—even lived in the dorms—and earned her bachelor's, teaching me that it's never too late to do anything. Clearly I've inherited some of her spirit.

I used to think I could control, not people, but the way things happen. Ron's death let me know. My mother's death let me know. They were two hard examples that there is nothing you can do to prevent some things from happening. Now, the whole idea of controlling the events of life is absurd to me. So, I've given that up.

Chaos is something that I thrive on. I love chaos. I'm good in chaos. I do my best thinking when I'm right up against a deadline with six other things in play. But I need to let that go too. Control and chaos are two C's that I'm getting rid of.

Now, I'm trying to focus on the C's that will help me get to the next step in my career and in my life. I can communicate, I can collaborate, and I can choose my path, rather than let it be chosen for me. I want to focus on my creative side. I've been working on the cognitive for a long time. The brain stuff I've mastered. So, I want to let my creativity in; I want to have the courage to step outside the box. It's also time to celebrate the things that I've done well. I have a tendency not to celebrate my successes. I tend to downplay them, or even turn them into something other than success. That's self-defeating.

There's probably a little bit of it in all of us. But I've found that is a common thread with women who've lost their mother. Not everybody has unconditional love from their mother but, assuming that you do, once you lose that, you lose that unconditional validation too. I've learned that no one else can give you that. You have to find it within yourself.

While I work on that, I'm blessed, because I still have my father. After my mother's death, I learned how to be a survivor through him. He started the Widower's Club and got another degree at 77. He has supported me through marriage, divorce, death, depression, and now, renewal. I still miss my mother, but Dad is here and that has made all the difference.

I also have wonderful friends. They'll say, "How many jobs did you turn down today? Girl, a year from now you'll be sitting pretty." Or, as my mother used to always say, "You'll be cookin' with gas!" I'm not worried. If I've learned anything it's that when one door shuts, another one opens, then another one shuts, but then another one opens. I can deal with that.

Without my mother, I think I would have been a very different person. My mother always thought—and made me feel as if—something magical was going to happen in my life, and that I was going to transcend any challenge that came my way. She thought that I had some kind of special birthright. She more than wanted great things for me, she really expected them to happen.

I was always popular growing up, and I think that was partly because I was always confident, *really confident*. My friends still talk about how when I pulled up on the first day at Howard, I got out of the car like, "Here I am!" Maybe that's something you're born with; I don't know. But I know that if anyone could *give* you that, it was my mother. I didn't realize it then, but now I know what she was doing. Her approach was a little bit over the top, but it worked.

A friend of mine's children are so secure and so together. I look at them—the way they carry themselves, the way they treat other people—and I'm just in awe. One day I said to her, "How did you do that?" She said, "Simple. I used the Ernestine Parrot method."

CHAPTER SIXTEEN

Richard D. Parsons

President, Time Warner, Inc.

It's a good thing Dick Parsons prides himself on his easygoing personality. Like a well-experienced and somewhat jaded pilot, it enables him to steer through the turbulence and unpredictability of business with relative ease, and few businesses seem to rock and roll like media giant Time Warner.

Parsons became a member of Time Warner's board of directors in 1991 and was elected president in 1994. Like his company, which is built of an unprecedented array of gold-standard assets (CNN, HBO, New Line pictures, the Atlanta Braves, Atlantic records, and several of the world's most profitable magazines, to name a few), Parsons' resume is stacked with gold-standard positions. He was chairman and chief executive officer of Dime Bancorp, Inc.; managing partner of Patterson, Belknap, Webb & Tyler, one of the nation's largest law firms; and senior White House aide under President Gerald Ford, in addition to other positions in New York state and federal service.

But Parsons, 52, has traveled in mighty circles long enough to know better than to define himself by his titles. He is that rarest of breeds, a serious businessman who doesn't take himself—or the trappings of life at the top—too seriously. Says Parsons, who is married and has three grown children: "It wouldn't bother me a bit if my obit just said, `He was a good guy.' That, to me, is the highest compliment."

I was Nelson Rockefeller's personal lawyer in the last years of his life. Before he died, he told his wife Happy, "If anything ever happens to me, call Dick and he'll take care of things." But I was around 30 years old; I was this kid and she didn't know me very well. She had this friend named George Woods who had been head of World Bank and First Boston. He had sort of adopted Happy as his charge and he said, "What do you mean? Who is this guy Parsons? I want to meet him and I'll decide whether he's right for you." So I was summoned up to Happy's apartment to be interviewed by this old tiger.

He starts going after me saying, "What have you done and why should this woman go with you? She needs someone who has some standing and some reputation. Where are you now? Where do you practice?"

"Well," I said, "I'm at Patterson Belknap."

He stopped and he looked at me and said, "You're a partner of Chick Belknap?"

I said, "Yes." The interview ended. He just turned to Happy and said, "He's alright."

To me it was the classic example of something my grandmother had always told me, which is that you are judged by the company you keep.

People ask me all the time, how did you—a kid from Brooklyn and Queens—end up here? Well, you never know the full answer to that. I mean, I think I'm a pretty good guy and I was a decent lawyer, but so are about half a trillion other people. I'm pretty clever, but I wasn't even the smartest kid on my block! Reputation, associates, friends, these are all factored into the mix that makes up a career. So the reputational value of the company you keep is very important.

I'm a Type-B personality. Type-As are driven. They have a need to achieve. They're intense, purposeful. I want to be relevant. It is important to me to matter, to count, to be able to affect what I want to affect in this life. But I'm relaxed, laid back. I'm easygoing. I don't have anything that I need to prove to myself or others. I love to play games. I like to win. But I know how to lose and I don't *have* to win. I'm relatively content to just, sort of, hang. There has never been a plan. There isn't a plan today. . . .

People have said to me, "When did you first think about going to college?" Well, I never thought about it. It was just expected. I am the second of five children, the oldest boy. I grew up classically: You *will* go to school. You *will* go to church. You'll do reasonably well, you'll respect your elders, you'll make your bed up in the morning. But it was not, You'll live this kind of life: you'll be a doctor, or a lawyer, or an Indian chief. It was, You can do whatever you want to do when you grow up, but nothing comes of nothing, so if you want to make something of yourself, you have to put in the time and be good at it.

The first job I had coming out of law school was something I had never even heard of two weeks before I accepted it. The rest of [my career] has been opportunity coinciding with interest and desire at the moment. People have asked, "When did you first think you could become the chairman of this or the president of that? When did it occur to you that you might?" It never occurred to me that I couldn't, or wouldn't.

When I think of my father I think of intellect and gentleness. When I think of my mother, I think of steely determination and grit. I was always much more like my father temperamentally, but I have my mom's willingness to try almost anything. I'm not fearless, because that would be foolish, but I have a lot of confidence in myself and I'm willing to risk failure. I have three children. If I could give every kid one thing, it would be a deep sense of personal security, because that enables so much else. I don't know, though, if that's something you can teach. There are some things you're born with. That may be one, and I have it.

Eighty percent of what makes people successful is believing in yourself. A lot of people don't try because they're afraid to fail. Most people would rather follow than lead because it's safer. That way, if it fails, they can say, "It's not my fault. Wasn't my idea." But if you don't try, you can't succeed. I will try almost anything of interest or that I think I want to do or need to do. If it works, it works, and if it doesn't, hey, I tried.

In many families there's one child who's always in trouble for doing stuff that he or she shouldn't be doing. That was my role in our family. So I managed to catch more spankings and disciplinary actions than my other four siblings combined.

I was a quick student but a lazy student. So I was able—this is sort of a good and a bad thing—I was always able to meet the expectations of performance in school without having to do brilliantly, because I wasn't really expected to do brilliantly. I was just expected to do well, and doing well didn't require all that much effort. So that left plenty of time to get into trouble.

In high school I had a lab bench partner in physics who was from Hawaii. Her father was in the Air Force and had been transferred to New York. She would talk about Hawaii all the time. And she made it sound so exotic. I didn't even know where Hawaii was. This is the truth: I took the SAT's in the fall of my senior year. In those days they gave you three free shots. In other words, you could put down three schools where they would send your SAT scores automatically. If you wanted more than three you had to pay a buck for each one. I wanted to go to Princeton since the seventh grade, because I had gone to a football game there and fell in love with the place. So I put down Princeton first, and I put down City College of New York, which was a natural. And there I was staring at a free third slot. And it just popped into my head: University of Hawaii. So I put it down. Those were the only three schools I applied to.

I didn't get into Princeton. I got into CCNY, but it was definitely time to leave home, so I went to the University of Hawaii. I had no idea what I was getting into.

I grew up there, which, I suspect, a lot of people think about their college years. I had to work, and figure out school, and put together a whole texture and context of life.

It was a big state school, but there were very few blacks; less than 1 percent of the population. But, it didn't matter because in Hawaii (this was the hoot) people of color—black, or Japanese, or Samoan, or Polynesian, or Filipino—are the majority, and the whites are the minority. What was interesting to me was that you were sort of adopted by all the other people of color as being aligned with them in a kind of global warfare with whites, and you were adopted by all the whites because you were aligned with them for being from the mainland. So, it was sort of an interesting juxtaposition of the traditional relationship.

The reality of the way I have experienced my life is that race has not often been an issue, period. Full stop. Having said that—I used to tell minority law students when they'd come into the workplace—racism does exist. It's never particularly bitten me in the ass, but I know it's out there. Blacks in the workplace are cut less slack, there's less tolerance for failure, particularly up front. If a white person muffs his first big assignment at a law firm—and I've seen this happen—the natural tendency of the partnership is to say, "Alright, well, he wiffed the first time, but he's a good man or she's a good woman, he or she went to the right law school. So give him or her another chance." When a black person wiffs, they don't say it, but you can see it in their eyes. It's like, "I knew they couldn't carry the load anyway." Subtle, but real.

So, it's a reality. But it's kind of like being short or tall or heavy or thin. It's just one of those things that you manage. And the management of that issue for me has never been particularly challenging.

I do think there's something to the notion of self-fulfilling prophecy. People who are quick to assume that anything negative that happens, or any different form of treatment, is racially motivated, are probably creating more barriers for themselves than they need to. Maybe some [motives] are [racist], but to assume that *all* of them are, creates a sense of your own reality that will take you down a bad path.

I've had people say things to me that are totally inappropriate, but if you just laugh and figure, it's their problem not yours, and move on, it does not become an incident or an impediment. It's a wonderful thing to be underestimated. It's much better to be underestimated than overestimated.

I don't get my feelings hurt or take that burden on. Let them feel or believe what they want. It's not my issue. My issue is this: Can I come out of this having achieved what I went into it hoping to achieve? Period. Full stop.

I went to law school in Albany because I got a full scholarship there.

One material thing happened between college and law school. After I graduated, I got married to my college sweetheart. I was 20.

So, I get to law school. I now had this wife who was working and expecting something of me. I had this scholarship that required something of me, and for the first time in my life, I kind of buckled down. I just brought some discipline to the way I approached things. I actually showed up at class. I actually did the assignments. I mean, in college, I became a *fabulous*, world-class bridge player. I started out as a physics major, but that required too much of my time, so I switched to history. Again, Type B.

I got drafted in law school, so I was gone from the last half of my second year until the middle of my senior year, and by the time I got back to school all the really good jobs were gone. A professor of mine was very close to a guy who had just been made counsel to the governor. He said I ought to talk to them, so I did. It sounded like an interesting thing to do, so I started working for Nelson Rockefeller.

Usually, people who got jobs in the governor's counsel's office had not just graduated from law school. They had been out for three, four years, so the average starting age was something like 28. I was now 23, so I was a kid relative to the people there.

The governor's counsel's office was the busiest place in all of Albany, particularly when Rockefeller was governor. He was a very proactive governor, always putting up plans and programs and initiatives. He was clearly the visionary of the state. So most of what was being done came out of the governor's office and most of that was constructed in the counsel's office. There were only eight of us and we ran flat-out all the time.

My first day at work, my boss sat me down and said, "Look, I'm glad you're here. You know, we're all stressed and busy, and we need some help. But you just sit here for right now because I'm too busy to tell you what you have to do." It was that kind of place. So I worked. I always had a lot of confidence. I always felt that I could do whatever it was that I was asked to do, but, for the first 18 months or more, I had absolutely no idea of how I was actually doing. I got no feedback. People would throw stuff on your desk. You did the best you could, put it back in the system, and hoped it worked. I had a sort of standing offer from my law school to go back and teach, which really appealed to me, so one day, I went to talk to my boss, and said, "You know my two years is coming up, and I was thinking about going back and teaching."

He said, "You can't do that."

I said, "Well, why not?"

He said, "Howard is leaving"—he was the first assistant counsel at the time—"and I thought we'd make you the first assistant."

Well, that was the first time we'd even come close to a job evaluation. And, I was stunned because, to me, I was just doing what everybody else was doing. I figured I was doing as well as the other guys, and that they were doing, basically, as well as me. I didn't, and I still do not, compare myself to others. I think those kinds of comparisons are almost always invidious. I don't reference my performance against what other people are doing. I usually just sort of give it my best shot and try to have some fun. As curious as it may sound, Type Bs, they're just kind of, like, "Tell me what I gotta do, and then let's all go out and have a burger."

Being first assistant counsel to the governor was the best, most fun job I ever had. Some would assume the best job I've ever had is this one. Time Warner is certainly the most interesting company. It has the highest assets, the most interesting set of businesses, and, through technology and globalization, they are morphing into other businesses. All of that is fascinating intellectually. And it's a hoot. Something makes me laugh everyday. But I have too much responsibility, too many people that I have to supervise and sit in judgment of, for this to be the most fun job I've ever had. The stakes are too high for that. You can have a lot more fun sometimes when you understand how you fit into the team, but you're not responsible for the whole team.

That's how it was in the governor's counsel's office. I was 25 and had a pretty significant set of responsibilities. I was the governor's principle spokesperson to the legislature. I was basically managing the relationships between the executive and legislative branches of the state government. I really enjoyed that. A lot of it relates to Nelson Rockefeller. I really thought he was a terrific human being, and we became very close over time. But it was a small office. There were eight of us. We worked together. We played together. We won together.

A wise man once said, success is 10 percent what you know, 10 percent who you know and 80 percent luck. Depending on how broadly you define luck—and I define it pretty broadly—that's probably about right. The who you know is just as important as what you know so, extend your reach. I've known too many people who just say, I have to deal with those people when I'm in the workplace, but then I'm running back to my clan, my crew, my posse and we can just hang together. Again, it comes back to personal security. It takes a degree of security and self-confidence to say, "It's a big world out there. Let me go out and see who's hanging around and what they're up to." But that will reap great rewards.

I followed Rockefeller to Washington. Then I worked for President Ford for a while. When I contemplate the lowest points in my career, one of them occurred during that time.

I was associate director of the White House domestic counsel, which was the White House policy formulating arm. The year was 1975 and there was a huge political flap around the re-extension of the Civil Rights Act. Not a lot of people know this, but, when the Civil Rights Act was first enacted, it had a five-year sunset provision on it, which meant it had to be re-enacted, or extended, every five years. So the Congress had extended it in 1970 and they had to re-do it in 1975. And the Republicans were not overly sympathetic toward this—remember I was working for a Republican president—so they had devised this thing called the Southern Strategy.

The original Civil Rights Act only applied, in terms of its teeth, to the seven southern states that had engaged in all of these voting rights deprivation activities. So the South devised this strategy that said, hey, what's good for one is good for all—let's extend this thing to all 50 states—knowing that by amending the act to extend it nationwide, the votes to get it through would fall away because a lot of the western states would then join with the southern states in voting against the whole act. So, it had the appearance of being fair-minded when in actuality it was a nefarious strategy designed to subvert the act. And Ford was sort of taken in by these crazy southern senators to adopt this strategy.

Well, I remember David Broder, who was a *Washington Post* writer at the time, came up to me one day and said, "Dick, how could you of all people be a part of trying to undermine the extension of the Civil Rights Act?" It really hit me in the gut, because I hadn't really done anything affirmative, to sort of grab the president and shake some sense into him. So this had happened on my watch.

I remember vowing to myself after that to never allow myself to be in that position again. You either gotta stand up and make a loud noise when things are happening that are inconsistent with your fundamental beliefs and with who you are, or you gotta move on. I felt like I had gotten co-opted a bit by needing this job and not rocking the boat too much. I became a little bit more of a boat rocker after that.

I came to learn over time that you're sort of always on stage. A lot of people are very correct in certain circumstances but in other circumstances, when they think it doesn't count, they're different. They will pay the price for that. What goes around, comes around. You try and represent yourself well wherever you are, whatever you're doing, and those wheels will turn in your favor—often times without your even knowing it. The story of how I made partner at Patterson Belknap is a perfect example.

Old white-shoe law firms—as they used to be called for the white bucks the lawyers used to wear during the summer—were nothing if not rigid in terms of how they were managed and how they functioned. You came to the firm, you spent so many years—always a measured course—you came up for partner, and you either made it or you didn't. They always made partners at the end of the fiscal year. In my case, however, I was called up in the middle of the year and told I had just been made a partner of the firm and I couldn't understand why. For the first time as far as I knew in the 70-odd-year history of the firm, they took someone off schedule and accelerated them. So I started digging around to find out what happened.

What happened was, at the time, Nelson [Rockefeller] was still alive and I was representing him. He had offered to donate some big sum of money to the Metropolitan Museum of Art and he told them he was going to send his lawyer up to negotiate the deal. So I went up there to meet with all these prominent lawyers and museum officials.

I stopped at the secretary's desk. She asked who I was. I said, "My name is Parsons," and she said, "Oh you're the governor's lawyer." I said "yes." She hit the intercom button and announced, "The governor's lawyer is here."

So the door flew open and I was ushered in and there were all these people sort of lining either side of the door. I walked all the way into the room, and I turned around and they were all still standing there, facing the other way.

I said, "What are you guys doing?"

"We're waiting for the governor's lawyer."

I said, "Well, he's here. I'm him." You talk about things that happen that might have a racial overtone, and you're better off laughing at it than taking offense! Now, I could get a case of the ass, or I could just get on with it. I got on with it, we were through in about 45 minutes, and I was gone.

Turns out, all these great old men—who were all big something or others back in the day—all hang out together at the Century Club. A couple of days after that meeting, Herb Brownell, who had been Eisenhower's Attorney General, had run into Chauncey Belknap—who was the titular head of the firm—at the Club and Herb says to Belknap, "You know, I met that new young partner of yours the other day and, boy, that kid's a crackerjack, and you guys are so lucky to have him, and I really commend you and the firm for making this young black American a partner. It's really what we need. . . ." I mean, he gave him this whole big thing while Belknap's sitting there eating his pasta, not saying anything.

Belknap gets up from lunch, comes back to the firm and says, "We gotta make Parsons a partner"—because *he* is *not* going to look like a fool in front of *his friend* Herb Brownell, the former attorney general—"and by God, I don't care that it's May as opposed to November when we normally make these decisions, we're making this kid a partner now." That was the deal. I was a partner.

So, you never know where it's going to come from in life. You never know who your champions are, or your detractors either. That story could've easily been told in the reverse. It could have been that someone came into the partnership meeting and said, "Today I heard that Parsons is a real asshole, so let's *never* make him partner."

What's important is that you have to understand how things work, and that it's not all about you. It's not all because you're a great guy or you're a shit. And it's not all just happening when you're in the focus of whomever it is you're trying to impress. I didn't have the foggiest idea who Herb Brownell was. He was just this nice old guy and I was there to do a job. You do the job, you do it the best you can, you try to treat people the way you'd like to be treated. And you do this *every* time because it's the whole package that counts and things can happen that you could never anticipate or predict.

CHAPTER SEVENTEEN

A. Barry Rand

Chairman and CEO, The Avis Group

When Barry Rand was growing up, his grandfather often told him, "If your mind can conceive, and your heart can believe, then you can achieve." Few have put such parables to conscious use in their lives as Rand has.

Throughout his 30-year career at Xerox Corp., Rand built a model reputation as someone who not only performed at the highest levels himself, but inspired others to do the same.

He rose quickly through sales, marketing, and management positions at the company, making waves and receiving numerous awards as he climbed. By 1998, he was second only to the chairman of the corporation and was viewed by many as not only the most natural successor, but the best possible one. When it became clear that he would not be made CEO, Rand opted to leave Xerox.

Unemployed for just under a year, he was single-minded in his resolve to lead a corporation. In fact, Rand rejected several highly lucrative offers in his quest to achieve that goal. At 56, he is now busily reorganizing and reenergizing the car rental company, and he's having a ball. Says Rand, who is married with two children: "You can only be successful if what you're doing is aligned to your passion. It was never `work' for me."

I thought I was going to be a professional football player. In high school I was all-metropolitan, all-Catholic, all-prep in football, basketball, and track. So I was used to being at the center of athletic attention. But a lot of people were all-everything from wherever they came from. Then, you get to college and the competition changes.

In my case, when I got to Rutgers the rules changed, too, so I couldn't play my usual position in football. I was an offensive end, and they made me a defensive end. I was really too small to play defensive end, so I was living on the bench, and I couldn't stand it. It changed my entire personality and, ultimately, it changed the course of my life.

I got mad, quit football, and went over to play basketball. There were some guys on the basketball team who were clearly better than me. But I started in front of them because I had a reputation as a great basketball player, and that reputation impacted everyone's perception, including mine. The coach made all kinds of excuses—"he's got his football legs; he's got his basketball legs; he hasn't practiced with us"—because of that reputation.

But, deep down, I knew these guys had more talent than I did, and it was a real lesson for me about how perceptions become reality. I got it both ways, because the fact was that I was really a better football player, but the guys with a better reputation in football were playing ahead of me. So I learned that this issue of perception and perception management is incredibly powerful.

I had an academic scholarship at Rutgers, and in the midst of all of my athletic angst, I screwed up the B average I needed to maintain to keep it. Once I lost the scholarship, my father said, "You screwed up, so I'm not paying a dime." I had to transfer to American University and work my way through.

That experience really changed me. I sat back and said, "What happened here is you couldn't control your emotions. All you had to do was hang in there—you would have started [in football] the next year. You caused your own failure because you couldn't stand what was happening to you and you just said, "Later with it." By making that decision, you automatically made yourself lose. As soon as you walked away, you failed. You didn't even give yourself a chance to win."

I've seen a lot of people who are very talented, who are very smart, but they can't cope with adversity. They don't have the ability to persist.

There are terrible situations where you can understand why they walk away. But the people who can handle the valleys in their lives are the people who ultimately make it, because no matter who you are, you're going to have a lot of valleys.

You have to look further than the immediacy of what it is you're not getting, and you have to focus on what you can continue to do. Fortitude, persistence, all those kinds of things become part of what I call the survival package that has to be incorporated into your character. If I had been more mature and looked at things with a long-range view, I would have been able to get through that valley.

Working through school taught me that there are consequences associated with your failures that you can't walk away from. It was a real lesson in accountability: I couldn't play any more basketball. I couldn't play football. All I could focus on was working my way through school. I had to just suck it up and move forward. In hindsight, it was therapeutic—even fateful—but at the time, it just felt bad, and it caused me to have a lot of questions about my future.

I had fallen from this pinnacle of being all-everything in high school. Now I started to watch the changing of the guard. I saw the lives of friends who didn't go to college going one way. Then, there were people, who I thought had made it to the next level in college, who fell off the track after college. So the issue for me became, how does someone keep accelerating? And as I was observing people, at various stages, fall *off* the track, I felt as if I couldn't even get *on* the track.

Then, one of my strengths started to pay off. I'm an only child, and I was a loner. So I grew up not having people that I would automatically share things with. I would always work through my own issues and then decide what I was going to do. In that sense, I was very self-directed.

As an only child, another advantage is that you don't get compared to other people. You're just compared to a standard, and either you're making the standard or not. My parents' expectations were expressed in things like, "Don't let people hold you back; don't dwell on the past." My mother in particular was always focused on releasing the blinders on what you're capable of doing. She was a school principal and was always clear about not letting anybody put limits on you.

If you are introspective, and if you understand your strengths and where you need to improve, and if you focus on your abilities, that is self-determination. I think that is critical to success: Focusing on me, what I've done and what I can do as opposed to making excuses. Also key is being able to control your emotions so that you can focus on moving forward as opposed to focusing in on the dire straits.

My philosophy in life is that you can't let events drive your emotions. Some of my friends will say, "Barry, we come to you because we want someone to be sensitive and do the mental coddling." I'm not the person to come to for that. I'm the person who thinks that as long as you are in the woe-is-me stage, you can't focus on what you have to do to get out of it.

We will spend a couple of minutes saying, "Woe is me," but then we have to put that aside and say, "What are you going to do?" You have to go from the paralysis stage to the action stage. My focus has always been on getting there as quickly as possible.

Those two things have helped shape my business perspective. I don't care where this role cuts off or where that organizational line ends, I see the virtual organization. You can't sit back paralyzed. You always have to assume that you are responsible for everything. Many people yield to these artificial barriers that people give them, like lines of authority, and they limit themselves because of these parameters that they think they can't get past. I have gotten into trouble at times because I tend to disregard those kinds of things. But it's paid off more often than not, both in business and in life in general.

I majored in political science and was going to be in a profession in which the currency was not knowing the exact answer but rather winning by having a philosophy built on sound logic and analysis. So, lawyer, political science professor, things like that appealed to me.

But when I went through this period of, "God, am I going to be one of those people who can't make it to the next level; great in high school, and then all of a sudden—Boom!—nothing," that scared me to death. I knew I had to figure out how *not* to let that happen. As I was trying to figure out what my strengths were and how I was going to leverage them, I started working in retail stores to pay for school.

Destiny here: I would have never worked in retail if I hadn't screwed up in school.

I realized that I could sell. It hit me that my skill was influencing people to do what I wanted them to do, so I switched my major from political science to marketing. There weren't very many black people in it, and I didn't know what to do about that, but I did know, from my mother and father, that you just gave it a shot.

When I got my degree, my boss at the men's store said, "Why don't you stay here?" I didn't want to be a big fish in a small pond, so I started interviewing with major companies.

I went to Xerox determined to do as well as I possibly could, but I also wanted to be an activist. Growing up in the middle of the Civil Rights era, you had to say (at least I did), that, wherever you went, you had to do something to contribute to the movement. So when I went into the corporate world I just said, "We're going to take this battle from the luncheon counters and the courts to the corporate board rooms. That's going to be my contribution to the movement." And that's how I could justify being one of the few brothers in the corporate world.

I remember that at the time you had to be at Xerox five years to get fully vested in the retirement program. I thought, well, there's no shot at me lasting five years because they're going to throw me out. Once people handcuff you financially, you have to make decisions based on what's better for you financially versus being faithful to your set of philosophies. I didn't want that to happen, so, for five years, I paid for everything with cash. I said, "When I walk away, I want to be able to do it with no financial burdens at all."

Because I didn't know how long I would last at Xerox, I was focused on getting all I could as fast as I could. It wasn't about titles. It was about getting assignments from which I could develop a portfolio of skills such that, whenever I left, I would have total confidence in my ability to run an enterprise. So I was always willing to take on new assignments, new initiatives, and tough challenges. I always looked at them in terms of two things: (1) what can I learn? and (2) is it something new, something that will add to my portfolio of skills?

I was focused on how to become the best salesperson in the briefest period of time and get promoted to sales manager. I quickly became first in my region and third in the country as a salesperson. In Washington, D.C., the gap between me and everybody else in terms of performance was humongous. But they made four promotions to sales manager, and they all went to good ol' boys. I wasn't even considered. I realized very early that you have to understand the system and how to get ahead in spite of it. It was clear that to get to sales manager, I was going to have to move out of D.C.. I quickly did both.

For a long time, I judged all of my achievements by age. It grew out of competing against older people because of my size. When I was 10 years old I was 5'10½". Because of that, I was always doing the same things older kids were doing—especially in sports, where I literally outgrew the teams with kids my age, and was forced onto older teams.

When you're 12, and you're hanging out with people who are 16, that's a huge difference. Socially, I had to try to act more mature than I was. And, as the only child of a mother who was an educator and a demanding father, who was a federal employee, I always had to excel. My father didn't care about any difference in ages. His thing was to be the best, period. I remember one time I brought home six A's, a B and a B+, so I was proud. His reaction was, "Why did you get the B?"

So I always knew that any thing less than my parents' standard of excellence was going to be focused on, and I got used to achieving things at an accelerated rate. Things went along fine until I hit 30. Fifty is an age that typically sends people into odd psychological states. Well, for me it was 30.

Suddenly, I had to sit back and say, "What do I do now? What's my next achievement? How do I keep it up?" I felt the pressure of having done a lot of things by 30, and being ahead of the game, but then of facing this range of 30 to 40 and no longer being a sort of wunderkind. I got over it largely by just focusing on my performance.

Performance has always been my badge. People used to say, "Why are you so interested in numbers?" When I was a branch manager, I had the best people in my branch, and I was the only manager who was interested enough to interview every trainee. But this was my life's blood, and I wanted to be sure that I was bringing people in who, philosophically, were like me. Black or white, male or female, I wanted people who—using today's terms—would both defend, and celebrate, diversity. My goal was to have the best branch and the most diverse branch, because I wanted to prove that diversity worked, that it was our strength.

I remember an incident in which another manager was trying to get me to give some of my people to other branches. Of course, I didn't want to, but when he insisted, I said, "You go talk to them. If they want to go, I won't hold them back."

He said, "That's not going to work because they will only do what you ask them to do. If you wink at 'em and say, 'Stay,' they're going to stay. I want you to convince them to go."

I said, "I don't know if I can do that."

Then he said, "Let me put it to you this way: If you don't share your people . . . budgets can sometimes be determined by who's cooperative and who's not."

I said, "Well, you shouldn't have told me that, because now that I know that there's some judgment in how you do these budgets, then I know that you can hold me hostage with that at any time. But the only thing that can outrun a bad budget is good people. Therefore, I have no motivation to give up my people. You can give me any budget you want, we'll figure out how to overcome it."

You know how in the Dracula movies people wear the cross? To me, numbers and achievement are like wearing a cross. And anytime they came out of the woodwork to get me, I'd just whip out my [performance] numbers and say, "Here's my cross!" And they'd kind of just shrivel up and go back into the woodwork, only to come out some other time and try again.

This guy tried to talk some of my people into going and nobody left. We were number one in the country for two years in a row. We crushed 'em!

Now, some people don't do things that way. They just say, "I'm not going to take it," and they bolt. But I say, once you make that choice you can't win. You are making the decision—you, nobody else—that you're not going to win, therefore, you're going to leave. That's what I did in college. I only had to learn that lesson one time.

Having said that, I must admit that I now know I stayed at Xerox too long. People have asked me, "Are you bitter about what happened at Xerox?" I'm not. People make their own decisions. I decided to ride the horse into a narrowing track and, as it got more and more narrow, I still thought I could get through. In the end I could say that I rode it as long and as hard as I possibly could. That was a plus. I didn't decide to give up. I rode it right through this narrow crack, and I just couldn't get through it.

I wanted to be CEO by the time I was 55. I set that goal when I was in my 40s. I wrote it down in very specific terms. I've always done that. At

55, I wanted to have freedom of decision. I wanted to be able to retire if I chose to, and I wanted to have a certain financial status, which I saw as a means to having more freedom of choice, more of what I call personal power.

I always knew that it wasn't going to be handed to me, but I chose to hang in there because, if I left, that meant that I wasn't going to win for sure. It became clear in 1998 that, in spite of my determination, it wasn't going to happen.

I was disappointed, but the reality was I made a mistake: My goal was too narrow. It was CEO at Xerox as opposed to CEO, what I could do as a CEO and where that could lead me. I was in danger of defining my success or failure based on one job at one company. There's a huge world out there. I lost sight of that.

I lost some of my objectivity because Xerox turned into a family and, once you cross that track, you cross out of the objectivity that is important when you're doing career planning and defining success for yourself.

The analogy is a fairly mundane one, but it works. People get attached to their first house. They don't want to sell it. It changes from a building, a destination, a form of shelter into home, memories, emotions, *family*. The reality is that it's an investment—one that should be used to get you to the next stage, the *next* house. It should be just one goal in whole-life planning.

When people see that house as "home," not "*a* home," they end up losing out on that investment. They don't leverage it. You see it a lot: Years go by, the neighborhood changes and they are still there in that starter house. That house becomes a symbol of something much broader than it should. That's what I did at Xerox.

The fact of the matter was, I never listened to the people who came to me and said, "Why don't you leave Xerox?" I could have left years ago and been a CEO of a very small company, then leveraged that up, because the CEO experience is what is necessary.

I didn't do career planning. I didn't do whole-life planning. I did Xerox next-step planning. And so, what I ask people now is, "What is *your* career plan? Not the company plan, not what is important to your colleagues. What's important to *you*?"

Most people face the question, Do I leave at the first sign of adversity or not? The answer, I think, depends on personality. I didn't, and I don't think most people do.

In fact, blacks have much longer tenure on average than their white counterparts. Because once we get in there, we think we've reached a safe haven in many of these companies. We've overcome the battles. We've gotten to this fairly balanced situation, and the thought of moving out of a comfortable situation into a new battle can be overwhelming. I think many people of color just get tired of picking the sword up and saying, "We're off to another holy war." You do get tired of it.

It's one thing to make the decision to leave, but, it's a completely different process to say, "Where am I going to go?" For a while, I was focused on just the trauma of making the decision to leave. Only once that decision was made could I then say, "Okay, what do I really want to do?" And that began the four- or five-month sojourn of trying to get to the answer.

Right away, I focused on my age-old goal of being CEO of a Fortune 500 company, but people kept saying, "Why are you focused on that? That's such a narrow segment of all the opportunities that are out there." Other opportunities were presented to me, but I wouldn't even listen to them. After rejecting the sixth or seventh fielder out of hand, I had to do some soul-searching. I came to the realization that I knew what I wanted, but I really didn't know why.

I wanted to be a CEO in the Fortune 500 because I'd worked at Xerox all those years and was on the boards of Fortune 500 companies. Was that good enough? I decided it wasn't. So I started looking at other options, like buying a business and becoming an entrepreneur.

At the same time, I became very analytical about developing a rational scheme—an architecture of thinking—about what I wanted to do and why. I decided that I like the complexity associated with scale. I like an international dimension. I like companies that are challenged in that I'd have to take them to the next level; that's what you have to do to be successful. And I like being able to leverage my experiences.

Finally, after assessing all of this, I came back to my original aim: I wanted to be the CEO of a Fortune 500 company. The difference was that now I could answer why to my own satisfaction.

I'm a Scorpio and Scorpios need to understand people and their motivations deeply, how they think, and why they think that way. I'm naturally introspective, but I think you have to develop that if you're not. If you are inner directed, your decisions really are based more on understanding who you are. The depth of your understanding of what your capabilities and fears and hopes are really becomes the basis for making decisions that you have to deal with years out. And so, as you get older, you go deeper, because that is how you make decisions, but all along the way, it's key.

There is an ancient saying ascribed to Aristotle that has actually been found in hieroglyphics thousands of years before he lived. It's one of the bases of intellectual learning and growth: Know thyself.

I read a book recently in which they discussed proof that what really separates people of excellence and achievement from the rest is not necessarily their confidence about the material or how smart they are or their rational skills. It's their ability to lead and influence others. Well, the platform for leading and influencing people is based on knowing thyself; knowing *you* first; being able to control *yourself*.

One of my basic platforms for living life is being really honest with myself, knowing my limits and what I need to do to overcome those limits, knowing where I need to grow. All that comes from knowing myself.

When I was presented with something so basic as, "Why do you want to be a CEO?" and I couldn't explain it to my satisfaction, I had to dig deep, because it's important to know, not just what you're doing, but why.

At Xerox, I was always determined to protect who I was by staying faithful to what I believed in and using that for change as opposed to getting comfortable and saying there's no need to be aggressive. My philosophy has always been that I was there to change the company, to make the company react to and reflect my set of values and principles. I wasn't there for the company to change me. But I'd gotten to the point where I was part of the establishment. I was becoming what I had been trying to change. It was an indication to me that it was time to move on.

Most people who have known me all my life say they are surprised that I'm still the same person. I value that. I may be more serious, and I may act a little differently, but that's maturity; my same basic set of values is there.

But in the year after leaving Xerox—I think of it now as my year of assessment—I had to double check that. An executive recruiter warned me that I would face a crisis around who I was, because unconsciously I would have come to think of myself in terms of my accomplishments and title. That's how you acquire power, and he was right. But I came through it pretty easily because I've always had a philosophy that there are two ways of having power. One is position power: what you do, your title, and all that kind of stuff. The other is personal power: your ability to influence people, no matter what your title is, if you have one at all.

I've always done my job based on personal power, and that's a better way to do it than to say, "I'm the CEO," or "I'm the executive vice president. Do what I tell you to do." It's really based on how you develop trust, whether people see you as honest, whether they see you as willing to help beyond any personal benefit. That's the kind of person I always try to be. Now, whether I live up to that is a different thing. But that is at least the goal.

Toward the end of my tenure at Xerox, I was disappointed in the fact that I was starting to see things through a set of expectations others had of me. People expected me to get to the next level. They expected me to do certain things. I have never operated on other people's expectations and, all of a sudden, they were powerful enough to start influencing me.

It occurred to me that I could, in some respects, meet other people's expectations by becoming vice chairman. I could have ended it in such a way that people could say, "Well, he got to one of the top two positions; that's a success story." Again, I had to ask myself, "Is that a good enough reason to stay? Does that decision reflect who I am?" No. That's not what I wanted. I wanted to go through this whole process, and if I failed, then I failed.

That represented a real turning point for me, because one of the driving forces in my life had been fear of failure. For me, there was always this dual motivation: I'd steer toward excellence, but there was an extra push from that internal voice that says, "I cannot fail."

Some people, when they're faced with failure, try to wiggle out of the situation. They'll say, "It's not really a failure because I didn't try hard," when, in fact, they did. Others truly just don't try, and, mentally, they are okay with themselves. I never got that. In my case, fear of failure makes me do extra things. It makes me stay up later to prepare. It makes me work harder in the gym. It makes me give at least 110 percent.

But sometimes it doesn't matter what you do personally. I've had things happen in my life that I believe are just sheer luck. It has nothing to do with how good or bad I was. It's just somebody watching and saying, "Okay, you tried as hard as you could, you fulfilled that requirement, so destiny is going to be good to you." I believe that.

During my career at Xerox, I did all the core things. I put out 110 percent, and in the end, destiny said that it was time for me to leave.

I learned a lot in the 12 months after I left. I learned more about business than if I had taken another two-year MBA course, and I became a better leader because of the process. I looked at various businesses and industries, assessed how my skill sets would translate in each, and gained a real understanding of the kinds of change that industries are going through today. It has been an incredible educational process. And, of course, I learned more about myself—the critical component in this mix.

Leaving Xerox and coming, ultimately, to Avis made me take a critical view of my business skills, reorient them, and make them much more focused on some of the more modern issues that we will be facing. I wouldn't have known it at the time, but the break was essential. If you've been in any company for a long time, like Xerox, you can find yourself able to think of things only in terms of the Xerox set of solutions. You need to get out of that narrow experience and refresh it, get a more global focus. I was able to do that and then some.

They wanted to make the announcement of my appointment at Avis on November eighth. I said I wanted it done on the fourth, but I didn't tell them the reason why. My birthday was on the fifth and I wanted the announcement to say I was 54, because my goal was to be a CEO by the time I was 55. That was my outer limit, and there was no way I was going to come so close and not achieve it.

Postscript
After implementing changes at Avis that led to a substantial boost in shareholder value, Rand sold the company in March 2001. He has since been exploring other opportunities.

CHAPTER EIGHTEEN

Robin Roberts

Sportscaster for ESPN and ABC Wide World of Sports

❖

Ever the realist, when a teenaged Robin Roberts accepted the fact that she was not going to become a professional athlete, she immediately switched mental gears. She would instead spend her life as a TV sports reporter.

If her ultimate goal—to host major sporting events like Wimbledon, NBA Finals, the Olympics—seemed unreasonable for a woman at the time, no one bothered to burst her bubble. At least, not while she was still at a tender age. But even when reality tumbled in, Roberts held on and achieved what she set out to do.

Now 40, this cum laude graduate of Southern Louisiana University has finally crossed over from being viewed as good *for a girl* to being widely regarded as one of sports' best and most versatile commentators, period. Having won the boys over, Roberts, who is single, is honing new and broader skills as a contributor to stellar news magazine shows including *20/20* and *Primetime Live*. She is also a substitute host on ABC's *Good Morning America*.

Of the latest challenges she faces, Roberts says: "If you play it safe, you may never know what could have been."

❖

My mother swears to this day that I marched in and said at a very young age, "I'm going to be rich and famous." I do not remember this and it just sends chills up my spine to think that I said it.

I don't know why it bothers me so much except that it just sounds so shallow. Not "I'm going to find a cure for cancer." Not "I'm going to solve world poverty." "I'm going to be rich and famous."

I grew up in an environment where wealth wasn't the goal, it was just doing your best. I remember in grade school, I went to career day and came home and told my mom, "I want to be a teacher, and I want to coach." She said, "No, you don't." Here she was, an educator herself. I thought she'd be thrilled. But she said, "You're just saying that because you think that's the only thing you can do." She was right and, in fact, I'd be a horrible coach. When it comes to sports, I like to do it and I like to talk about you doing it, but I can't tell you how to do it. I'm really grateful for having parents who never let me sell myself short.

The truth is, I never gave serious thought to any career that didn't involve sports. For a long time, I wanted to be a professional athlete. I was a state bowling champion when I was younger (girls weren't allowed to play much else), but tennis was my passion. I would go to the local tennis court and just stay there all day long. My parents took it seriously. I had a coach, got a ranking, even won the state championships in mixed doubles with Pat Barnes.

But, if you're a true athlete, you know when it's not going to go beyond a certain level. I realized that in high school, and that's when I turned my interest to communications. It was traumatic in a sense, but I've always been a realist, and because I had a plan B, I wasn't devastated.

My older sister, Sally-Ann, was a news anchor—still is—for a CBS affiliate in New Orleans. We didn't have internships back then. So, I tagged along with her to work and was able to see firsthand what it was like.

I knew there would be barriers for me as an aspiring sportscaster that my sister didn't have. I knew that people would look at me first as a woman, then as a woman of color, because it's sports. It's men going, "Can't we have something for ourselves? Do women always have to try and hone in?" I had already fought those battles. Back when little boys would want to play ball with me, it was my little girlfriends who gave me a hard time, saying, "You don't want to play sports!" So I already had dealt with that. My answer then and now, was simply, "Yes, I do."

Knowing that it was going to be a challenge didn't turn me off, but it was definitely not anything that I relished or looked forward to. I am, by nature, a pretty conservative person, so I didn't want to bring a lot of attention to myself and I knew that just being involved in sports as a woman would automatically bring its share of attention. I would find out that the biggest hurdle was just getting hired.

I've had a boss or two who was very difficult to deal with, and, of course, every woman in this business has had her encounter with the Sports Information Department not allowing her into men's locker rooms. But I haven't had to take a lot of stuff from male athletes. They've been cool. If I ask a stupid question, they're going to give me crap like anybody else. But male athletes never gave me smack for being a woman, because athletes know athletes. They would say, "You walk like an athlete." I'd say, "Is that a good thing or a bad thing?" I never was quite sure about that, but their recognizing me as an athlete really helped.

I ended up being really fortunate because I graduated from college in May of 1983, and by August, I was working at this $5.50 an hour, 30-hour-a-week job on air in Hattiesburg, Mississippi, doing sports. It was the same station where my sister started out. In fact, she was the one who helped make it happen for me. They brought me in for an interview and basically, because I was Sally-Ann's baby sister, they created a part-time position for me.

I had actually received an offer to be a news anchor/reporter at $18,000 a year in Biloxi. But I said no, because, as a woman, you can't do news and then, all of a sudden, become the sports reporter. Your credibility is damaged. So I had a game plan and an innate sense of what to do. I have always trusted my gut, and I know that I'm ahead of the game in that regard. I think it came through my athletic background of always knowing how to position myself.

I was in Hattiesburg nine months when I got another offer to join the Biloxi station. They called as soon as they had a sports opening. I did well there and I liked it, but I was really anxious to get to a major market and, the more I tried, the more frustrated I got.

Every time I got a foot in the door, news directors would say, "I don't think my audience is ready for this." I kept making cold calls and sending out tapes and hearing that over and over again. I call them my reject tapes. I felt as if they just had a big rubber "Reject" stamp. They'd get my tapes and—BOOM—stamp them, and send them right back. It was very discouraging and very hard not to take personally.

But I had to caution myself and say, "Okay, I'm young. I haven't been doing this very long. Don't play the victim. Don't automatically think it's because you're black or a woman." I tried to find out why I didn't get certain jobs or assignments. I purposely projected this image of confidence, and I was very persistent.

Meanwhile, the news director in Biloxi asked me if I wanted to be the news anchor because I was very popular. That was a real turning point; had I done that, I probably would have stayed right there, and I might not have had the courage to continue to look for sports jobs. I was about 25, and they would have doubled my salary if I became the news anchor. Again, I said no.

That was the first time that it was hard to turn down an offer. I didn't even have a nibble from any major markets, and it was the first time that I questioned myself—the first and only time, really. I talked to my parents and to friends, and then the ultimate question was posed to me: What is going to make you happiest? I didn't want to cover murders and fires. Even though it was a difficult decision, I knew deep down, it just wasn't what I wanted to do with my life at that time.

I kept getting raises in Biloxi because their Q-ratings said that I was well received. And yet, in looking for other jobs, I wasn't getting any callbacks. In this industry, so much depends on the person who's watching your tape and how they happen to be feeling that day. That's the scary part. It is *so* subjective, and you have *so little control.*

It's like figure skaters or divers, whose success or failure is judged by a panel just sitting there, watching them. If I'm playing basketball, and I score more points, I win. I don't have some judge going, "Well, that jump shot wasn't quite a flawless 10." Are you crazy? I could never compete in a sport where somebody else is telling me if I'm good or not. And yet, that's largely the reality of my career. Even when I do my best, the results are often out of my hands and that is still hard for me to deal with.

I talked to my sister about it and she introduced me to a talent scout from a major network. He suggested that I send tapes out and just ask for advice. So that's what I did and it took people off the defensive. I realized, people like helping people. They can't necessarily give you a job, but if you're asking them for a critique, and making them the expert, they like that.

I was living at home, so I made sure to send tapes to markets where I knew my parents would be traveling. That way, I had a ride and a place to stay (obviously, I was not making big bucks in those days). My folks were planning to go to Nashville for a convention, so I sent tapes up there to news directors and said, "I'm going to be in the area and would just love to come by and say hello." I didn't ask for a job. They didn't have to pay for me to get there. I was just going to be in town. Only one station agreed to meet with me. It was the NBC affiliate.

I met with the news director. He liked me and said, "Let's keep in touch." I called him every couple of months until, finally, he said, "How about if I create a position—life-style reporter—but you'll also work in the sports department?" Great! But the catch was, he could only pay me $17,500.

At the time, in Biloxi, I was making almost $30,000, but I didn't hesitate because it was a larger market with more prestige. I would be able to send my tapes out from a station in Nashville as opposed to Mississippi. So, again, I was focusing on the big picture.

That was really my first lesson in the power of "let go and let God," not that I got it at the time. I mean, honestly, sometimes the harder I try and the more I want things, the more difficult they get. When I release, it's amazing. I've had to come to the realization that some doors are shut for a reason. That's very hard to admit, because we all feel that we know what's best for us, and the unseen is so difficult, especially for people who are driven by tangible results. But you can't say, "Okay, if I make five calls, or if I exhaust everything, then that means it's not to be."

I have had to accept in the last few years that God's delays are not His denials. Everything is not going to happen in my time frame.

By many standards, I did well. I was out of school in 1983 and working at ESPN by 1990. I had worked in four markets in the seven years in between. But we all have a feeling about where we should be and, half the time, by my game plan, I was behind and frustrated because I still had so little control.

That's why I like Oprah so much. No one decides her fate. I can't wait until I can *make* the calls and not *take* the calls. In this business, that's something that comes with time, position, luck, and a lot of other things. Or it may never come. I don't care if you're black, white, or purple. It's an industry that's very difficult to crack in that regard.

I'm not a control freak, but I do have a military background. My father likes things a certain way, and I am his child, so I do like a sense of control and routine.

I always start the day off by reading positive material. Even before I get out of bed I have my little books set aside. They're devotionals like, *Streams in the Desert*, which is something that we've read in my family for generations, and *Simple Abundance*. It's always about 20 minutes of reading culminating with a passage from the Bible. Only then do I get up, because once you get out of bed, there are so many other things that you know you should do and want to do, that it gets away from you. I just want to be able to hit the floor, and go, "Alright, I've reinforced myself; I can meet the day."

I'm a big goal setter. I love to make my to-do lists and to be able to check them off. There's a sense of power in being able to say, "Did that, did that." I don't do it all the time, but I do it whenever I know that I'm going to have a busy day. I'm more efficient that way.

I don't call them New Year's resolutions, but I'm very big about reevaluating at the end of the year, looking back, and seeing what I achieved and what I didn't. But I don't focus on new beginnings only at the start of a new year. If I feel like I'm in a rut at any time of the year, I get very focused on the idea that each new day offers the chance for a fresh start. Somehow, within myself, I can get very fired up about tomorrow.

My motto has always been "Think big, dream big, but focus small." Sometimes you can get overwhelmed when you have a massive vision, like, "I'm going to be running the network in three to five years." I know the day-to-day things ultimately will get me to my ultimate goals.

There are so many misconceptions about success. The biggest is that it solves all your problems and makes you somehow better than others. Another is that it's unattainable, that it takes too much hard work, that it's for other people.

In reality, getting ahead is as simple as getting started. So many times we just don't get started. Once, when I was in a rut, I did some work with Tony Robbins, the motivational speaker, and it really helped me. It was very basic: Take action. So many of us want to be successful, but we won't take action, we won't pick up the phone and make a call, we won't do whatever it takes to get to the next level. It's easier to stay comfortable, so we won't take risks.

When I first got to ESPN, I never stopped asking for the assignments I wanted—no matter how many times they told me no—and I never stopped asking how I could improve. I got my big break there—hosting *NFL Prime-Time* along with Chris Berman and Tom Jackson—by asking for it.

I was there for about six months when I found out that one of the hosts of *NFL PrimeTime* was leaving. This was *the major football show*. I very innocently went to the managing editor and said, "You got somebody in mind for the *NFL PrimeTime* show?" I remember John Walsh kind of looking at me as he said, "What do you have in mind?"

I said, "Well, I'm doing the Sunday morning show. So I thought it would be just good, you know, because I'm already here. I could just stay and do the nighttime show." This was a really plum assignment. He just kept looking at me a bit strangely and he said, "Well, uh, give me a few days."

He called me back into his office at the end of the week, and his exact words were: "I'm going to take you up on your offer. You can do *NFL PrimeTime*."

I was cool: "Well, great. Thank you." I walked out of there going, "Yes!"

Sometimes we sit there and go, "I'm going to get this job. I'm going to get this assignment. They're going to come to me," and we're disappointed when they don't. I was taught to go in there and ask questions and put myself in a position for good things to happen to me. And it's not always asking for a job. I'm big on just getting input—from *anyone* who can be helpful. Heck, I'll even call the head of a network.

After I had been at ESPN for a year or two, I was asked to be the host of *American Gladiators* and they were throwing a ton of dough my way but I was worried that doing it might prevent me from ever achieving my big dream at the time, which was to host the Olympics. My agent said, "Call Dick Ebersol. He's the head of NBC, they have the Olympics, call him."

So, I called him. I told him my situation and said, "I value your opinion," and we hit it off from that point. He knew who I was—which thrilled and amazed me—and he said that while he didn't think it would hurt me, because I had already established myself, it was not necessarily going to help. So, I took a pass on it.

When I told my family and friends what I had done, they were like, "You called Dick Ebersol!" I thought, what's the big deal? All he could do was not take my call. But he did. So I'll take chances—and the athlete in me is willing to fail.

If you want to be successful, a willingness to take risks is mandatory. If I hadn't walked into John Walsh's office and asked about *NFL Prime-Time*, would I have gotten that position? I don't know, probably not. If I hadn't called Dick Ebersol, would I have made the best decision? Again, I just don't know. What I do know is that to get ahead, you have to be willing to put yourself on the line.

Michael Jordan did this great commercial where he talked about the thousand or so free throws and game-winning shots he missed over the years. We always think about him *making* the winning shots. We never think about all the shots he *missed*. Some of us play it too safe. Here was Jordan saying, "I'm not going to sink the winning shot every single time. But if I don't take those shots, who knows?" That's how I look at myself. If I don't take that shot, I won't know.

I have no regrets. The lifestyle that I lead is similar to a professional athlete: the travel, going to the sporting events, even though I'm not participating. I've been to the Olympics, Wimbledon, WNBA and NBA finals, SuperBowls. So I'm living the life that I wanted; just not on the playing field.

It used to be totally fun. I have to admit that in recent years it's become work for the first time. But now I'm filling in for Diane Sawyer on "Good Morning America." I have an hour special that I'm working on for ABC. I did a piece for *Prime Time Live*. I'm working on pieces for 20-20. It's the big leagues, and I'm still a little bit out of my element.

When I'm dealing with sports, I can almost floss at the same time. It's a challenge in itself to remain challenged by it and upbeat about it, and not feel like it's old hat. But, in the past three years or so, I've become really comfortable with what I'm doing and how I am perceived. I'm not stopped in airports anymore by people who say, "You're really good—for a girl."

I know that people now see me as a sportscaster. I don't feel like I have to prove anything anymore. At the same time, I still know I can never be average (not that I would want to be). I always felt that if I did well, other women and other minorities would be given opportunities, which has been the case. We have a number of women now on-air at

ESPN. There are only a few, but it's continued to grow. I don't take full credit for that, but I do take partial credit because I knew if I stunk up the place that they would have been less apt to hire us.

I do feel that now, when people are hiring women for these jobs, they're not thinking that they're taking a chance. I'd like to think that some of that is because I've been successful. But I don't think you ever feel like you've made it in this industry. It's so fleeting. I don't care who you are, or how much money you're making, you can be gone tomorrow, we all know that. So it's much more important to feel good within yourself, and have that be your measure of success, as opposed to needing other people to say that you're successful.

Early in my career we had consultants that I called "insultants," and I would act or dress this way and that way because they said I should. Then it finally dawned on me, they *have* to make suggestions or they're out of a job. Once I realized that, I eased up on myself and used more of my own common sense.

This is a business where the input about everything you do never stops. Some of it is constructive, but some of it is just downright vicious. Imagine how you would feel if, with everything you did, you had, literally, a million critics. It wears on you a little bit. But as I've gotten older and more comfortable in my own skin, I've realized that what people really see is my genuine self. The more comfortable I am with that, the more people respond to it. The vast majority of folks that I work with are the same when they step into the studio as they are outside. There are a few people that take on a different voice or a persona, but, frankly, that's too much work. I believe less is more. I've got enough going on in my life not to complicate it with silly stuff like that.

What matters is being accurate. Being respected. Being credible and knowledgeable and just doggone good. I also like to be entertaining. But today in sports there are some really sad stories. The violence right now in sports is very troubling. So it's important that people see me as a real journalist—no bells or whistles.

While I never wanted to do news when I was breaking into the business, it's time to branch out now. As you get older, the issues become more important than, "How 'bout those Yankees!" It's all about evolving as a person. There's so much more I know I can accomplish, so many more people I can touch.

There's a young woman who went to Virginia Tech and she was a production assistant at ESPN. She came into my office several months back and said, "You're the reason why I'm here. I watched you, and I felt like, 'Yeah, it can be done.' It gave me hope." I was looking at her and she was so sincere that she was trembling, and it hit me that somebody is now out of college who saw me doing this from the time they were in junior high.

I never consciously thought about being a pioneer or anything even approaching that. That wasn't my motivation by any stretch of the imagination. I was just out here, doing my thing, and that gave this girl a point of reference that I didn't have growing up. Unintentional as it was, that really made me feel good, and I think that the older you get, the more you need to have that component in your success. You become less focused on yourself, and more on your impact on others.

I am who I am. I don't act any differently now than I ever did. Fortune and fame accentuate the person you are to begin with. If you're a good person and you come into a lot of power and money, you do more good. If you're a terrible person, with money and fame, you're even worse. Whoever you are, I think the most important element in your life is your inner circle of family and friends.

My inner circle would never allow me to lose myself. When I saw Darva Conger, the woman who "won" on, *Who Wants to Marry a Millionaire*, I thought, Where are her friends? She needs a new set. I see it with athletes every day, and it's very disturbing.

My father was a Tuskeegee Airman who never boasted, never bragged, even to his own children. I come from a long line of achievers who've stayed very grounded and very true to certain basic beliefs. Talk about humility. When you have that kind of blood running through you, you can't help but keep things in perspective. That's something I was blessed with.

I have learned that it doesn't matter who you are, or how good a person you try to be, or how well you do your job, some people are going to flat-out be threatened by others. I have no control over that, so it's their problem, not mine. What I can control is who I am and what I give, what I put into it—work, life, all of it. At the end of the game, that's got to be enough.

CHAPTER NINETEEN

Joyce M. Roche

Former President, Carson Products

In her much celebrated career, Joyce Roche went from one groundbreaking opportunity to another. A trailblazer in the marketing arena, she was the first black woman vice president at Avon Products Inc. During her 19-year career there, she rose to become vice president of global marketing. When she hit the glass ceiling in 1994, she decided to leave the company she loved.

In 1995, Roche joined Carson Products as executive vice president for global marketing and was promoted to president in less than one year. During her tenure as president of the African American personal-care company, total sales increased by more than 130 percent, its market share rose from 13 percent to 20 percent and international sales increased from 20 percent to more than 35 percent of the company's revenues.

In addition to being featured in *Black Enterprise*'s "21 Women of Power and Influence in Corporate America," and "40 Most Powerful Black Executives," in 1998 Roche was selected as one of *Business Week*'s "Top Managers to Watch." Roche, who is 52 and single, sits on the board of directors of SBC Communications, Inc., Tupperware Corporation, and Anheuser-Busch Companies. As for what the future holds for her, she says, "I have learned to let the future unfold, and to not try to rush it along. In the meantime, I'm just enjoying right now."

Ever since I was little, I wanted to attend Dillard University, but it seemed like it was going to be an impossible dream. I just didn't have the money. I enrolled at Southern University in New Orleans, but Hurricane Betsy radically changed my plans, flooding my house and keeping me out of school for a year.

By the time I entered Southern in the Fall of 1966, I had made up my mind I was going to Dillard, no matter what it took. I applied for and received a National Defense Loan, and started there in 1967.

Dillard proved to be the right place for me. It enabled me to set realistic goals, and gave me the tools I needed to achieve them. I received the education, the values, the support I needed to deal with the world "out there." That support made all the difference. It gave me a strong sense of who I was and what I wanted to accomplish. It awakened a belief in my ability to compete and succeed anywhere. I learned that I could take risks. I could go beyond my present dreams and seize new opportunities. For me, the motto of the university, "From Confidence, Courage," became a reality.

Of course, I received a good strong basis of values at home, from my parents and family, but it was the reinforcement of those values—all of that uncompromising emphasis on respect, on believing in yourself, and on looking to help somebody else, not making it just a "me" thing all the time—at Dillard that enabled me to achieve my goals in graduate school and in corporate America, in spite of some pretty big challenges.

Dillard—and life—taught me that every single one of us has the power to shape our own future, and our people's future. But, to do that, we must define success in real terms and on our own terms. It's an individual definition of success that determines one's goals and one's actions.

By the time I graduated in 1970, there were opportunities available that I had never even dreamed existed. The civil rights movement and affirmative action were changing the consciousness of the country and opening new doors to African Americans.

Ivy League schools began to seek minority students for their MBA programs and two friends piqued my interest in the idea. I pursued it, even though I didn't have a clue of what I would be getting into, since I had never taken a business course in my life.

I applied to Columbia University, they gave me a full fellowship, and I accepted, but it was scary. Columbia was a fiercely competitive school in a strange environment, far away from home. Needless to say, I wasn't exactly one of the crowd. Women made up only 10 percent of my class and African Americans, less than 1 percent. I had no choice but to put what I'd learned at Dillard right out there on the line, and it served me well.

At Columbia, I not only gained the business training I needed, but I discovered my niche in marketing, a field I hadn't even known existed! By the time I graduated from business school, corporate America was opening its doors to women and minorities, but the economy was taking a downturn, so I left without a job.

After a few months of sending out resumes, I landed a position at City University [of New York] in their business office, but it wasn't what I really wanted to do. So, after a few months, I began sending out resumes again and by then corporate America was opening its doors a little wider. I stepped through those doors into a world that challenged me and my values to the core.

When I began at Avon, in an entry level position in marketing, there were only three other women in the entire department, and one of them started at the same time I did. As pioneers in a basically white-male world, we had virtually no role models.

Our mistakes were legendary. At first we dressed like, talked like, and, to a great extent, acted like, the men who were in power. I'll never forget a woman who came into Avon as a vice president. This woman had the worst mouth I had ever heard on anyone in my life. Obviously, she was emulating more of a rough male demeanor, and this must have worked for her at her other company. But it was so offensive that it ended by tripping her up in the end. Ultimately, she was ejected from the culture because at Avon it just wasn't acceptable.

It's very difficult when you're not part of the network and the network doesn't share, and, as women, that's the position we were in. Her strategy—to emulate those in power—was on target. The problem was that she picked up the wrong characteristics.

Early in my career, I watched and learned to pick up the characteristics of the people who succeeded, but you always have to be careful; if those characteristics suit the company culture but don't fit within your core values, then you need to question whether that's the company for you. If they don't fit, you'd best get out.

During my tenure at Avon, I was often the first or the only black person or woman, and my fear of being wrong or looking silly paralyzed me. Not only was I worried about how my mistakes might affect me, I had a fear about the implications that my mistakes could have on others coming behind me.

I can remember sitting in meetings and silently working out an idea in my head, trying to get the wording and expression of it perfect in my mind, and I'd be just about ready to speak when I'd hear someone else—usually a man—say what I was going to say. He'd just spit it out, clearly not trying to make it flawless, but it would be fine, totally well received, and my opportunity to make that contribution would be gone.

Women and minorities often don't speak up for fear of being wrong. What they don't always realize is that that hesitancy is often viewed as ignorance or incompetence. I finally realized that I had to just open my mouth. Once I did, it was clear almost immediately that it was going to be okay. I wasn't going to die or get laughed at or get fired on the spot. The confidence that comes from that builds on itself over time.

The other thing we tend to do is try to almost preempt other people's negative responses to our ideas. Another woman at Avon, who was either the first or second female VP, couched everything she said with, "Now, this might sound silly, but . . . " She demeaned herself every time she did that. There are better ways to hedge your bets.

The first time anyone ever did let me know they thought I was stupid was after I left Avon to work at Revlon. At Avon, I had moved quickly from that entry level position and was promoted four times in four years. But then I got my first glimpse of the glass ceiling.

I was manager of merchandising and my next step would be a big one—to director. Suddenly, there just didn't seem to be as many people or as much willingness to say, "Let's give her a chance and see what she can do." Luckily, fate stepped in, and I was offered a director of marketing position at Revlon. It represented a big risk because, as companies go, Avon and Revlon were like night and day. At Revlon, I would have to prove myself all over again, but I decided the risk was worth taking.

It was the first time I worked for a woman. I had been there a couple of months and my boss asked me to do something that had to do with "SKUs." Well, every organization has their own lingo, and I had no idea what an SKU was. At Avon, we called them units.

I looked at her dumbfounded and asked what an SKU was and she looked at me as if to say, "You are the stupidest person I have ever seen." I knew at that moment that I would never allow myself to be put in that position again.

There was another woman at Revlon who had come in from Avon shortly before me. From then on, I would always listen to my boss' instructions as if I absolutely knew what she was talking about. I would write it all down then go to this other woman and say, "Okay, please translate this into Avon-speak." And she did. She was enormously helpful to me in that way.

I tell people all the time, mentors are great but you can get wrapped up in finding one person, more senior to you, who has the time and desire to help you get where you need to be, and that can be hard to find, especially within an organization. You can still get a lot of what mentors provide through networks of people at your own level or even under you. I always did that.

By the time the 1980s rolled around, women and minorities were a permanent presence in corporate America. We hadn't reached the top of the ladder, but we were moving up, learning as we went along, and we were making a difference. After two years at Revlon, Avon called to ask me back. They held out a carrot, which was the potential to become an officer in a short period of time. I took it.

Then, the environment changed again. The new decade brought in a whole new concept of success. Biggest and most expensive became the best. Materialism was rampant. What you owned became more important than what you contributed. The value of education and long-term growth were replaced by lots of hype and short-term glitz. The goal became winning at any cost. The motto: Me first.

It was a game with everything turned upside down. Milken, Campeau, Trump, Boesky, and hundreds of others won big, and the media trumpeted their successes. On the surface, it looked so appealing. Then the cracks started to appear. The same newspapers and magazines that had praised their victories were soon full of their failures: Campeau was bankrupt; Trump was in trouble; Boesky, Milken, and many others were going to jail.

For most blacks, the excesses of Wall Street seemed pretty remote from our daily lives. We hadn't become the big inside traders or corporate raiders or junk bond dealers, but those false values affected all of us. They challenged and in some cases changed our deepest beliefs.

Think about it. For some, it was simply a feeling of dissatisfaction, of inadequacy—even failure—that we could never achieve the status symbols that the world now equated with success. Others became workaholics, putting their families and personal lives on hold as they sought success. For others, it became a continual pursuit of material possessions, leading them deep into debt for the right house, the right car, the right clothes.

The same warped sense of values that destroyed some of the big shots contaminated us and our children. We forgot the value of education and our educational system slid into disrepair. We forgot the difference between self-worth and material worth, and our humanity and sense of community were compromised in the process.

When I was growing up, people just cared about each other. It wasn't a question of, "I have and you'd better get . . . ," it was a question of, "I have. What do you need?" Everyone understood that today they might have, but tomorrow they might need, so you'd never risk turning your back on anybody else. More of us thrived as a result. Even in a business environment, keeping and nurturing that sense of humanity is a plus.

We were all damaged by the unrealistic, morally corrupt concept of success that says, "Money is all that matters. Greed is good. It doesn't matter how you get what you want, as long as you get it."

As 1990 began, the mood of the country changed dramatically again. Disillusioned with the empty promises of the 1980s, frightened by the high-profile failures, people began to ask some good questions: "What is it that really matters? What is the point of it all? What does success really mean in terms of my own experience?"

For me, such soul-searching led me to take the biggest risk of my career. After being back at Avon for about 14 years, that old glass ceiling found its way back. I was an officer by then and I had held every marketing position in the company. I had to decide between continuing to do some of the same old things or jumping out with my knowledge and experiences and with no job in sight. I decided to leave Mama Avon again.

Again, the risk paid off. For one thing, in the months I had between jobs I learned a lot of valuable lessons. I learned that our goals can't be dictated by other people. Each of us has to define success for ourselves.

We each have to discover our own purpose, our own mission, our life's work, and pursue it to the best of our ability. And, I mean, the *best* of our ability. And I learned that sometimes that requires jumping out there into the vast unknown and taking a risk.

After fielding a number of positions that were not for me, I was introduced to the investors who were in the negotiation phase of buying Carson Products, a hair-care company based in Savannah, Georgia. They were looking for someone like me. I joined the management team as executive vice president of global marketing and, in less than a year, I became the president and chief operating officer. I was finally able to move beyond the glass ceiling.

My three years there were a whirlwind experience. We set out to completely redefine the company as a personal-care company—and a global one at that. We did acquisitions. We went from concept to market with new lines and new products at warp speed. We went public on the Johannesburg stock exchange with our South African subsidiary and also took the parent company public on the New York Stock Exchange.

We had a great strategy and we had some great successes, particularly abroad. But there was a lot of frustration, too. The problem was in implementation. We bit off too much. We tried to do everything at the same time; the learning curve was huge and the juggling process was extremely difficult. The financial community kept challenging us, but the investors kept insisting that we could do it all. In the end, we disappointed the market and the shareholders.

I probably should have gotten tougher with the investors and said, we can't take on everything. But some of that old fear came back—fear that if I said that, maybe they wouldn't want me. You should always have enough confidence to take those risks.

In 1998, we brought in a new CEO. I figured we'd be able to have an effective divide-and-conquer approach between us, but we had trouble with the division. Within three months we were stepping all over each other and we had to have a come-to-Jesus discussion where it became clear that I had to go. There was no power struggle; it was amicable. But, at first, I was quite disappointed.

Then I was relieved. It had been so hard. I had been on the road for three and a half years, and I was exhausted. After I left, recruiters would call and I couldn't even talk to them. I just needed a break.

And it wasn't as if I had nothing to do. Being at Carson got me on radar screens that I probably would never have been on otherwise. I was asked to be on three boards in three years, which opened up a whole other role for me. I've also been able to do a lot of volunteer stuff that I never had time for. I've done an advertising campaign for my church, and a marketing plan for a local music festival. I never thought I'd enjoy that sort of thing, but it's beginning to feel pretty good.

The world has changed radically since I graduated from college in 1970, and, now that we've entered a new millennium, that change is accelerating. It has made many of us uncertain about the future and how we can succeed in it, but every age has had its challenges. We have dealt with and overcome so many of them. I believe we have the power to do that now.

Why am I so optimistic? Because the times are forcing us to stop and examine who we are, what we want, where we are going, and what it will take to get there. I believe that as we do this, and take it seriously, we'll find ourselves moving forward on a much firmer foundation, with aspirations that are more realistic, long lasting, and ultimately, more satisfying.

In this new information-based era, leaner, smaller corporations will need top talent with advanced skills and higher education more than ever before. People who have this training, who really perform to the best of their ability, will *always* be in demand. Corporations will compete for them, and help them develop. We must make sure that we are among those people.

What will that take? Money? Power? Extraordinary brilliance? Social contacts? It never has before.

If you take a hard look at the executives and successful entrepreneurs and professionals profiled in *Black Enterprise*, you'll find they weren't people with extraordinary talents, extraordinary brilliance, extraordinary wealth, social positions, or extraordinary advantages of any kind. They are ordinary people from widely different backgrounds with different talents and different goals.

They each had good educational backgrounds, set high standards for themselves, and worked to the very best of their ability. Each seized the opportunities at hand and charted his or her own personal path to success.

Education—not only top-notch classroom training, but the teaching of strong values and reinforcement of a sense of true self-worth—is still the key for African Americans. It will continue to show us the way out of limitation, the way to achieve our individual goals for ourselves, our families, our world.

As we look ahead, there are so many bends in the road. We can see but so far. That's how life is. I certainly had no idea that Hurricane Betsy would change my college plans and, ultimately, my life. Or that the civil rights movement and affirmative action would provide opportunities I never imagined growing up.

I couldn't make a five-year plan for success then. I still can't. And I'm not sure anyone really can. Over the next five, eight, ten years, who knows what new opportunities will emerge?

One thing is certain: If we are to succeed, individually and collectively, we must hold on to those same values that enabled so many of us to survive and succeed in white male-dominated academia and business so far. Those same values that prioritize education, respect, belief in oneself, and service to others will see us successfully through anything this new era throws us.

They aren't old fashioned, they aren't about to go out of style. They aren't just nice-to-know sentiments. They are need-to-know rules for living. If we live by them, they will separate us from the pack. And if we do our best, we will have no regrets.

I don't regret anything in my career because it has almost been as if there has been a hand guiding it. At each instance of disappointment, I ended up having an opportunity to do great things that would bring me a lot of personal and professional satisfaction.

I had an interesting conversation last year. Someone made a comment about me and all the people who were featured on a *Fortune* magazine cover about successful African Americans. She was saying that a year or so later, most of those people weren't even at the companies they had been at. The gist of her comment was that getting all that exposure can be the death knell for a career.

I think that's absolutely ludicrous. If I can be an example to kids coming up that there are alternatives to the often questionable quick-buck lifestyle; that you can be a success in working hard and being a part of the system as opposed to working outside the system, then great!

I don't care that some people may end up punctuating my name with "she used to be . . . ." Hell, I never thought I was going to be in the first place. There's nothing for me to feel that I have to shrink from or prove. And that's a great place to be.

Postscript

Just a few months after this interview, Joyce Roche accepted a position as president and CEO of Girls Incorporated, a New York-based organization that seeks to build confidence and capability in girls ages six through eighteen. Girls Inc. has 130 affiliates throughout the country and 70 percent of the girls involved in its programs are minorities.

Hotly pursued by executive recruiters after leaving Carson Products, Roche ultimately turned down two offers from major corporations in favor of this move to a non-profit. "I kept getting corporate inquiries, and I finally realized that at this point in my life, that type of opportunity just wasn't as appealing to me," she says. "When this came along, and I started talking to people about it, and learning more about our programs—which relate to everything from basic education and sports to preventing teen pregnancy to teaching young girls money management—I knew it was right for me.

"For the first time, I'm in an organization where I can impact real lives, and not just the bottom line. It's just proof once again that you never know what's around the bend."

CHAPTER TWENTY

Ruth J. Simmons

President, Smith College

In 1995, Ruth Simmons shattered the glass ceiling in higher education when she became the first black woman to head a Seven Sister college or university.

She was the youngest of 12 children born into a Texas sharecropping family that was poor in material resources but rich in self-respect. Early on, she began her love affair with learning and surpassed even her parents' expectations, attending Dillard University on scholarship, graduating summa cum laude.

After a year of study as a Fulbright Scholar in France, she earned two postgraduate degrees from Harvard, then began her career as an assistant professor at the University of New Orleans in 1973. She was vice provost at Princeton University when Smith came calling.

The liberal arts college has enjoyed some of its most critically productive years during Simmons' administration, leading her already distinguished reputation to flourish. According to her friend, the philosopher Cornel West, Simmons, 55, is "perhaps the most visionary leader in higher education." She is divorced and has a grown son and daughter.

When I first became president of Smith College, I didn't think of myself as being particularly unusual. I had been a faculty member who, like many others, had come up through the ranks and had been in training for this for a long time. And, my own life, like the lives of many women of my era, could not be called planfully charted.

When I was a teenager, my teachers took an interest in developing me. What I did that was unremarkable was that I stuck with it. I got into [college], and kept going and when an opportunity presented itself, I'd take advantage of it.

So, I was at a loss for what to say when suddenly I began to be questioned by puzzled people: "How can someone like you," they said, "become president of a place like Smith?" Was there a particular course of study that was fruitful (surely not the romance languages I studied)? Were there work experiences that I skillfully arranged to build a reservoir of knowledge useful to a college presidency? How did I identify the right professional and educational mentors?

The first few times I got these questions, I was rather perplexed; as it continued I became a little annoyed. Eventually, however, I started thinking very seriously about them in order to be able to say something meaningful about what I consider to be the major influences in my life.

In fact, the things that I thought as a young person would serve me well in my life and career have not necessarily been the things that have served me best. What has helped me most in this position is in many ways distinctive from what helped me get to this position.

When you have a job like this, that is all encompassing, and you are subject to constant scrutiny and very heavy criticism for almost anything you do, there has to be some bedrock that gets you through it all and keeps you pointed in the right direction. That doesn't come from your Ph.D. training or your Harvard education or your experiences as an administrator or in the classroom. It has to come from deep inside. It comes from who I am fundamentally, as shaped by my mother and my family and life circumstances.

I was born the youngest child in a large sharecropping family in a little town in east Texas called Grapeland. Whenever you're born into very limited circumstances, it creates a desire in you to have a comfortable life and to have a life that is without those limitations. But shaped by the social limitations of the pre-civil rights 1940s and 1950s, my preteen and teenage years held little promise of great accomplishment.

Most of my eleven sisters and brothers before me had gone into military service or early blue-collar work as soon as their ages allowed. I had a lot of ambition, not to do what I'm doing now, but to get through school and get a job as a secretary to support myself and help my parents.

I am convinced that my parents shared these relatively modest goals for their children. No doubt, from their own interactions outside the all black neighborhood where we lived, they knew we would eventually face bigotry that would undermine our sense of self and community. Thus, they admonished their children to retain always a sense of themselves and their worth.

My parents' values were clear: Do good work; don't ever get too big for your breeches; always be an authentic person; don't worry too much about being famous and rich because that doesn't amount to too much. In short, just try to be a good person. And so I went about my life trying to take advantage of opportunities as they came along, trying to do good work to the extent that I could.

Of course, it took more than just that, and more than my parents ever could have foreseen. Growing up in the Fifth Ward in Houston, we were close enough to downtown Houston that you could see the skyline from the area. My parents insulated me from that world because they believed that I would never have to make the leap into that alien culture. And, what could they tell me from their bitterly segregated world that could truly help me make that leap? How could they adequately prepare me for the world that lay ahead?

There was one way for certain: My mother and father taught me some basic values that they believed would help me survive, wherever I found myself in life. My mother, particularly, took the time to tell us stories—about the woman who had made the mistake of having too much pride, about the man who had made the mistake of betraying a friend, about people who had fallen to great depths because of other flaws of character. Not well-educated people—my parents finished eighth grade, probably equivalent to about two grades today—they were very, very wise.

For me, my parents are evidence enough that we really do not need sophisticated answers. What we do need is to focus on the education, the formation of children from the time they come into the world, and we need to inculcate values that allow them to live their lives decently and with great integrity. Our primary task is to teach our children fundamental respect for other people.

I learned about this from a very modest woman who was a maid: My mother, Fannie Campbell Stubblefield. Like most housewives of her day, she assumed the primary household responsibilities in our family, but because it was very expensive to rear a family the size of ours, she sometimes worked outside the home or took in ironing for extra income. And from time to time, when she went to clean houses on Saturdays, she would take me with her.

Too young to be able to do anything useful, I was given the chance to watch her as she worked. I was given the privilege to observe a remarkable woman take great pride in her work and carry herself with extraordinary self-respect, and with extraordinary kindness.

We see many people today—young and not so young—who are very angry at their lot in life. If there is a person who had a right to be angry about her lot in life, it was certainly my mother. The sharecropper system was one of the worst imaginable, but the woman I observed went about her work as a maid with the greatest dignity. When she had to interact with her employers, it was with remarkable equanimity. I learned at a very young age then, that interacting with others on a civil basis, a respectful basis, depends not only on how they were raised; it depends mostly on how *you* were raised.

My mother taught me to value no person on the basis of their material worth. She handed down stories of courage in the face of bigotry. She suggested a way for me to survive in the midst of the acute intolerance of our society. She showed me how she could, with grace, magnanimity, and aplomb, carry out the most difficult and most unfulfilling work.

My mother died weeks before my sixteenth birthday, leaving me bereft and confused. In my quest for formal learning, I overlooked for many years the greatest source of inspiration and learning in my life. Eventually, alongside the course of study that I followed in high school and college, I began to try to retrieve, understand, and integrate her teachings.

Over time, as her example came into stronger relief, I developed an understanding that what I had learned from this simple yet elegantly informed woman held as much value as all the books I had read, the courses I had taken, the colleges I had attended, and the degrees I had earned. I learned from my mother, and the way she worked, how to care about my work—how to care about everything I do.

I will always remember the ironing she used to do. There was no permanent press then nor steam irons. She would build mountains of ironing, and I would help her sprinkle every garment and roll each one up in a ball to keep it moist. Then she would begin the long and tedious ironing process.

I remember her careful labor on the piles of cotton shirts: Ironing the collar, ironing the horizontal piece across the back of the shirt, ironing the top and all around the buttons, one by one.

Always, I think of this scene when I speak with parents who worry that they may not be able to give their children the so called best. This is what I tell them: When I watched my mother iron those mounds of clothes and move the iron around those buttons, absolutely insisting that she do the very best job she could, *that is how I learned to be a college president.*

We have had the strongest fundraising years in the college's history since I've been president. Alumnae have reacted well to my appointment, and that's an opportunity for every private institution to feel encouraged that race is not an impediment to leadership.

Leadership is about staking out an area where you can do a good job and caring enough about that job to take chances, to put your skills on the line, to put your viewpoints and vision on the line, and then to see what works.

Frankly, I'm surprised by the courage that you need to handle such a leadership role as this. I don't mean the kind of courage you need on a battlefield. I mean the courage to stand up to opposition, the courage to say what needs to be said to a well-heeled alumna who disapproves of the direction in which you think the college should go. I'm talking about the courage to make difficult decisions at critical moments when you know that the burden for success or failure will be yours alone. I'm talking about real fortitude.

I didn't learn that in the classroom or in previous positions. I learned that from my parents, from watching how they handled the difficulties of their lives, from the model of strength and dignity they provided.

The spiritual underpinnings of my culture have also made a big difference. The reality of a job like this is that it's hard, the pace is grueling and there's a tremendous loss of personal time and, to some extent, personal identity. There are things I can't say or do as the president of Smith because I have become representative of the institution. When you represent a place, something of yourself gets lost in the process. I have ten years during which I must basically set aside many things that I might say or do if I were pursuing only my own interests and representing only myself. That's a tremendous loss and that is sometimes hard to handle.

What do you call on in times of stress? What do you call on for the courage you need? A great many people have the requisite education, but it's those personal qualities—the fundamental and spiritual aspects of your character—that really make the difference in what you can achieve.

Often, women and minorities think they have to imitate to be successful. They think they have to do what their white peers are doing or that they have to be invisible and quiet and that will get them someplace. If there's anything that marks my career, it is that I never believed that, and I never cared about that. I don't believe in disturbing things for the sake of disturbing them. At the same time, I'm not a person who's afraid to take on a challenge and to do something useful and different.

When I came out of college, I had no plans for a grand career. I didn't know exactly what I would do. What I did know was that I would get married, have children, and work in some capacity. That was not unusual for the time.

Women today tend to want the same kinds of things. But they worry more about marriage, children, work, and the balance of the three. They've seen the radical shifts of the last 30 years and the challenges imposed on women and on society as a result.

My mother's model for me was pretty simple. She was a mother and wife; she worked, basically, from home. My model for my daughter has been very different from my mother's model for me, mainly because my time and options were so different. My daughter has seen me work all of her life. She's seen me move around the country for different opportunities. She's seen me lead in several circumstances. She's seen a very independent woman.

But, I did sit down one day when my children were small and I said,

"If I let my career take over, my children will never see me." So, I decided, very consciously, that I would not allow my career to stay on the track it was on. I got off, side-stepped, and slowed it down until my children were at the high school level, which really wasn't that long. Too many people believe they can set aside their personal relationships to make their careers go faster and farther. You can't without paying a very high price.

Clearly, those balances are at times hard to strike. We're going through a major shift in the way that women work and create a life, and society has not yet grasped how to adapt to that. Coming out of college, I expected to get married and basically to be taken care of by my husband. I knew that I would work if I chose to, but that I could choose just as easily to be home with my children.

Women today know that they are more responsible for their own futures than they have ever been. Most young women understand that they will work because they will have to work. My greatest concern for them — and for anyone, really — is that they will not have a balanced life.

As a child, I was surrounded by people all the time. I was a part of my grandparents' lives. Teachers were involved in my life, ministers, all of my neighbors were involved. As the youngest of 12, what I longed for more than anything was solitude, and if you asked me at any given moment, "What do you want? What do you need?" I knew. The answers are ever changing, but I have never in my life not known exactly what I wanted.

Most children today don't have the deep connections I've had. They haven't known the closeness of extended family, the sustaining joy and shelter of strong, long-term relationships with neighbors and other members of their community. No wonder they lack connectedness.

Young people fill their lives with busy things and with a lot of noise, but they are deathly afraid of the silence of contemplation. I ask my students all the time, "What do you need? What do you want?" They stammer and look uncertain. They can't answer.

This generation has had lots of *things* — television, soap operas, videos, video games, computers, things — but they haven't stopped long enough to just think. In this life, you need to know who you are and what you need. The answers to that can't be found in the clamor of a too-fast, too-busy life. They lie in the heart and in the home of human connection.

In this country, we say that if you work hard and persist, you can do anything, but it's almost inconceivable to people that it's truly possible to succeed on persistence and good, hard work. In a sense, Americans don't believe their own hype. Well, I believed the rhetoric. The reason I'm here is because I believed what people told me, and they told me it was doable. They said, "It doesn't matter that you grew up a sharecropper's daughter. What matters is what you offer."

I tell young women not to put a lot of stock in what they read out there about the issues that will shape their lives, and all the discussion surrounding the question, "Can women have it all?" I tell young women that their lives will be shaped by what they put into them, just as mine has been. Whatever societal shifts have occurred and will continue to occur, it remains true that what matters is what you offer—and I'm not referring to one's credentials.

Postscript

On October 14, 2001, Ruth Simmons was inducted as president of Brown University. In doing so she became the first woman president of the Providence, Rhode Island university as well as the first African American to head an ivy league institution.

The November 2000 announcement that she would be leaving Smith four years shy of her anticipated—although unofficial—ten-year tenure came as a surprise. But Simmons' indelible mark on Smith College will remain. On her watch, the Picker Program in Engineering and Technology—the first undergraduate engineering program at a women's college—was established, as were several programs in the humanities; the college launched its most ambitious and successful fundraising campaign to date; and admission yields and selectivity increased, as did minority applications and enrollment. Smith's current first-year class is its most diverse in decades.

In Simmons' first address to the Brown University community, she lauded its reputation as a bastion of idealism, independence, creativity, and humaneness. "I will be intensely interested, you can be sure, in improving both the capital and operating funds of the University," she said, "But I hope never, *ever* to lose sight of the fact that Brown's core values, and *not* the size of its endowment, will forever be this university's greatest asset."

A similar statement can, of course, be made about Simmons: She is keenly aware of her core values. She remains glued to them, guided by them, and unflinching in her resolve that they will carry her through life's greatest depths, and its heights as well.

CHAPTER TWENTY-ONE

Frederick O. Terrell

Managing Partner and CEO, Provender Capital Group, LLC

Rarely are top-gun investment bankers with the guts to become entrepreneurs noted for their humility and kindness. But it's tough not to include such attributes in describing Fred Terrell.

First featured in *Black Enterprise* as one of the "25 Hottest Blacks on Wall Street," in 1992, Terrell was then a rising star at CS First Boston Corporation, where he headed the Mortgage Finance Group and became a senior member of its Principal Transactions Group.

But even making partner at the venerable, old-line firm did nothing to diminish Terrell's identification with disadvantaged black kids in struggling neighborhoods like the one he grew up in in La Puente, California. It was in part his commitment to black empowerment that led him to exchange the prestige and security of First Boston for the risk and responsibility of running his own venture capital firm.

"I tell my sons and other young black kids all the time: Get your feet on the ground and know who you are," says Terrell, 46. "You can't be attached to being partner at such-and-such. Who cares? It's got to be about who you are. Make yourself something to be proud of, and get attached to that." Terrell is married and has two young sons.

I remember traveling with my father to his hometown of Millington, Tennessee when I was about ten. It was 1965, because we were there when the Watts riots were happening back home.

We went to a church there one Sunday and a lot of the people knew of him, because our family had been prominent in the town. In this room there must have been 250 people or more. We were sitting there, and all of a sudden he just stood up and started talking about politics and about what was going on in California. "You know, everybody thinks California is so great," he said, "but California is going 30 miles an hour and Tennessee is going 60 miles an hour." That's the only line I actually remember him saying.

But what stays with me very clearly is my sense of amazement that my father—who was a janitor in a drug store in La Puente, California— had the ability, the instinct, and the confidence to stand up in front of this crowd of relative strangers and just speak. I thought it was just re-markable.

My father died when I was a freshman in college. He was one of those classic guys who didn't finish sixth grade and didn't quite know how it all fit together, but he definitely had his eye on the ball. He had a lot of personality and he was a leader because he was comfortable in his own skin. He was not constrained by his position in life. He didn't let it be what he was about. He didn't let it keep him from being proud and having an opinion, which, I think, is something we need so much more of in our community.

He cared a lot, in his own way, about being entrepreneurial. He would do things like go out to the desert to buy a bunch of watermelons, bring them home, and then sell them to our neighbors out of our garage at this incredibly discounted price. He brought home shoes from people at the store for us to shine. On weekends, we'd go to people's houses to clean them. Sometimes we'd wash cars.

Today, I know some people would say, "how terrible." But we were doing all this stuff together and so, I never thought of it that way. We were all doing something together. And that made it fine. And I think he wanted to give me and my brother the sense of what it was like to sell stuff and have a business. What he managed to succeed in doing, was teach us by example the value of having a strong work ethic. That, and we needed the money.

He had a tough job. He wanted a lot for his kids, and we didn't have a lot. But, like people say these days, "We were rich in family."

I like to tell people who think that my father was just a janitor, that they couldn't be more wrong. Whatever your job is, it's your choice whether or not to let that define you. My father taught me that you define you; your character, your values, your actions define you. And doing those so-called menial jobs, and watching my parents and brother do them, has been the most important facet of my life, because it's given me a deep appreciation for people who do that for a living—especially those who do it with pride, as my father did. If I can instill that in my kids, whatever they end up doing in life, it will be mission accomplished as far as I'm concerned.

For as long as I can remember, I wanted to be a lawyer. I didn't know a single person who was one, or anything near that. I just thought it was a neat thing. I was very interested in news and politics since the third grade and, I suppose, I connected law to that. But in our neighborhood, nobody went to college. My parents cried at my high school graduation, because in their minds I had made it.

I got to be known pretty early as a smart kid. I tested very well, so I got elevated in people's eyes as somebody with potential. But, by junior high, I was having problems with teachers. This was when the Black Panthers were all over the news and I was really into it. From my own limited perspective, I saw all the racism around me. I was reading everything and bringing books to school that would talk about people being hung in Mississippi, and I would take on any teacher who implied that everything was great. They were voting for Ronald Reagan for governor against my candidate, Pat Brown. California was really changing, and I was aware of it even in the sixth grade.

My parents were also very political. They were union people and proud of it. We would sit around and just chop up the world, the way all African American families do in their home. So, I had a point of view, and I wanted to express it. In other words, I was just a smart-ass who would go after people, even a teacher and they really resented it.

I remember that there was a competition to write a speech for junior high graduation. We had to write a theme around the title, "Our Quest, 1968." Mine was about leadership and pursuing a law degree. And politics was in there, with my dream of pursuing public office. I won the competition, but the teachers didn't want me to be allowed to deliver the speech at graduation, which probably fueled my fire a bit.

This was the era where you didn't stand up for the national anthem. You made open protests, like [black track stars] Tommy Smith and John Carlos at the 1968 [Olympics]. We were marching around the high school, and there were police cars on the campus all the time. There was just a lot of stuff going on, and we were a part of it. As smart as I supposedly was, my grades were just okay. My freshman year in high school, the teachers were saying to me, "You know, not everybody goes to college," and I was just blowing them off.

But as a sophomore, I was diagnosed with severe scoliosis, a condition characterized by dramatic curvature of the spine. I was a football player and suddenly I had to have surgery and then, literally, lie in bed in a body cast for a year. You know, I sort of lay in my bed crying and feeling sorry for myself because the world was passing me by. But I learned how to play guitar enough to play bass in a band for many years after that, and I had a lot of time alone with little else to do but think.

Around the same time, my father was diagnosed with cancer. He had an operation, and for a while we were both laid up—him in his room, me in mine.

When I went back to school after being bedridden, I started getting focused on trying to go to college. I had completely flipped. I got straight A's from that point on. I don't know what exactly happened. Something went off in my head that there was just no time to play around anymore. My father was dying. My mother was dealing with it. It was hard, and I just couldn't afford to screw around anymore.

But even though I would go to class and do all that academic stuff, I could also really hang with my homeboys, and I never lost sight of the importance of that. I think I earned their respect for hanging, but for doing well in school, too. I had some different interests, but I didn't feel I was different from them, and I wanted to be accepted. Consequently, I went through everything they went through—and I do mean *everything*. I went through the whole hoodlum thing. I had friends who got killed, not just by rivals, but by police. My parents knew none of this.

How did I not get stuck in it? There were moments when I just snuck off or begged off. Something would be about to go down, and I'd say, "I can't quite do that; catch you tomorrow." But I *would* catch them tomorrow. And it kept me in the loop. I didn't try *not* to be one of them, but I'd draw the line when I needed to. I was class president, but I didn't let it get me too far from being in the mix. Even today, I don't ever want my own success, or what I do professionally to take me out of the mix of what all black people care about and think about. Today, the thing people say that's most flattering to me is, "You don't ever change at all."

I went to La Verne College, a small, liberal arts college about 30 miles from where we lived. My father died my freshman year, my mother was diagnosed with cancer my sophomore year and she had a mastectomy. She couldn't afford to keep our house, so there was clearly no money for school. But the good news was, I always got free money from some scholarship, some fellowship.

I had good grades, and I always had a lot friends and people who wanted to help me. I think some people identified me as a worthy cause because I worked full time from the time I was a sophomore. Here I was, had never known anybody growing up who had a white-collar job, and as a student, I was wearing a tie, working in local government every day.

It started as an internship, but I loved the work. I really cared about it and did a good job, so they hired me full time. I just got lucky. I impressed the right people. I was making as much money as I would have made if I had already graduated. I even bought a car, a shiny new MG Midget. My life wasn't bad.

By the time I graduated I was known in local government as a real standout. Part of that was just because I was black and a kid—20 years old. The city government was all white and significantly older. I was working for the city manager in a power slot that had me going to city council meetings and doing reports for the most prominent people in West Covina, a place that was both literally and figuratively across the tracks from La Puenta. I was also selected to participate in a national fellowship program involved with leadership training. It was with the Coro Foundation, and it was a great opportunity for me.

I have never had a problem talking to an audience. That's something that comes very hard to a lot of people, but, like my father, it's something that comes easily to me. People pick up on that, and it helps lead you into leadership positions. It wasn't as if I was promoting myself. I don't remember going around looking for ways to get people to care. But I was different, so different that the newspapers wrote stories about it. I remem-

206 *Take a Lesson*

ber one said, "city manager's smart aide does city policy during the day and plays in a rock band at night." It was great. It was a terrific time that led to one of the most important transitional periods of my life.

Around that time, I met these guys who would become great heros of mine. Virgil Roberts had gone to Harvard Law School and was an emerging black lawyer who was taking on school desegregation cases. He was a star in L.A. I met him because his sister-in-law at the time and I went out for a hot minute. His roommate, Art Frazier, was a lawyer who had gone to Yale Law School. They had two other friends, a guy named Gilbert Ray, who was first in his class at Howard Law School and then became the first black partner at O'Melveny & Myers, and Charles Harper, who had just finished MIT's Sloan School of Management.

This was a whole new thing for me. I had never met black people who had gone to first-class schools. They became my closest friends. They turned me on to excellence and doing things a certain way; they made me look at achievement and politics from a different perspective. I'm sure everybody has had people who, if they weren't there, their lives would be really very different. Not because they wouldn't have been good guys, but they wouldn't have been given that critical break that changed everything that would come after it. That's what these guys did for me. Because, although I saw myself as a person who had a lot going for me, they just raised the bar to a whole new level and exposed me in a way that altered the entire course of my life.

They wanted me to be like them, and I wanted to be like them. Very clearly, they all said, "You gotta go East," but the lawyers in the group didn't think law school was the thing to do. They thought it was business school. But they were patient with me. I ended up going to UCLA law school for a year, then took a leave of absence to go to the Yale School of Management. But I had no plans to stay on the East Coast. I really wanted to be on the West Coast ultimately, and, in my mind, I was definitely going back to finish law school and then run for office.

But at Yale, I got sucked into the whole East Coast thing. I had no idea that Wall Street was happening; then I spent a summer working at First Boston. I loved it. I didn't think I could do it, but all of a sudden I was doing it. Still, I stayed on plan. I graduated and went back to L.A. to do two things: finish law school and pursue a political career. I wanted to run for city council.

I remember standing in line for readmission at the UCLA registrar's office and my mind started racing. It was thinking, "What am I going to do: East Coast, West Coast?" I really liked the Wall Street thing, and First Boston had made me an offer. I was also pretty much schooled-out. And all of a sudden I just thought, "I'm getting out of this line. I'm going to see if I can do this political thing, and if that doesn't work, I'm going to go work on Wall Street." So I walked out. It was, literally, just like that.

I pursued the city council slot just long enough to find out that I couldn't get elected. A lot of people thought I was a bright guy, but I wasn't connected enough to get the votes I needed. I really struggled with the decision, but finally I accepted the job with First Boston and came back East.

I wanted to succeed, I wanted to compete, but I was scared to death. I was scared because I was a fish out of water. I was calling my mother, saying, "Mom, you can't believe how these people dress." I came to work one time in a sport coat. When I told a friend of mine, he said, "You might as well have been naked." People were wearing cuff links everyday. Given my background, that alone was frightening to me.

At Yale, I had dealt with some of that—feeling different. I knew that my upbringing was very different from the average guy in class and that I had missed a lot and there was no way to make up for that. But it didn't bother me because I knew that my upbringing gave me a set of things that he didn't have, either. I just recognized the difference. It was maybe a disadvantage vis-a-vis pursing a Wall Street career and feeling comfortable on the first day of work, but I thought I had something valuable to offer too.

By the time I got out of Yale, I was getting a lot of offers. So, it wasn't that I wasn't feeling needed or wanted by these big firms. But inside them, there were virtually no black people. The black guys who are considered powerhouses now were just starting their careers. So, I thought I'd do as well as I could but I never thought that they would allow me to be a partner in the firm. It just never crossed my mind back then. I thought I would check out at some point or get checked out.

Ron Gault was the first black guy to make partner there. He joined the public finance department a year before I joined. He had been in city government and had a great reputation. Ron made the transition as well as anybody ever could, but it still wasn't clear whether anyone [black] could make it from associate on through [to partner]. It's a distinction few can appreciate, but it was a distinction nonetheless.

I started out in public finance and I brought in a piece of business in the first two weeks. It was through my political contacts in California. It was a big piece of business, it came out of nowhere, and they were blown away, because associates just don't do that. So, that got me noticed pretty early.

I went into public finance because I thought I would like it. But I didn't. There were great people to work with, but I thought it had a diminished presence inside the firm, and I couldn't handle the corporate finance guys thinking they were better. It was sort of an ego thing for me so I got out of there.

On my one-year anniversary I got asked to start this derivatives group. It became the first group of its kind on the Street. What that did was to allow me to be an associate who knew more about this very complicated new, emerging area than most senior bankers. I mean, they just didn't get it. I got it, and I used it to let them know that I knew more than they ever imagined I might. It allowed me to play a card that we don't get to play very often, which is, "Well, he's the smartest guy about it." Nothing's better than that.

I was coheading this group, (although I didn't have the title) and I was making presentations to the firm's largest clients. I'm not saying I'm the smartest guy around, but all of a sudden I was in a position in which this very senior managing director would be forced to call me—an associate—and ask would I, could I, go to Ohio to help him get a piece of business. Talk about something that humbles somebody on the other end. That was something they were not accustomed to.

I did a deal that was Deal of the Year. I got promoted to vice president in two years (it's usually a four-year track). I was on a fast track.

I don't know if anyone can pinpoint when they actually knew for the first time that they might have a shot at something that they had always thought was a pipedream, but you do know when you're making a lot of money for the firm, and I was. I was also not shy and retiring about telling people. At one point, my group was producing the lion's share of the firm's profit. We were not only doing well, we were hitting the ball out of the park. And I started to think it would be just impossible to ignore that kind of revenue contribution coming from anybody.

I have often thought that if they could have foreseen the promise of the derivatives market, I probably wouldn't have gotten the same opportunities. But the guy who asked me to do it happened to be one of those color-blind white people who just didn't see me as a black man.

There are a lot of them, but I've come across four for whom decisions encompassing color just wasn't their first instinct. So, because of him, I was put on this track, and I had no more idea of where it was going to lead than they did.

I didn't get promoted when I expected to—even though everybody said it was a sure thing. It is never a sure thing for us. But this was as sure a thing as possible. So much so that the guy I was working for had asked me about my new business cards. This guy, who was a partner, fell behind in the process. He wasn't sophisticated enough about the maneuvering that goes on and he even acknowledged that to me. In fact, he felt almost as badly about it as I did. Anybody will tell you, when they go to make partners in these firms it's not a casual thing. "You want that guy? You have to give me 10 reasons why my guy's not making it, because your guy is." It gets to be very personal.

So, he told me I was going to make partner. And while I was telling people on the outside that I didn't really care, it was very important to me. It was a big moment, the biggest in my professional career. And when I didn't get it I just went home, got in bed, and pulled the covers over my head. I didn't want to cry or anything. I just wanted to wake up the next day and have the moment be over.

When I did wake up, I faced a whole day of people who would come by one by one to tell me that they thought I should've made it. Then there was the obligatory meeting with the CEO, who told me, "You know, usually you get turned down one year." I was angry in that meeting as I was told what a great thing it was that I was made managing director and was basically assured that I'd make partner the next year. In the scheme of things, I still made it relatively early. I was a nine-year guy. But to have been an eight-year guy would have been unequivocal. I wanted that. I believe I deserved that.

Was I tempted to say, I'm just going to take my little marbles and go? Sure. But that's not so easy to do, particularly as a black man. They know they have you. You're one year away from partner. You're at a first-class firm. What are you going to do, take your trip on the road? You can find out very quickly that your phone is not ringing. And also, as I've often said: Once you break in a couple of white people, it's no small task to go break in a whole other group of white people. After all, it took eight years to break those in.

At First Boston, I'm walking around on the trading floor like I own the place. I'm out there getting, "Hey, Freddie, what's goin' on? Hey, babe! You know, ba bop, ba bop, ba bop!" I walk over to a new place as the new black guy on the block and a managing director? I don't think so. That'd never work. In general on the Street, they don't like outsiders coming in laterally. It isn't great to go in where people are out to get you, and being black does not improve your odds.

Bottom line: At First Boston I felt like I belonged and I wanted to stay. At First Boston, in the end, I did better than break them in. I think I won them over. And, they won me over too.

The institutional racism still bothers me, and the lack of black presence in these firms still galls me. But I have gone through a complete philosophical shift over the last 10 years, and the shift is from thinking a lot about the political process to believing that it's all about capital.

If people have money, they can build businesses, they can hire their own people, they can shape culture, they can build better schools, they can do the whole thing. I hate to make it so simple, but it's incredibly powerful to be able to invest in people who you think need the money and who you know are going to do great things. Whites have had that for a zillion years. But it's a great void for the rest of us.

First Boston was, at the end of the day—with all the achievement, with all the accolades, with making partner—just my job. At First Boston, I was helping make people rich, and one of the reasons I got out of the firm is because I got tired of doing it for others. I wanted to do it for my own. I now know that that power can change the world. The other stuff we fight about, as important as it is, is a little bit of a distraction. The real guts of it is, How do we put dollars in the hands of businesses and entrepreneurs who want to grow, and shape a culture that we want to be a part of? That's what every other successful group of people have done, shape it for themselves, and their power comes from their ability to finance it.

Look, I'm walking into a corporate suite at a sporting event out in Los Angeles and I have a sports coat on. Some woman was trying to show me her ticket before she went into her suite. Why? Because she assumed I worked there. There's just a presumption in the world about our role. There's a presumption about our class, and where we fit in. So, if I'm dressed in a tux, they're going to think I'm a waiter. And we all laugh about this, and we joke. But when we're not laughing, we're thinking it's amazing, isn't it? And it will continue to happen until we have enough access to capital to change the culture and, thus, change the perception.

There's nothing more powerful, and there's nothing that will end racism faster, than walking into a room of white people who have the idea that they want to build their company, and you and your black colleagues are the people who can do it.

We have this experience now frequently: walking into companies where they've read our stuff, they're anxious to meet us, and the red carpet is rolled out because we're the money. Then, all of a sudden they find themselves sitting there having to explain about their company that's doing well, but could do better, to *black people* and asking if *black people* would care to *own* it. Racism? It all breaks down right there, not because they're going to get over racism. I've given up on that one. I don't ever think that certain people are going to ever like black people and maybe, in their own world, they have good reason. But who cares if you like me? Just respect me, and then we'll do business all day long and if we become friends in the process, all the better.

I know I'm preaching to the choir, but that's the great epiphany. That's the great thing that I've learned in the last 10 years.

I tell young black people: Get your feet on the ground, and know who you are. I do live my upbringing every day. You have to get grounded about who you are. If you're not quite sure, you'll get bounced around and get your heart broken, because the institution knows what is, and it knows where you fit into it. Your black face tells it all. To make even a dent in those age-old presumptions, you have to start by being real with yourself and comfortable in your own skin.

Who you are, the essence of you, I can't tell anybody how to get that. But I know that it's got to come from something other than what you become. You can't be attached to, "Well, I'm a partner for this big, exclusive firm." Who cares? It has to be who you are if all of that gets stripped away. It's what allowed my father to be proud of himself as a janitor. Even now, in the safety of prosperity, I'm not sure I got it as deeply as my father did. But I have enough to survive and to know what I have to do from here on out. That's my parents' legacy to me.

As corny as it sounds, I care about my tombstone. I want people to think that I really cared enough to try to make things better for more people.

There are kids growing up now who are going to be running big conglomerates that, hopefully, I will have an opportunity to help with. That will be my proudest accomplishment, second to raising my own kids. Career-wise, it brings you full circle to have an opportunity to influence the success of others.

A group of young black guys came in for a meeting the other day and one said, "You don't remember, but you returned my call a while back. I couldn't believe you returned my call and gave me some advice. We stayed on the phone for half an hour." Well, now I'm feeling pretty good. I mean, it makes my day to think that these guys think that I'm a good influence.

But I always try to remind myself of just how little I've accomplished instead of how much. At 45, I'm still thinking of myself as a younger guy, sort of seeing all the stuff I want to accomplish and not feeling really like I've gotten anywhere near where I want to. So, I said to this kid, "Now look, we're a small firm, so don't be confused by Provender Capital Group versus what's really going on out there. We're not [financier Henry Kravis' mega-firm] KKR."

And one of them said to me, "Don't say that anymore because you're what I want to be." What can I say? It just doesn't get much better than that.

CHAPTER TWENTY-TWO

Lloyd D. Ward

Former Chairman and CEO, Maytag Corporation

❖

Few in business—or any arena—are as driven, as disciplined, as charismatic as Lloyd Ward, and few are as openly proud of their own accomplishments as he. But then, he has good reason to be.

A college basketball star and Michigan State-trained engineer, Ward excelled his way through the ranks at some of the world's best known companies (Procter and Gamble, Ford, Pepsico) before joining Maytag in 1996.

A born leader and master motivator who listens as carefully as he speaks, Ward, 51, seems ruled by passion for his family (he is married with two grown sons), for sports (karate, basketball, and golf), and for his ambitious corporate pursuits. His intensity is fueled by his absolute belief in the potential for growth and change. Ward believes every individual has that; despite several pointed encounters with racism during his career, he believes every institution has that potential as well.

Ever quick with a powerful turn of phrase, he says, "The oppressed have to overcome the prejudices of society. Knock on the door, pull on the handle, and, if you have to, dismantle the hinge."

❖

Over two decades ago, I interviewed with a Fortune 500 company in an effort to get into their management training program. After very little consideration, the busy personnel manager said, "It's impossible now. Come back in ten years."

So, I thought for a minute, looked him straight in the eyes and responded, "Which would be better, sir, the morning or afternoon?"

My point is that, as far as minorities are concerned, the key to success is determination. And I speak from experience.

In 1966, I was told that I couldn't carry the necessary credits and courses to be an engineer at Michigan State University because I was black and on an athletic scholarship.

In 1970, I was hired into corporate America under the stigma of "qualifiable" because it was assumed that regardless of grades, leadership, and achievement, blacks were simply not as qualified as whites.

In 1971, I had to spend the night in a Kentucky jail because it was alleged that I left a restaurant without paying the bill. Little did I know at the time, it was a for-whites-only restaurant lacking a sign to that effect. They wanted to teach us to avoid their neighborhood, their establishment, their food.

In 1972, the first day on a new job in Albany, Georgia, I drove up to the plant for the first time, a proud, young, black management executive. An armed security guard stepped forward, actually drew his gun, and ordered me to get out "'cause ya see, ain't no *niggers* supposed to be on company property."

I could give you countless examples like that if I thought about it. Even today, as one of the CEOs of America's top business enterprises, strangers continue to regard me as the subordinate to any white traveling companion. And throughout all this—the frustration, the fear, the outrage—I've arrived at what I think is a most important conclusion: Racism is not a problem in America.

Sure, it's real in its impact, and real in it's consequences. But problems seek cures, and there are no cures for this. Getting racism to go away is like trying to boil the ocean. So, we are better off as individuals and as a people when we view racism, not so much as a problem, but as a situation, because situations beg to be managed, not cured. And managing *any* situation is something that is absolutely doable.

The most important thing, it seems to me, is what you bring to the

situation: your attitude. They say that the foundation of success is preparation, the realization of success is courage, the limit on success is imagination. What they don't say is that the *engine* of success is *attitude*.

I believe that in large part, the outcome of a racist situation is driven
by the attitudes the parties themselves bring to it. If I had been as confrontational with that armed security guard as he was with me, I could
have ended up with a serious problem. Instead, I kept saying to myself,
"Lloyd, forget winning and losing. This guy's got to get something he
wants or I'm history. All you got to do is figure out what he wants."

Looking at him with his uniform, his gun, and his badge, it came to
me that here's living proof that Aretha was right! What this man wanted
was a little r-e-s-p-e-c-t. And in that situation, tough as it was to hide the
rising heat under my collar, that's what I gave him.

Before I told him who I was, I told him how much I respected his
conscientious follow-through on local plant policy. Then, later that afternoon, I was happy to personally witness that he was just as compliant
with our *new* plant policy. In other words, this "nigger" got to stay, but
the guns and racists didn't. You see, I could affect policy *and* who ser-
viced the gates.

The lesson here is clear. Racism is not my problem. It should not be
any black person's problem. For us, it is a situation that can be managed
quite purposefully. Remember: Attitude. Life's a do-it-yourself proposition. Don't let it drive you; you've got to drive it.

But there's a larger lesson here. My story includes all those difficult experiences I mentioned, and others. It wasn't only white men
who questioned and judged me. After college, when I'd go back home
to Romulus [Michigan] to hang with my buds, I got, "So, hey man, so
you sold out, huh? Look at those clothes. You don't even talk like us
anymore." You know, this was the late 1960s, early 1970s and the di-
chotomy of being black in corporate America was very real. So, this
was the space they were in, and these were the choices I was called on
to make.

But my story also includes a first-class college education, athletic
achievement, outstanding mentors, loving family, and business recognition and success.

All these elements, the positive and the negative, are pieces of the
plot, sometimes even themes. But they are not my story. My story lies in

how I have *responded* to the events of my life. It lies in how my values shaped my response, in how my response created meaning, and in how I used that meaning to invent my future.

Year after year, I had to think about, who am I? What do I want to become? I've taken a lot from role models and business associates—black, white, Asian, Latino—but within that process, I was always sure that I had to define who I was for myself within whatever space I was in.

This is true for everybody. The events in our lives form the outline of our stories, but not the content. We complete our stories by the way we respond, the way we learn, the way we interpret. Every response is a prism that separates the meaningful from the mundane, and every response adds to our story.

I often tell this tale of a black man who, 40 years ago, wanted a $300 loan to start a business. He wanted his own auto mechanic shop, and he needed seed money for tools and equipment. Just $300. It was a small step toward a big dream locked in a vault; a promissory note unpaid.

He went to more than a dozen banks and got smarter and more polished with each encounter. But in the end, the answer was always the same: No.

A year later, still holding onto what were now just pieces of his dream, he was given this advice by a friend: "Don't tell them you want the money for a business. They don't want to help us help ourselves. Just tell them you want to borrow the money for a vacation."

Well, the man was suspect of the advice, but he tried it. And he got the loan and went on to build a successful business. That man was my father.

I think about that often, and ask myself, "How could he not seethe in righteous indignation? How could he not rise up in anger and disgust?" Yet, what I remember most—and, more importantly, what I *learned* from his example and use to this day, every day—is how he responded, how he played his part in the American dream, how it became part of his story and, by extension, my story.

Over my entire career, I've been working hard at finding myself and realizing my full potential. You know, the absence of slavery is not the same as the presence of freedom. I've been in pursuit of my freedom—the freedom to create my own destiny, to stand empowered by my own strength, not by any outside assessment of who I am or what I ought to be. I've been busy writing my own story. It's something I believe every person—and surely every African American—needs to do.

But as you go about your journey, I believe you have to have a plan and develop an approach that works for you. The approach I use today began back when my career began. It worked then; it works now. And it always starts with my having a specific destination in mind.

My very first day in my very first job out of college found me walking into the headquarters of Procter and Gamble in downtown Cincinnati. I was excited to be there; I was humbled to be there. On that day, all I wanted in the entire world was to be good at whatever I was assigned. I didn't care what the project was. I'd do it, and I'd be good at it. That was my destination. But it didn't take long until just being good wasn't good enough.

Early in my career at P&G, I was exposed to an intellectually stimulating and highly complex technical project. It opened my eyes. It was led by a section head who was two levels higher in the organization. That project helped crystallize my own aspirations, and it transformed my destination. Now, I wanted to lead a project of similar size, scope, and impact. I accomplished that in record time at P&G.

Soon after, I was a section head in engineering when, once again, my destination was transformed. I can clearly recall it to this day: Another project, another eye-opener. This time I was exposed to a category management team that worked on business issues, not just technical projects. Specifically, I was intrigued by a very capable vice president and general manager. I could see myself running a business meeting like the one he was running. I could see myself looking for business solutions— not just technical solutions. I could see myself with a new destination that represented a fundamental shift. Before this, I envisioned being a vice president of engineering. Now, I could see myself running a business, and, I mean, I saw this destination with clarity.

No matter what organization I've been in or where in the hierarchy I've sat, a specific destination has been fixed in my mind at every moment, and I was committed to it, no matter how long it might take to reach it, or how difficult, or how seemingly improbable.

As important as it is to have a destination, though, you have to also enjoy the journey. By 1987, I was vice president and general manager at P&G. But the journey to that destination took me, literally, out of P&G,

into Ford, and then back to P&G. It took more than a dozen years. It required lateral moves, even steps backwards. It took more work than I had imagined, more learning than I realized, and brought more fulfillment than I expected because I *enjoyed* the journey.

If I hadn't, I would not have performed as well as I did during the journey, and I would not have hit the destination with as much impact as I did.

Key to both the destination and the journey is always to add value and to make a difference. But performance alone isn't enough. It's like success in isolation: It's still success, but it's not linked to something bigger.

It takes learning to sustain performance. It takes learning to inspire performance the next time, and the next, and the next. Learning *and* performance linked together make the journey infinitely more enjoyable, and the destination infinitely more reachable. But I'm not talking in mere platitudes here. Learning—true learning, lifelong learning—are so key. You cannot take this concept for granted.

Early in my career, I learned *how* to learn at a level I had not experienced before. I was a group leader in engineering at P&G and I had the opportunity to interface regularly with the director of engineering. He stayed on my case and tied my stomach in knots until, with the help of external mentors from my college days, and an internal mentor named Floyd Dickens, I came to the realization that the central goal wasn't about being right. It was about being able to learn, to grow, to take feedback and do something with it. It was about networking, and that meant connecting with others regardless of their level or job title.

It was about learning *how* to learn, it was about maturity, and it was about *confidence*. It's that confidence that enables you, once you reach your destination, to celebrate. But as you raise the glass with one hand, reach up and raise the bar with the other hand. It's confidence that makes you look for that next level, then reach for that next level. And it's confidence—an unwavering belief in yourself and your potential—that enables you to be excited about the challenges—even the enormous ones—along the way.

I've spent a lot of time studying leadership. I've taken a long, hard look at why some people with the most promising credentials fail to make the grade while others, who may start out disadvantaged, succeed.

This has produced in me a leadership framework that serves me in everything I do. I've identified five elements that produce a special kind of leadership. I call it "unassailable leadership," leadership that can't be duplicated, denied or diminished.

The first is so simple: Dare to dream. In other words, as I've said, always have a destination in mind. The second: Operate out of your imagination, not your memory. This goes to the issue of learning, but it's a bit broader.

It seems to me that, no matter what your color or gender, from birth everybody's got at least one choice: the choice of living life or memorizing it; the choice of making every year a new experience, or a repeat of last year.

Managers get paid to work out of their memory; leaders are rewarded for working out of their imagination. Managers discuss how; leaders talk about why. Managers are controlled by history; leaders write tomorrow's history with their actions each day. Managers are analytical, careful. Leaders are intuitive and more concerned with *progress* toward a goal than with making *mistakes* along the way.

Don't get me wrong. The world needs managers *and* leaders. But it helps to make the most of your moment if you are clear on which you are, and how you can perhaps transcend your current position, if your destination lies elsewhere. The bottom line is that thinking in conventional terms produces conventional results. And too often we only realize that we have been thinking in conventional terms after the fact.

To succeed, you have to continually operate out of new paradigms, and you do that by tipping the scales in favor of what's right, not who said it; what's needed, not who approves it; and what's effective, not has it ever been done before.

Third secret: Walk with elephants. This idea references an old fable about an elephant and an ant crossing a bridge together. As they crossed, it rumbled and creaked. When they got to the other side, the ant looked up at the elephant and said, "We sure shook that thing, didn't we!" My point is, when you team up with an elephant, you can make things happen that you couldn't on your own.

The fourth secret is just as simple: Be a maniac with a mission. In other words, trust in your own individuality and go at your purpose with all the energy, focus, and resolve of someone who can see no other way.

Finally, and for me, this has been the most essential: Love adversity.

You know, if you're a weight lifter, the only way to build muscle and strength is to lift the heaviest weights you can every day. If you only lift light weights, you don't make any progress. Growing up, I was—and still am—a big basketball player, and, to improve, I'd always look for the best basketball players to play against. I'd literally go from playground to playground looking for guys better, stronger, taller than me to play one on one. I was lifting weights.

Today, as a new CEO, still in my rookie year, I've already dealt with more issues than many CEOs face in their whole careers. We're currently off 50 percent in our stock price; we have to retool our business model and regain the volume that our stockholders deserve. The level of personal engagement, time commitment, stress management that this position demands is like nothing I've ever experienced. You talk about loving adversity! But I am compelled to take it to the next level. And so I see myself at work, lifting weights every day.

How can African Americans in particular get anywhere if we don't love adversity? Like our "situation" with racism, adversity is a fundamental part of our story. There's no way around it. It's part of everyone's story. So why not see the opportunity, even the beauty, in it? The fact is, success makes you complacent, while adversity calls out for your deepest strengths and best abilities. And we face adversity even in the midst of success, so we must use it to our benefit. By that I mean, we must embrace it.

Now, I know, it's easy to talk, but hard to live; simple in concept, but complicated in execution. Over the years, I have watched good and decent people, bright and capable people, energetic and dedicated people lose their creative zeal, their desire to excel, their courage to compete and make a difference. Everyone goes through those moments when we question ourselves, and self-renewal is hard, especially when there are daily reminders that the more things change, the more they stay the same. It's like the age-old optimism test: Is the glass half full or half empty? The answer lies in your attitude.

The fact is, we *need* to continually remind ourselves that despite considerable achievement to date, our work is far from over. And we *need* to be clear that it will stay unfinished until the cruelest hoax in business—the gap between hype and hope, between the promise of equality and the practice of equal business opportunity—is over. We *need* to see the adversity, because only then can we *deal* with it.

Right now, American enterprise fights harder for minorities as customers in the marketplace than for minorities as colleagues in the boardroom. That is reality. And, if that reality is to change, it will be because of the action we take, the results we deliver, the value we add, and the way we see ourselves in the context of everything outside ourselves.

I have learned to look at the world this way: The more resistance there is to my ideas, the more excited I get, because then I know I'm onto something big!

So, if you ask me, is the glass half full or half empty? It's both. It *is* half full. It *is* half empty. And it is also the wrong way to ask the question. The question we have to ask ourselves is: How large is the glass, and how full can we make it? You see, I believe the best way to *predict* the future is to *invent* it.

Postscript

Citing fundamental differences with Maytag's board of directors over the company's strategic outlook and direction, Lloyd Ward resigned in November 2000, having spent four years with the company, one year as chairman.

CHAPTER TWENTY-THREE

Patrice Clarke Washington

Captain, UPS Airlines

When Patrice Washington decided as a teenager that she had to have a career that would enable her to see the world, her first notion was to become a flight attendant, since it was the most realistic option for women at the time. But Washington quickly decided it was actually more logical—and it would be far more fun—to be flying those planes to the destinations of her dreams instead.

Once she got it in her mind to become a pilot, there was no turning back. The Bahamas native earned her BS in aeronautical science from Florida's Embry-Riddle Aeronautical University in 1982. She then began her steady rise through the pilot ranks, graduating from smaller planes to large commercial jets. In 1988, she became the first black woman to fly for United Parcel Service when she was hired as Second Officer on the DC-8. In 1994, she was upgraded to Captain, becoming the first black woman to hold that rank with a major airline. (UPS is the ninth largest U.S. airline.)

As passionate about flying today as she was as a child, Washington's success embodies the inspirational lyric, "I believe I can fly!" She began the new millennium by receiving Turner Broadcasting's Trumpet Award and recalling how her high school classmates laughed at her ambition. Now it's Washington, 40, who's laughing—all the way to the sky. She is married—to a pilot. They have two young sons.

*I*t was career day. I remember we were all assembled in our high school gymnasium. The guidance counselor sat us down and gave a little talk. I have no clue what she talked about at this point, but one of the things she did do was ask us all to state what we wanted to do after high school. I said I wanted to be a pilot, and everyone started to laugh.

Had it not been me who was saying that I wanted to be a pilot, I probably would have joined in the laughter, also, because, truly, I didn't know anyone who was involved in the airline industry—not as a pilot or flight attendant, not even as a ticket agent. All I knew was that this was what I wanted.

Throughout my childhood we would fly back and forth between the Bahamas and Miami. That created within me a desire to travel and see the world. In my teen years, I decided that the way to combine that desire with work was to become a pilot and have a bird's-eye view of the world from the cockpit.

I never gave it a moment's thought that I didn't see women flying airplanes. If it did occur to me, it didn't stay with me. I simply said, that's what I want to do. But as we go along in life, we all get laughed at for something at some point, and when people laugh at us, there is always a little bit of a question: What am I doing? I had those moments. However, I knew that I didn't want to do some of the more popular things that my classmates were going to do.

I had no desire to be in the medical profession. A lot of the females from my high school class are nurses. I had no desire to teach. I didn't want a desk job because I didn't want to shuffle paper all day (of course, I hadn't a clue that I had to deal with so much paper as an airline pilot). So, by a process of eliminating the things I didn't want to do, I was able to stay very focused on pursuing what did interest me. There were many other things that, I suppose, would have come a little more easily to me, but I didn't even know enough about aviation to know that at the time.

I didn't think at all about how my race might affect my becoming a pilot either. Growing up in Nassau, I was part of the majority, so I didn't grow up with a thought in my head that because of my race I was limited in any way. I wasn't told from the time I was a little girl that blacks do certain things and whites do certain other things. That was a huge advantage.

I also didn't grow up seeing all the negative images of blacks on television that you're just absolutely bombarded with [in the United States].

I can't say we don't have race problems in the Bahamas, but, certainly, it's nothing like it is here in the United States, where everything seems to be so racially divided. There, people were people. If you stole, you weren't seen as stealing because you were black. You stole because you were a thief. So, minority wasn't a word that was part of my vocabulary, but in college it became very apparent that I was in the minority.

Leaving home and going to school in Daytona Beach, Florida at Embry-Riddle was the first time I was really on my own and it was the first difficulty I faced on the road to pursuing my dream. I was not very far away from home, but in terms of the people I was meeting, and the setting, it could have been 100 million miles away.

Here I was, a girl from the Bahamas, at the biggest school I'd ever been a part of. There were no other Bahamians there and, in most of my classes, I was the only female. Certainly, in the flight program there were very few females who were taking flying lessons. There were some other people from the Islands with whom I could feel somewhat comfortable. But I had no other real peers or people who understood my way of life. It was a great big culture shock for me, and that made it extremely difficult.

In that first year in particular, I remember calling home every weekend. I couldn't wait. I'd talk to my family, and once we were done telling what was going on for the week, and who was doing what, when it was time for the phone conversation to end, I would start crying. I did that for the first eight months.

There were times when I thought, "What am I doing here?" But the temptation was never great enough to do anything about it. It was "What am I doing here," and then I dried my tears and went on. I had to stick it out; there was no other choice if I was going to reach my goal. My outlook on life has always been if it's doable, then why can't I do it?

In retrospect, I suppose I was pretty bold, or stubborn, or strong willed, but at the time, I would never have described myself that way. I would have said I was very shy, which I still am, but I'm bold in that I like a challenge; I like things to be very different from the status quo. And I have a real strong-headedness, a desire to succeed, and to not be a quitter. And, despite my tears of homesickness in college, I have always had a real drive to be independent and self-sufficient.

To become an airline pilot, you have to really want it, because the road to getting a job with a major airline is not an easy one. First of all, the schooling that's required is tough and it costs lots of money. And once you have the basic certificates to do the job, then you have to spend a few years at a measly salary trying to get the experience that you need before a major airline will even look at you. Lots of people are pilots, but a whole lot fewer of them are airline pilots, and even fewer are captains. You have to really love it to get to where I am. It's got to be in your blood.

I've only had three jobs in my adult life. The first was with a small charter company, Trans Island Airways, in the Bahamas. I worked long hours and got paid so little that I had to live with my mother and drive her car. If I didn't have that available to me, I'm not certain what would have become of me because, starting out as a pilot, you just don't have enough money.

My employer, I remember, was very eager to hire his first female pilot. Not everyone was as excited about the idea as he was. One day, a family came in for a chartered flight and an old lady was a part of the group. When she learned that I was going to be the one to fly them wherever it was that they were going, she said that that was *not* okay with her. I think what she actually said was, "Oh, no. No woman is going to fly me anywhere!"

My colleagues were more upset about it than I was. I just thought, "Hey, there you go." That was the first time I didn't have to guess about how someone felt about the situation. She came right out and said it. I really don't recall whether I took them or not. I just remember that little scene where she expressed that it was not okay for a woman to fly her around.

I suppose by that point in my life I had come to the awareness that sometimes we, as women, are our own worst enemies. We have set limitations for ourselves many times, and if you cannot envision yourself doing something then it's hard to envision someone else like you doing it. I have not had a similar experience with African Americans. Black people are always very excited to find that I'm a pilot. They may be surprised, but the blacks who have approached me about it always think it's great that I'm doing this.

I believe that what we expect of ourselves is what we achieve. If you expect that you will achieve greatness, then chances are you will. If you expect that all you're worth is to clean house in service to someone else, then that is probably what you will realize in your life. Knowing that, I was not particularly surprised or bothered by this woman's attitude. I saw it as her problem, not mine, and because of that, I really didn't have any response to her.

I remember one of my friends started to say, "You know, she is a really good pilot. She has trained me," and blah, blah, blah. And I said, "Really it's not important. We all have our thing. Just let it be."

If you answer every person who has a gripe with you, that would be your full-time job. Sometimes you just have to let things pass. If something moves you so deeply that you can't let it pass then, yes, maybe it is appropriate to respond in some way. But you have to choose your battles. That was not powerful enough to elicit a response from me.

The Bahamas has a very small aviation industry, so by the time I interviewed for Bahamasair, the interview process was really more of a formality. They knew me. They knew what my training was. They knew before I got there whether I was good. I recall flying my first jet there and feeling: I'm finally doing what I always wanted to do!

When I first got on with Bahamasair, I flew a two-engine turboprop. It seated 48 passengers, but by jet standards it was relatively small. I went from that to the Boeing 737, which is a small jet.

First you get in the simulator and do all these procedures that teach you how to fly the airplane. Then you get in the airplane and do what we call a line-oriented experience. The first four or five flights, you're just concentrating on what's going on in the airplane. I remember the first time that I thought, Okay, I've figured this out. I had reached a level of comfort at which I could actually look outside and really enjoy the scenery. We were flying from Nassau to Miami, and I remember sitting back and feeling the yoke in my hands as I looked out the window at the Bimini Islands, and I was, like, Yes! This is cool. *This is cool.*

It wasn't about feeling successful, per se. It was just that I was actually doing the thing that I had always wanted to do. It felt so good. I truly at that moment felt I had arrived. I was Queen Bee.

Since that first, wonderful time owning the cockpit of a jet, there have been occasions when I've known that my presence was not appreciated or desired, and people have tried to make it difficult. Usually, unfortunately, it's other pilots.

Our cockpit is a very, very small, enclosed environment, and if you have someone there who's got a gripe with you or your presence, it's very difficult to hide that. There were times I had to stand up and say, "Hey, I will not put up with this. If you've got a problem with me, let's take it to management, and let's deal with this on that level, but, you won't mistreat me. You don't have to like me, but we have to work together professionally in this environment."

Because flight crews are usually small, that testosterone-driven environment gets minimized. It's not the locker-room mentality found by [female] sports reporters or women on Wall Street. There are usually just two or three persons in the cockpit, so if I am there, I have already significantly reduced the number of males on board. Sometimes the guys do have their little thing where they sort of leave you out, or they talk at you, not to you. But the nasty talk—the swearing and so on—for the most part, does not happen.

There is still a need to be aggressive, especially for women. And there have been times when I should have said something and I didn't. If you're viewed as being a little too nice, you can be trampled. Some people will look at niceness, and take it for weakness, and if the impression is that I'm weak, it's followed by, "She has no business being here." But if I remember to put on my aggressive hat and say, "Hey, this is what it takes to get the job done and I won't put up with any foolishness," then everything goes well.

Unfortunately, one of the things that has happened, if not to all of us, to most of us blacks, is that there is the assumption on many people's parts that we were hired simply because the company had to meet a quota of some sort. Then the thinking is that we're not here because we're qualified or equal, we're here because the company was forced to hire blacks. God forbid you're not aggressive and you don't stand up to somebody who suggests that or who is just basically being a bully. That helps to solidify in their mind that you don't belong.

My race was never identified on my resume. It wasn't purposely omitted, it was just that, having grown up in the Bahamas, where the emphasis put on one's race is so very different, in my mind it was never important. It was not until I took the job with UPS and joined the American work force that questions of race started to become something I had to address on a frequent basis.

My personal life decisions have always been consciously made to accommodate my career. I love planning and organizing. I have to have something that needs to be accomplished, some little goal that I set for myself, all the time. I always have a plan for accomplishing it and I write it all out.

In my 20s I was not interested in anyone in particular, and didn't want to be. I had set a goal for myself that, by the time I was 35, I would be married. I also wanted to be a captain by 35, and I had to be captain before I would allow myself to have children.

It all worked out beautifully. I got married at 33 and I was made a captain the same year; I had my first child at 35. So I set those goals early and they all fell right into place on time. Now that I've accomplished the marriage, captain, and children, the goals and time periods are getting less and less specific because I'm still in the midst of figuring out how to juggle this family/career thing.

The airline industry has changed tremendously from when I was 13 years old and saw this job as oh so glamorous and grandiose. With deregulation came lots of changes. Thirty years ago they probably had more time to go and take in some of the cities on layovers, so the job probably was more glamorous. Now everything is on the time clock. People will hear that I spent a night in Chicago, another night in Toronto, another night in San Francisco, and they'll say, "Oh, that is so grand. I never get to travel. I would love to be able to do that." In a way, it is grand, and I love it, and that's why I do it, but it is work. Because I slept the night in Toronto, Canada doesn't mean that I really got to see much of Toronto.

I've flown the DC-8 for 12 years. Flying an airplane, particularly the one I fly, is truly a challenge. I love a challenge. I love the ability to "be gone," is what I call it. It's hard to explain, but I love being literally here today and gone tomorrow. I love the sense of moving across the ground at 650 miles an hour. I love arriving in a different place and having a chance to take in a bit of it before arriving back home.

At UPS, we have six different airplane types now. Although the skills required to fly each of them is generally the same, each airplane presents its own group of challenges. And so right there you've got a whole list of things to accomplish if you so desire. I would like to move to a different airplane. I haven't because the schedules on the DC-8 enable me to do my job as a pilot and my job as a mom.

Prior to having children, I flew the trips to the Far East, to Europe, and so on. Right now we have a sequence of trips that goes entirely around the globe, and if I didn't have children I would be on whatever airplane's doing that trip. However, things change in your life and you need to prioritize. Right now it's more important to be close to home, so

I fly the Midwest United States on what we call "reserve coverage," where we're on call, much like a doctor or a nurse.

You come to a certain point in your career where your goals are not just about the job anymore. The first 10 years in this profession were all about making the grade and building the flight time to get the major airline job. Now that I've settled in, it's a question of: What else do I want to do with my life?

I've always had a desire to own lots of real estate, so I would like to get my real estate license. I'd also like to go back to school to get an MBA in finance because I like numbers and I like money. My stepfather owned a liquor business while I was growing up, and I've always had a desire to be an entrepreneur, and own a small restaurant. My sons are three and four now. As they become a little more independent, I will do what I can to make some of my other dreams happen.

I got into aviation purely out of desire. Somehow I had the wisdom to do the things that I needed to do to succeed. But in retrospect, I think we can follow one of two formulas: the formula for success or the formula for failure. The formula for success starts with first having a dream or a vision of something that you want to do. Once you have the dream, you need to set goals for yourself. Then, once you've set those goals, you need to embark upon a plan to make them happen.

Typically, that plan has to include: (1) an education; (2) stick-ability; and (3) patience. I've met people who change jobs at the drop of a hat: "Oh well, I didn't like it there today so, you know, I'm going over here." They get employed all the time but they never stay anywhere. You can't be successful if you're just hopping around without a plan. You also need patience. You have to be willing to wait so that your craft or whatever it is that you're working at has the time to mature and settle. Then you can reap the full benefits of your effort.

If I had been impatient to make money or become captain, I would have quit a long time ago. Sometimes, just having patience can be challenge enough, but if you combine it with a good plan and hard work, you'll get on the right track and it will pay off. When it does, you can think back on all of those who laughed at your dream and say, "Hey, who's laughing now?"

CHAPTER TWENTY-FOUR

Maxine Waters

Congresswoman

❖

She is one of the most powerful women in American politics today. Now serving her sixth term in the U.S. House of Representatives, Maxine Waters represents a large part of South Central Los Angeles and the surrounding area.

Garnering a well-earned reputation as a fearless and outspoken advocate for women, children, people of color, and the poor, Waters works continually to refocus the national spotlight on the plight of inner city communities. In recent years that has included uncovering evidence of CIA involvement in drug trafficking in her district.

This former chair of the Congressional Black Caucus (1997–1998) honed her no-nonsense approach to politics during 14 years in the California State Assembly. Operating in an arena that can turn hope and optimism into cynicism and despair very quickly, Waters, 62, remains a fighter poised for victory. "I believe in the power of the second wind," she says.

"When you feel put-upon, disgusted, and angry, if you succumb to it, you may lose out on a lot. But if you suck it in real hard and say, 'I'm going to do this; I'm going to make myself keep moving forward,' you can do what you need to do." Married for the second time, Waters has a grown son and daughter from her first marriage.

❖

I was always taught that in order to advance, you had to make people like you. So, you didn't say anything that might cause people to be upset. Consequently you often didn't really let people know what you thought at all.

It was an approach that was encouraged more because of race than gender. When I was coming up, we had evolved from a point in time where blacks were grinning and scratching their heads, but they had taken on a new way of being accepted—and it was by not making waves. The general rule for us was, "Don't act like Uncle Tom, but be very nice. Don't say what's on your mind. Whatever anybody tells you to do, just do it. Be quiet. Look good. And get along."

So, that's what I did. I was obedient. I did not question or defy authority. I did not make waves.

The rules were largely born out of the desire of African American parents to keep their children safe, and I suppose it did that, but it denied us something very important in the process: our true selves.

My career in public service began when I became a teacher and volunteer coordinator in the Head Start program in Los Angeles. In a way, my life began then too. It was a very important turning point for me. Ultimately, it's what happened there that most shaped my personality and paved the way for whatever I've achieved since. That's when I discovered who I was.

Head Start was one of the programs of the War on Poverty, and what it did was open up opportunities for people like me who had ideas, as well as some sense that they had more talent and could do better things than their situation was allowing them to do.

This was in the early days of integration and there was a lot of time and energy put into developing consciousness-raising groups, in which you had confrontations with people from all different backgrounds and you basically learned about each other by battling it out. Participating in these encounter groups was actually part of our training to work in Head Start.

I just loved those groups and what I learned from them. I learned to confront people and have people confront me. I learned that I had strong, solid opinions, and I learned how to express them. I discovered that I was very angry about having been contained, and I felt that I had lost a lot by not expressing—or even having—an opinion. So I went off into the other direction of making sure everybody knew how I felt, and having something to say all the time.

For the first time, I could say to people, "I don't believe you," or, "You said one thing yesterday and you're saying something different today. What do you really stand for?" And people could say things to me. I had very thin skin, too, so I had to work on that. In the end, all of that open exchange between blacks and whites in the Los Angeles area at that time really helped to shape who I became.

Working at Head Start, I came to grips with who I *really* was. I discovered that I had been in the shadow of myself, trying to act out what I was taught about expectations of human behavior, instead of just being myself.

Because of Head Start I was able to reflect on my early childhood years and to understand more of the people who had great influence on me. There was Miss Johnson. She was a striking woman, a hard teacher, and she was very stern. Everyone kind of admired her because she looked great, but she was tough on you.

In her class you got seated based on your grades. The better your grades, the closer you'd sit to the front, so we were always competing for the first seats in the first row. I mean, we fought like dogs to sit in those seats. I was always in seats one, two, three, or four. If your grades went down, your seat moved immediately, and she would make you feel bad by marking your paper all up. But it was good. She taught me to compete.

There was also Miss Carter and Miss Stokes. Those teachers thought that I had something. I was always in the play, or the oratorical contests, or something, so they thought that I had potential. I don't know where they thought I could go with it, but when I graduated from high school, the prediction in my yearbook was that I would be Speaker of the House of Representatives one day.

I always had a sense of politics in some way, shape, form, or fashion. I was always the president of some club or another. My mother, even though she was uneducated, had a real sense of politics. She worked at the polls, knew the elected officials, and talked about the presidents and what they were and weren't doing. So I kind of had a scent and feel about politics and government from a young age, but I had no plan.

I floundered largely because I got to make too many of my own decisions too early, without having any basis for making them. I think that's problematic even for young people today.

I was the fifth of 13 children and I was about 12 years old when I got my first real job working in Thompson's Restaurant in St. Louis. It was segregated, so the black employees could not eat lunch in the dining room. We had to eat in the basement.

We were not treated well, or fairly, but I learned at a very early age that if I wanted to have nice clothes when I returned to school in September, the way to do it was to work during the summertime and earn that money. So I was anxious to work. I loved pretty clothes and being able to buy them for myself; it made me feel like I was in control of my own destiny. Really, I was too young to truly appreciate how bad the situation at the job was.

I went on to later work in a clothes manufacturing factory, which was much worse. All of the operators were white and the people who had the worst jobs were people of color, like myself, who were shouted at and talked to badly. You ran around all day, lifting and dumping these heavy bundles of clothes in a factory full of dust and dirt and terrible conditions. Did I learn anything positive from it? Oh yeah. You learn from everything in life.

It's good to learn what you don't like. It's good to learn what people think of you, and why they think that. It's good to know what racism is. And it's good to know the difference between hard work and easy times. I learned all of that.

I think that because of that whole lifestyle, my parents considered me kind of grown up early on, so I got to make a lot of decisions. But I didn't know what I was doing. I didn't have enough knowledge about what was really available to me, and what it took to get there. Exposing young people to opportunities and helping them to understand what's out there is extremely important. Counseling is important, and I didn't have any.

For years, I didn't even think in terms of things I'd like to do. I was kind of an observer on the outside, just watching and looking. But at Head Start, I was learning so much so fast, and things started to gel for me. As I started to share what I was learning with the parents of the Head Start kids, I really began to understand what you could do for children. Even though I had kids at that time myself, I hadn't really thought about what was most important in the rearing of children, and how to make them feel good about themselves. There was nothing in the experience of the poor children in my neighborhood that really made them feel good about themselves.

My parents had not been good at that particular part of it. My mother was a hard-working woman who, during tough times, was on welfare. My stepfather was all right. They tried hard to do right. But they were not parents who said, "I love you." They were not parents who hugged and kissed you. They weren't into building self-esteem. But a lot of black parents weren't. They were into building kids who got up every morning, went to school or work, and kept clean and out of trouble. There was a reason for that.

But, at Head Start, learning about this business of building self-esteem in children so they can feel good about themselves helped me to learn how to feel good about myself, and that was the most important experience of my life. After that, things made good sense. Things flowed. I was in charge.

That's when I locked into this crippling experience of wanting to be liked. Up until that point, it had been very important for me to be liked by everybody. At Head Start, I finally realized that the need to be liked can be very controlling, and so I went from one extreme, of wanting to be liked by everybody, to the other of not caring whether anybody liked me at all. When you get to that other extreme, you tend to make enemies easily.

When you're just not mindful of other people's feelings, you interfere with your ability to get things done. People will not only resist you, they will attempt to stay away from you. I had a lot of that in the early days of my career with Head Start, and then I learned to temper it a bit after running for the California state legislature.

This business of politics really teaches you to temper everything. You have to take a lot. There are so many different personalities, so many different orientations, and different points of view, and no matter how stupid you may think some of them are, you have to suffer them. Out if it, you learn to respect people's differences and the experiences that shape those differences. You have to tolerate and respect them in order to be effective.

In dealing with colleagues, this is particularly important because these are interdependent relationships; we've got to work on a lot of issues together over a long period of time. I have to be very careful to contain my anger. Some people can have a falling out and then come back together easily. I don't, so I have to be very careful. I can't afford to make enemies by mistake and lose out on the opportunity to get something done because someone is mad at me. I don't make very many enemies among my colleagues, but when I do, it's serious. When I decide that I'm going to part ways with someone, I try to know exactly when it's happening and why, so I can prepare to handle everything that's going to come from it.

I have really come to believe that if you basically respect people and you have integrity, that's all it takes. It doesn't take any additional act of thunder or lightning. If you show respect for people and honesty about relationships, it will be just fine. And, if that's not good enough for people, that's their problem. That's not your problem. You don't have to do more than that.

That's my philosophy about people voting for me. I will work for my constituents; I will fight for my constituents; I will confront the system and the establishment about injustices and inequality. I respect my constituents. I respect people in general. But I don't have to do more than that. I try to do what the Ten Commandments teach you to do. That's all that's required in life.

I got into politics because I really have a great sense of fairness and a strong sense that this system has not been fair to everybody. There was a need to confront that, and for elected officials to work for people who don't have fancy lobbyists in Washington, D.C. on their behalf. I thought I could do that, but I must say that, when you talk to elected officials, most of the time you will find that they think they are driven by these very altruistic ideas. Maybe they are, but I also know that there's something in the personality that finds it very satisfying to have wins: wins on the campaign trail; wins on legislation; wins on the competition. The competitive nature is very much satisfied by being in this arena.

I love the win! And I get great satisfaction from tackling the impossible and confronting the ills of society that other people find it difficult to confront. One of the things I like most about what I've done is that I'm a little bit on the radical edge. At the same time, I'm able to play it in the mainstream. I like the idea that I haven't had to conform to the norm in order to move into leadership.

I didn't have a great plan for any of this. I didn't even have a great plan to leave the Assembly and come to Congress although I saw that my Congressman was getting older and was not going to be there very long. People would say to me, "Why don't you just run against him? You know you could beat him." But one day I sat down and wrote him a letter that said, "I will never run against you." When he decided not to run, I was the first person he called.

It wasn't that I liked him too much to run against him. I just think the price of ambition is sometimes too high. Ambition is a good thing, but unbridled ambition is *not* a good thing. To run against a sitting Congressman who had integrity, who was doing the best job that he knew how, just because I wanted it was not good enough. In general, I don't do things by any means necessary.

I have never had designs on my career in the sense that I know exactly where I want to go and that I'm going to do such and such. I believe that your work speaks for itself and it'll take you where you need to go. If you do your job well, not only do opportunities open up, but you create unforeseen opportunities that might never have even occurred to you.

In the California state legislature it was just unthinkable that a black woman with a black agenda and a liberal edge could be the chair of the Democratic caucus or could be the whip or could be just about everything that I am now. I like being able to embody the message, "Oh, yes you can." Even here in Congress, I've continued to keep my radical edge and move into the leadership. I like the contradiction of that, and the ability to exemplify the notion that you don't have to accept or conform to a centrist position in order to achieve the ability to be in the back room and to negotiate on behalf of those people and issues that you care about. You can operate a little bit outside of the box and still have the inside track.

I'm told by people who disagree with me that they respect me. And sometimes they are in awe of how strongly I feel about poor people, how strongly I feel about some of the women's issues, how strongly I feel about issues of inequality, and the fact that I will say what I believe and then stick to it.

On the other hand, I know that some people start out being very worried about their ability to work with me. But they will find that at very difficult times I'm an extremely reasonable person and I confront crisis. No matter how difficult a crisis is, I think it can be worked out. I never think a situation is so untenable that you can't do anything about it. In crises I have my best spirituality, whether it is a physical accident or complicated legislative issue, and that has helped keep me in good stead.

I have not always been this way. It's come with learning to trust my instincts and learning to listen to my entire self. It's hard to explain, but you will find that once you get in touch with yourself, you're almost being directed on a constant basis, if it's no more than understanding why you do this or why you feel that. The earlier in life you get that, the better off you'll be.

I have grown not only to trust and pay attention to myself, but to get quiet and reflect on what happened in a given situation; to examine how it could have been handled better. I still work at trying to deny the quick response, and I have my clearest thoughts at 3 A.M. Somehow, at that hour, the answers are all there. I've had time to sleep and rest, and when I awaken at about that time, I start to reflect on the day and to think about the future. This quiet, thoughtful time, has helped me to make better decisions and to better understand how the world works and how this business works, and why people do what they do.

I learn something every day of my life. I've learned something from every experience I've had. It's a continual, never-ending process. And through the years, you keep learning why you do what you do. I believe that that, eventually, is the key to success. I don't mean success in monetary terms, but success in terms of managing yourself and being on good terms with yourself.

I strategize constantly, mostly in my head. I may have thoughts about projects for three, four, or five years but, by the time I move on it, I know exactly where I'm going. So, I've been a planner, but not in the traditional way. As a matter of fact, traditional plans, I think, are void of insight, because the way we're taught to plan is more or less to put down on paper, between 9 and 5, kind of where you want to go with a project. I think planning requires a lot more than that. I think before you move from one step to the other with a plan that you should understand whether you started out with a theory that makes good sense. It sounds so fundamental, but you'd be surprised at how many people don't do this.

There are a great many frustrations in my line of work. The system moves so slowly, and I am not a patient person. Sometimes the wheels [in my head] are turning so fast, and I have seen so much and understand so much and I just want to get on with it. My husband will tell me, "Slow down," but the older I get the less I want to slow down. I have things to do.

It's very hard to create meaningful change. My main frustration is that most people don't know how much power they have, and so they don't act on it. They get socialized in the ways I might have if I had not had the good fortune of discovering myself in the way that I did.

There are so many people who are scared of their own opinions, who suffer injustice because it is too difficult to confront, who have the potential to make change, but are satisfied that they're doing okay and it's not necessary to endanger themselves or their acquisitions by speaking up on behalf of a better life for all people. There are people who, literally, mortgage their ability to create change because they don't understand their own potential.

I'm disappointed that people think that there's a person who can do it for them. People tell me all the time, "*You go*, and *you* make those people do right," when, in fact, our collective power could create tremendous change much more quickly.

I am not nearly as frustrated by attempts by certain people to deny us power or access or equality, because that's how the world and our country have evolved. People have become rich and powerful because they've denied others the opportunity to share in the wealth and the possibilities. I expect that. But what I can never be comfortable with is people who accept it as a *fait accompli*, who believe that they have no choice in it and no power to do anything about it.

One of my great disappointments has been the discovery that whites oftentimes, no matter how close you are to them, really don't understand the similarities and the differences between us. I thought at one point that close proximity and interaction over a period of time automatically led to certain kinds of understandings. But even today, I'm surprised by whites who work with, live with, interact with, and have what are considered to be good relationships with blacks, when they suddenly reveal through their actions or words that they really still don't get it. They haven't quite seen you or your people. They still view you as something quite different and confounding. That continues to be very disconcerting for me.

But the worst among us are those people who seek power, get into positions of power, believe in and even are boastful about the power they have, and do nothing with it except enhance themselves.

I had an interview one time and, after talking to me, the reporter said, "You really care more about what the people down in your district think than your colleagues." I said, "You got it." She thought that was strange, because her idea was that I should care more about what my colleagues think about me. I guess she figured that's how you make it in this business. I know that many people these days believe that. I don't.

I work with many of God's children who have been dropped off of America's agenda. These are young people who are disillusioned and may not understand much about the system. When something that I'm doing opens up the opportunity for discussion and interaction, and they respond positively, that reinforces me.

I take great satisfaction from working with people who others don't feel are worthy of a lot of time and effort: women in drug rehab, the children of welfare, ex-gang members. When I can see that my work is not only appreciated but changing lives, that reinforces me.

There's a school that's named after me—The Maxine Waters Employment Preparation Center—that I helped to found in a Los Angeles Unified School District. A lot of young people there stop me on the street and say, "I go to your school and I'm learning a lot." I have a program in public housing projects to connect young people with job training opportunities. When young people see me and say, "I went through your program and I want you to know that I'm working, I'll never go back to jail again, now I'm taking care of my kids," these things reinforce me. This is why I do what I do, and, while the frustrations and disappointments are real, the satisfaction is real too. The rewards outweigh the sacrifices.

I don't think you have to compromise your feelings about your constituency, even if it means you have to confront your colleagues in order to get along with your colleagues. Confrontation does not intimidate me.

What does intimidate me is that this business can get vicious. You're always under scrutiny, but it's not simply the scrutiny of your constituents or the press about your work, it is the underlying vicious scrutiny of people who make it their life's work to say, "This person has stepped on too many toes; it's time to take 'em out." I know legislators whose lives and families have been devestated by the viciousness. That's very intimidating.

But policy and politics are a part of me. It's a way of life for me now, and I love it, although I still struggle with parts of it.

This job requires scheduling every inch of your life, and that is not good for what I consider wholesome and healthy relationships. You have friends because you're there for them at special times in their lives. You're there for them for the births and the deaths and the celebrations. But when you're saying to your friends all the time, "Sorry, I can't. I've already committed to . . ." or when your friends call and say, "Hey, let's go to a movie," and every time you're saying, "Eh, can't do that . . . ," it's a problem. What happens is, you begin to isolate yourself, and I've seen it happen in this business more and more.

Whatever career you have, and however successful you might be at it, when you don't have time for the human things in life—the things that help you to bond with family and friends—it's very detrimental. You'll end up a lonely person who's sitting there ready to be friends now that you have stopped your busy life, but your friends will have bonded with others who were there when they needed someone. That's a very, very troubling thought.

It is very tough to be here and have to decide whether you're going to miss a vote on welfare reform or healthcare or something that you know is important to people, to go to the funeral of somebody you care about. This past week I had a conflict between [the Banking Committee], where we were holding a hearing on drug money laundering, which is a big issue with me, and [the Judiciary Committee], where we had some equally demanding and interesting issues going on at the same time. I've learned to live with the conflicts, but I still find it stressful to have to make decisions that require me to say no to something important.

I have a lot of faults, but I think my greatest strength is my courage. I'm not a deeply religious person, but I think that my sense of fairness and justice comes from the spiritual. I think I am rewarded for being fair.

I think I'm rewarded for respecting other people. I think I grow and gain from that, and that belief gives me courage—the courage to be fair even when it's not easy to be fair, and the courage to not only work hard, but to try different things; to walk into difficult situations; to be at risk, and believe I'm going to come out alright.

I don't see me being in harm's way because I take so-called risks. I just think that, because I believe deeply that what I'm doing is so right and so fair and so purposeful, that no harm can come to me.

I don't think fearlessness quite describes it, because fearlessness means, to me, that you just kind of blindly go into situations with no fear. I go into situations with the belief that I know enough about myself, I've thought enough about the issues, I care enough about us all that positive things are bound to come of it.

If you're going to take risks, know what you're doing; walk into them wide-eyed and understand the consequences, because when you fall into them backwards and by mistake, you're often surprised by the outcome. And those kinds of surprises, no one enjoys.

CHAPTER TWENTY-FIVE

Clifton R. Wharton, Jr.

Former Chairman and CEO, Teachers Insurance Annuity
Association—College Retirement Equities Fund (TIAA-CREF)

❖

For anyone who knew Clifton Wharton's life story, his 1993 appointment as the first black Deputy Secretary of State seemed a glorious way to cap a career marked by pioneering leadership positions in the worlds of economics, academia, foreign affairs, and big business. The U.S. Department of State appointment was especially fitting because Wharton's intention while growing up had been to follow in the footsteps of his father, who had served as U.S. ambassador to Romania and Norway, among other foreign posts.

Given that background and a sterling track record marked by integrity and high performance, when Wharton walked away from the position less than a year after accepting it, it was clear that he had good reason. Although he chose not to discuss it much in the press, since then Wharton, 74, has been working on his memoir.

"In taking a detailed look back at your life, and in interviewing others about their recollections of it, you realize not only that there is quite a bit that you've forgotten, but that there's so much you didn't really see at the time. It's been quite extraordinary." Married almost 50 years, Wharton has two grown sons.

❖

One of the fun things about writing your autobiography as I'm doing now is that you find out things about yourself. You see patterns in your life that you didn't know existed.

For example, I was the first black to become a member of the student radio station at Harvard. Because of World War II and the high turnover of students in and out of the service, I was elected production director. I think I was 17 years old.

The radio station had what they called comment books—long, legal-sized, bound books—and all of the members of the radio station would write notes to each other. If I wanted to leave a note for you about doing something on a program, I would use your code name, and I'd tell you such and such, or, if I wanted the whole station to hear about something, I'd write it out for them.

I went up to the archives at Harvard, and fortunately, they'd saved these comment books. I went through all of them for the years I was involved in the radio station. In there, I found that soon after I was elected production director, I think it was two full pages where I described in a highly detailed memo to the whole staff of the radio station the changes that I wanted done. I came back and said to [my wife] Dolores, "My God, I was a CEO at 17!"

Now, at the time, I wasn't thinking "I'm in charge" or "I'm naturally good at this." I was just thinking "This is the way you have to do this." And it was so funny to come across this, because until I did, I was totally unaware that I had a certain style of operating, a certain consistency of approach, that I have used over and over again, from my earliest days. I have also responded to situations repeatedly that I consider to be a creative challenge for change. In other words, I always like to get where there's something I can really do.

Although I was born in Boston, I spent most of my earliest years in the Canary Islands. My father was the first black to pass the Foreign Service Exam, and, eventually, he became the first black career U.S. ambassador, and he was posted to Romania and Norway. The simple fact that those years were not spent in the United States, I believe, made a very big difference in my life.

A friend who I grew up with recently reminded me that when I came back home with my parents, all the kids in the neighborhood thought I was like somebody from Mars, because I'd been in these foreign countries, I spoke all these languages, I didn't know any of the local games or anything. But I had no idea they perceived me that way. I was having a great time. So I've always been very comfortable in my own skin.

When I came back to the States to live full time in an environment where I was exposed to and experienced racism, I was 10 years old. By that time I was, to a certain extent, perhaps, inoculated. It's not that it could not hurt, but it had a different cast to it. I had not experienced it on a constant daily basis, which is one of the greatest evils, as far as I'm concerned, of the whole process.

I'm quite convinced that whites do not understand what it's like to live as a black in a discriminatory society for 24 hours a day, 7 days a week, 365 days a year. *It does have an effect.*

I was given an extremely secure home and family environment, and I was, in effect, told that I could, if I worked hard, do anything I wanted to do. But to have been away from that [pervasive racism] for that formative period of time helped me enormously. It gave me the ability to say [when faced with a racist] there's something wrong with *them* instead of there's something wrong with *me*, and I still feel that way.

I had intended to follow in father's footsteps to become a U.S. diplomat. When people ask me why I didn't go into foreign service, I always tell this story: One day while I was in Washington, my dad took me down to the state department to meet his friends. There were three of them, and they all said upon meeting me, "Oh, you're Clif's son. Well, when are you coming in?" *That* for a 21 year old! I said to myself, "I don't want to be my *father's* son. I want to be my own man!" Now, the story has probably changed several times in the telling, but in essence, it is true. I decided I wanted to be my own person. That's why I didn't go into the foreign service.

But my father kept after me. Every time I made a career turn, he was there, saying, "Well, that's not such a good idea. Why don't you make a lateral entry into the foreign service?" Then, when I became president of Michigan State [University], he said, "President? Well, you've done much better than I ever did."

I don't think one expects to exceed [their parents' level of success] as much as to be able to exploit a much wider range of alternatives than were available for them. I had absolutely no thought about becoming a university president. I was doing well and enjoying myself in the foundation world when Michigan State came along. That had never been in the plan.

There is in most people's careers an element of serendipity, but there is also a certain amount of knowing broadly what you would like to achieve and where you'd like to go, and then there is the ability to recognize when the elements turn up with the right mix to achieve it.

Looking back, the turning points are more obvious than at the time you made your decisions. For example, I wanted to go to Bowdoin College and my mother wanted me to go to Harvard. That was that, but it probably changed my life in ways I will never know.

I really did not have a specific quality of life that I aspired to. Rather, I thought about the kinds of components that I would find rewarding and enjoyable, that would make a difference: a job, a happy marriage, a life with children. I was not focused on earning a lot of money. It was not that kind of a conception.

The one thing I did expect was that I would be a useful pioneer, and, as it turned out, I was. I was the first black to graduate from the Johns Hopkins School of Advanced International Studies; the first black to head a predominantly white university, Michigan State, back in 1970; the first black to head a state university system—I was chancellor of the 64-campus State University of New York; the first black to chair a major U.S. foundation, the Rockefeller Foundation; the first black elected chairman and CEO of a Fortune 500 company, (in fact, it was number 19 last year) TIAA-CREF; and the first black to become deputy secretary of state, in 1993.

I've been the first black in many jobs, but I've never taken a "black job" in my life. What I mean by that is that I've seen numerous cases in which corporations need to have high-profile, highly visible blacks or females, and they'll almost create jobs and put the people in them. They'll give them beautiful offices and all the rest of it, but no power, no nothing. That, to me, is a "black job."

When I was chancellor of SUNY during the Reagan administration, I was approached about an ambassadorship to South Africa. Now, what did I know about South Africa? My geographic experience is Latin America and Southeast Asia, so why would I not deal with South America or Latin America, where I have some competence, and go to South Africa?

I learned this from my father early on. His first post was Liberia, [West Africa] because that's where the blacks were always sent. Later, when assigned to other traditional black posts, he went to the state department and he said, "You're exporting U.S. racism."

The converse is true also. There are times when, in spite of your obvious competencies, you *won't* be offered a position because the person in charge simply can't envision a black in it.

I had an interview years ago at Exxon, and their representative said, "Well, I don't think you'd be happy at the company."

I knew that Exxon had operations in Latin America, so I said, "Why wouldn't I be happy in Latin America? I'm bilingual and I spent my childhood in Spain."

"Well, no, you wouldn't be happy. . . . " So I just let it go at that.

Years later, the then CEO of Exxon called me and wanted to know if I might be interested in joining Exxon on the corporate board of directors. I told him that I couldn't because I was on the Ford Motor Company board and there was a problem of conflict, but, at the same time, I couldn't resist telling him my story. "You know," I said at the end of it, "times change, life is funny . . . ."

He was absolutely mortified to think that years before I had been treated that way by a recruiter from Exxon Co., but again, that was then.

There was a speech I gave at Howard University, in which I talked about the problems experienced by black social scientists and how they are seen as competent only when they are doing research on black issues; they're not expected to be competent in collecting data on anything else. So the moment that you are put into what I would call a "black job," that automatically excludes you from being viewed as competent in anything else, and your quality of success in that field is not going to be viewed quite the same way. In fact, you can be badly injured by being put in that spot, under that label.

That's why, as a rule, I just say that I'm not going to take the black jobs. I'm not denigrating people who do, but if it doesn't truly fit me, why would I go after it? No. The job has to suit me or else my ability to make a significant contribution becomes moot. You have to be who you are, and you've got to maintain a sense of humor, because if you don't you can become torn and depressed. So, two things: If it doesn't fit, get out, and if you're not enjoying it, get out.

To a certain extent, I came along at a time when the environment and the whole context [of U.S. race relations] was dramatically different from today's. It was clearly harder for my generation [to succeed] than it is now, but, coming along, I was very much aware of how much easier it was for me than for my father. When he was in the department of state [in the 1920s], he was the only nonmenial black in the *entire building*, and there was only one white person that ever went out to lunch with him—twice—the entire time he was there.

But whether you're talking about his day, or my early career, or what it takes to be successful today, certain elements remain unchanged.

I'd begin with preparedness and persistence. And when it comes to being prepared, the young people coming into academia and corporate positions today are generally very well prepared. They've gone to great schools, had great training positions, and they've had more role models in many industries than my generation ever had. So that's one.

But on the persistence side, I'm struck by a certain shift. I've often said that the blacks who attended college in the 1930s, 1940s, and 1950s were blacks who *aspired*, and if their aspirations sometimes seemed unrealistic to an outside observer, well, he'd better just stand aside and watch. We knew we had to be twice as good as our white peers to compete successfully, but we had the self-confidence to respond to that challenge. Really, what choice did we have?

Years ago, my wife Dolores founded the Fund for Corporate Initiatives (FCI) which developed a Young Executive Program, designed to nurture the advancement of women and minorities in corporate careers. When I look at the early FCI fellows from Dolores' program, virtually all of them are at the senior-officer level now, and it is tremendously impressive and very gratifying to see that.

At the same time, I think that there are some young blacks who are so anxious, ambitious and, at the same time, turned off by the persistence of real or perceived discriminatory treatment, that, to a certain extent, they quit. They quit the job, or they go someplace else rather than doing what some of us used to have to do, which was, just fight right through it, just don't give up.

Having said that, I know that for every one of [the blacks like] me in my generation, there were others of us who were just as good or *better* who were not able to break through, even though they fought very hard at it.

As to the question of whether you still have to be twice as good, I would say that the further up the ladder you go, the more it's true.

If you take the Fortune 500 companies, how many are headed by women and how many are headed by minorities? Very few. I mean, you can think of them by name, and that tells you something about where we are. The more measurable the performance in a particular industry, the better are our chances for reaching the top within that industry.

I remember when John Rogers started Ariel Capital [Management in Chicago]. I know him because his mother was on the Equitable board with me. John was good. And when he started, a number of us tried to see to it that he got a fair shake in terms of having access to people to talk to about his investment firm. But there was still a lot of questioning and unspoken doubt about him. Then he started performing, and you couldn't stop him because his performance was *measurable*.

The one thing that I have regularly said is that the pool of top talent is always small, and if you perform the role that you're in right now in a superior fashion to anybody else in that same role, you're going to move, one way or the other. It's not that you spend your time thinking, "Ooh, I'm going to get this, and I'm going to get that." Just *do* it, and, bingo!

My experience at Michigan State is a good example. The risks posed by that position were probably the biggest of my career, primarily because of three things. One is that it was such a visible pioneering slot. Dolores and I had always functioned as a team and everybody was watching the two of us like hawks. We lived in a glass house for the first couple of years. Every word we said, every thing that we did was under the microscope, so that even the slightest stumble could be perceived as our falling off a cliff. There was a lot of pressure.

The second thing was that it coincided with massive student unrest nationwide. I mean, we had *massive* student demonstrations with four and five thousand students tearing up the campus. Other campuses like Kent State had people getting killed. In Michigan, the legislature passed resolutions that the presidents of the top universities ought to be fired because of the student riots.

Thirdly, for some people who didn't know me and my background, there was a serious question about whether I knew what I was doing in running a university of that size. But, I just kept going until I showed them what I could do. Having gone through it so many times, I always find it slightly amusing.

At the time you're doing it, you don't stop to think about it. During the riots, every university president had to question whether he or she was going to survive. But that's out of your hands. We found unexploded pipe bombs on our campus a couple weeks after [the riots] were over. If those bombs had gone off, I might not be here today. But you can't control that, so you don't think about that. You focus on what you *can* do, and you go at it with the utmost integrity. That's something I learned from Theodore Schultz, the Nobel laureate in economics, with whom I worked as a research assistant while pursuing my PhD. He was a tremendous teacher—just a great person—and he was a person who invariably stood by what he knew was right. That's a very impressive quality and it had an enormous impact on me.

Key to my success at Michigan, and throughout my career, has been my wife Dolores. We've had an extremely successful marriage, a very happy marriage, a very loving marriage, and it has been that way for 50 years. There is nothing I would ever do without the full advice and counsel of my wife. And there has never been, that I know of, any instance in which she has not been willing to tell me personally, privately, what she thinks. She's levelled criticisms and comments about speeches, actions, ideas, you name it, she will always tell me what she thinks, and I will, if she asks me, tell her what I think.

I've often said that when you're a CEO—or a leader in any setting— you have to have at least one or two people around you who will tell you the truth. I've been very lucky in that regard. In addition to Dolores, I've always tried to have at least two business colleagues like that, and I could always rely upon them to tell me *exactly* what they thought.

With Dolores, the value of that counsel and the depth of that honesty is intensified. *No one* knows me better. That has been absolutely invaluable: to have someone who not only knows me and shares it with me, but is also part of the process, *understands* the process and is there with me—whatever comes.

The partnership role that Dolores played at Michigan State was incredible. When I wasn't there and the kids came over to the president's house—three or four *hundred* of them—she'd be out there talking to them. They'd be yelling and carrying on, and she'd be right there dealing with it. It was one of the reasons why she eventually became a corporate director—she became so well known. She was the first woman and the first black on most of the corporate boards she serves on.

Over the years, we have learned to shift gears. She will play the role of the "spouse of . . .," and then I'll have to switch and play "spouse of. . . ." It's a very interesting process, and one that is still, despite all the years and changes in the business landscape, a very difficult one for women and men.

I can remember when she went on the Phillips Petroleum board, and I would go to the annual meetings. She would be the only female there to work, and I'd be the only male there to go off with the wives of the other board members to enjoy these great trips. I must admit, it has never really been a problem for us. My feeling has always been, if she is willing and prepared to play that supportive role for me, why shouldn't I do it for her? It is the least you can do, and it's really quite meaningful.

There is nothing worse than seeing a situation in which you've got a dynamic male who's moving up the corporate ladder, or whatever the ladder is, and the spouse is stuck and nothing happens for her. That is very, very difficult, and it produces all kinds of trauma in its wake. That situation frequently leads to the breakup of the marriage, because she has nothing but the children, the soccer games, the ballet lessons. She's a college graduate and she has just never had the opportunity to develop at the same time as the male spouse. When the spouse has an opportunity to grow at the same time—it doesn't have to be at the same levels—then there's a meaningfulness of the interaction in the relationship, and a sense of worth on both sides. Then, you're really a team, and that can be very powerful.

It's hard to explain because it's subtle in the way in which it happens, but there's no question that I would not have been able to accomplish what I did without Dolores.

Besides having a close and supportive spousal relationship, I'd say one should always have an activity in which you try to help the next generation, not necessarily because you get recognition or credit, but more just because it's something that's important. The presidential fellows program I initiated at Michigan State involved their spending one or two semesters in the president's office; there were 13 of them total by the time I left. Recently we had a reunion to catch up on what had become of them, and 11 of the 13 were able to come. In this group were two college presidents, a vice president of research and graduate studies, a chief financial officer, vice president of a community college, a few professors, two government officials, and so on—just a stellar group.

The stuff they remembered that I told them I didn't remember telling them. They remembered when I did or said certain things, how I handled situations, and this had been helpful to them. They had used their experiences with me to evaluate and handle their own experiences as they moved forward. Now, I am never going to get a front page story in the *New York Times* for that, but I know that there are 13 people who, in one way or another, I have had a positive effect on individually and on their careers. That is good.

Finally, trust your instincts. When I resigned as deputy secretary of state [in 1993], I didn't feel it was proper to comment on it in any great length at the time, but I've had two cabinet members call me and say, "They tried to make you a scapegoat. You sure were right to get out when you did." I trusted my instincts completely about getting out; perhaps I should have relied more on my instincts when I decided to go in.

I had been approached by previous administrations for various cabinet posts, and I always said no. I just didn't want to get into that life. They play a lot of games in Washington that I had no interest in playing.

What changed my mind about this option with [President Clinton] was that, before my meeting with him, I had participated in the economic summit held at Little Rock in the fall after the [1992] election. It was a gathering of about 200 to 250 people for a couple of days. I watched him operate, and I was impressed.

He sat there and chaired the entire meeting, except for one session. He had a briefing book that was about two inches thick; never once did he open it. He engaged in discussions with the leading experts in a variety of fields *in depth*, and it was clear that he knew the subjects. It was a tour de force. So, when I was approached this time, I said to myself, "Well, if the president thinks I can be helpful, and he has these qualities, this would be a great opportunity to make a contribution."

When the first leaks came out that the White House was unhappy with me, they just had no factual basis at all. They said that they were unhappy with me because of the failed U.S. policy toward Bosnia. I thought, What are these faceless people talking about? Anybody that knew anything, knew that I was not involved in the policy at all.

Then it was modified, and the leakers said that I had no foreign policy experience and that I was just a university president, or something like that. I was baffled by it.

When I raised this with [then Secretary of State Warren] Christopher, he basically had no satisfactory response. When he issued a kind of bland supportive statement, and Clinton didn't say *anything*, I said to myself, "I know how that game is played: The gradations occur in how they express their level of support, and people read those like they read tea leaves. So the moment they take on a certain tone, your effectiveness is undercut." And I just said, "No way! I came down here to help, not to play some game or be a scapegoat."

I could've stayed and had a big brouhaha and fought it out, but that was not my goal. There are a lot of people in Washington who will hang on until their fingernails are gone. But I said, either the president and his staff appear to give me their full 100 percent support or I'm out of here. So I submitted my resignation on Monday, and I was back [in New York] the following Monday.

What did I learn from that? Probably that I should have trusted my initial instincts. For anything more, you'll have to read my autobiography!

CHAPTER TWENTY-SIX

Terrie Williams

CEO, The Terrie Williams Agency

❖

A social worker by training, when Terrie Williams decided to launch her own public relations firm, she didn't play around. With basic grit and humility, she managed to land comedian Eddie Murphy and the late jazz great Miles Davis as her first two clients.

Since then, Williams has built a name for herself as an author, lecturer, and master of the ability to reach out to her broad list of clients and contacts in a highly personalized fashion. A graduate of Brandeis University, Williams is in constant self-improvement mode, gathering helpful advice and information wherever and from whomever she can. She is known as much for the inspirational tips she copies and then sends around the globe to friends and associates as she is for her hard work and accomplishments as one of today's leading public relations entrepreneurs.

"Have I made it? I'm not sure what 'it' is," says Williams, who is 46 and single. "And I don't really think about that. I just think about getting it done."

❖

*I*t has always been in me to save the world. I wanted to be a nurse, until I realized I couldn't stand the sight of blood. Then I was going to be a clinical psychologist. I wanted to get a PhD in clinical psychology, but you have to take statistics. I can't even pronounce it. I got a D in statistics twice, so I said, "Okay, I don't think this is for me." I did some research and saw social work as a viable alternative, and I'm still doing social work, even though my job everyday is to run a public relations agency.

When I decided to leave social work and start my own business, I really didn't have a choice. I couldn't do what I was doing anymore. I couldn't take working on a day-to-day basis with all those souls who needed so much help. There are so many things that you can't do anything about: The pain that people are in, the things that these kids have seen, abuse that's been visited upon them. I took too much of that home with me, so it was time to begin the next phase of my life. I had no choice in it. I was going to have my own company because I just *had* to get out and get on to something else.

It was scary going out on my own, but what I've come to learn over the years is that the less risk you take, the less you gain in life.

It was at a screening that I did not want to attend, that I dragged myself to, that I got [comedian] Eddie Murphy to sign on as my first client (and his first publicist). It was hard to throw myself out there, but by forcing myself, I ended up being where I was supposed to be that night. That's life. Sometimes you have to force yourself to do things that you don't like doing, but usually your life is enhanced when you do that.

When I was working at New York Hospital, I was the only black social worker out of forty in the department, and I was the youngest. When people would ask me to go to lunch, I would make excuses. Everyday, I would go get my lunch and then sit in my little office, eat lunch, and take a nap. I was depressed, obviously, and overwhelmed by the sadness of the job, but I was also just shy—always have been.

I forget how long that went on, but it was too long. Finally I realized that this was really pathetic, so I decided I was going to start going out to lunch. When someone asked me I would go, at least once a week, then more often. I just kept up that conscious effort—again, kept forcing myself—and that's how I came out of this shell that I was in.

If you get up in the morning and you have a knot in your stomach because you're going to do something new and different, it's a good thing. You're scared or nervous or whatever, but you're going to come to a better place. It was a major, major coup to land Eddie Murphy and [the now deceased jazz musician] Miles Davis as my first two clients. And I felt a little charge when I signed [talk show host] Sally Jesse Raphael and [author] Stephen King, because that represented somebody saying that we could do more than just black projects. None of it ever would have happened—*none*—if I hadn't forced myself to step out there.

If you *don't* get up in the morning with that knot in your stomach, it means that you're just going through life being kind of complacent. So don't run from the knot, don't run from the fear. Just go ahead and run to it, embrace it, and know that it's going to take you to a better place.

We are all bound by our childhood experiences. They affect who we are today. Because education was something that wasn't easily attained by either one of my parents, they really wanted to make sure that my sister and I got the best. They sent us to the Young Mens and Womens Hebrew Association [nursery school] in Mount Vernon, NY. We were lower middle class and grew up on the south side of Mt. Vernon, which was predominately black. The school was on the north side.

I was a very bright Little Miss Goody-Two-Shoes. I was always driven to succeed: president of the graduating class in eighth grade, president of the sophomore class, graduated high school a year early. But, underneath all that, I didn't quite know where I fit because I was the only one in my neighborhood who was going to a north-side school.

There were three upper-middle-class black families that lived on the north side; they were not very welcoming. It was some of the white kids and/or their parents who invited me to have lunch at their homes and to play with them.

Now, my mother, aunt, and I see members of one of those black families who never gave me the time of day when I was there then. Because I have arrived, because I have achieved a fair amount of success, now it's cool to talk to us. It's very interesting to me how I wasn't good enough back then—or my family wasn't good enough—but my success changed things.

Experiences like that have made me very, very mindful of class distinctions. I don't understand anybody thinking that they are better than anybody else. I'm very passionate about that. It matters not who you are.

The safety net could be gone in a heartbeat and you could lose every-thing you have today or tomorrow, and you would want to be treated the same. The only way you can ensure that is to treat everybody with re-spect and courtesy. If the truth be told, a lot of times it is the janitor, the secretary, or the person you *think* of or *treat* as unimportant, who can be really helpful to you.

Back then, I think I probably felt intimidated by folks who had more than I did, who were considered upper class, or upper middle class. Now, in many ways, I know that I was and am better off than a lot of those people because their mindsets are so limited. If I only knew then what I know now!

I've worked with some of the most powerful people on the planet—folks who impact millions of people's lives. For me to have an idea of the inner workings of their minds and their lives is a blessing. And I think it's made me more enlightened than the average person about what all that fame and fortune is really like.

People often think that if they just get to a certain place, if they ac-complish their goal, suddenly everything will be perfect, all their prob-lems will disappear. Well, I'm here to tell you to learn to enjoy the journey along the way, because when you get to "it," it's not always what you imagined. Sometimes, all you can do is get through one day at a time, and it's not about what your position is or what the world thinks that you have. It's about your heart and how you feel.

The misconception [about someone who is successful] is, "She's successful, she has no problems." Just because one appears to have it all, doesn't mean it is so. In fact, it rarely is. I'll be talking to somebody and they'll say, "I think that so-and-so is so incredible," and I'm sitting there saying to myself, "You have *no idea* how much pain this person is in, or what an ass this person is. No clue!"

For me, working with people who don't have integrity or honor has been the most challenging part of this business and the most disappoint-ing to me over the years.

In recent years, I've made a conscious effort to redirect my business in the area of corporate marketing because of the unique challenge of working with individual personalities. Too frequently that has meant dealing with people's outrageous demands, babysitting, hand-holding. I no longer have the tolerance for it.

I can think of situations over the years in which I was trying to protect clients, because I didn't want the world to know how difficult they could be, but they would just continue to do things that would make them seem like a jerk, which made all my efforts kind of futile. I decided that futility is just not one of my goals, so I had to stop putting myself in those positions. I would have to love and care for them from a distance.

Two individuals that I worked with in the past were outrageously late for photo shoots—I mean, *hours* late! Then they would come in unapologetic and arrogant. I don't understand that. You set the time for this, and you come in five or six *hours* late with an attitude, telling folks that they have a half hour to get the photo shoot done? I don't think so.

I tell clients all the time that as they forge ahead, they must make sure they are aware of how they come across. If they are not sure, they should find out. It may be a painful lesson, but it's worth enduring.

A few years ago, I took a human awareness course called LifeSpring. It was one of those things I had to force myself to do because I knew I needed it. At one point during this intense five-day program, we were asked to pair off with another person. One exercise we did involved having the other person act out what they thought about their partner. My partner took my pocketbook, flung it over his shoulder, and walked around the room with his nose up in the air. His observation was that I was arrogant, distant, and aloof. I thought, "Whoa, wait a minute." I always considered myself a pretty friendly, down-to-earth person. Where was this coming from?

I asked a few other people in the class what they thought about his impression, and they agreed with him. They pointed out that when we took breaks I would go off by myself and not mingle. The truth of the matter is that I'm just very shy, and I was afraid (and still am) to walk up to people and introduce myself.

Had this been a business situation, I would have had no qualms about "working the room." I have trained myself to do what I have to do when I'm making a presentation or dealing with clients or working on an event. But this wasn't work and my inhibitions implied to others that I was distant. My feelings were hurt by the experience, but it was enlightening and important to me to know how people perceived me. Perception *is* reality; it didn't matter what I thought.

My shyness is something I have always had to work on, but it's been empowering to learn that a great many people who are in the performing business are very, very shy. Look at somebody like Bobby DeNiro who is *painfully* shy, but he does his craft. Michael Jackson becomes another person when he's on stage. Johnny Carson—the King of Talk—used to talk about how, when he was at a party, he'd be off in a corner. Being famous or rich or admired doesn't make it any easier for them to make conversation. Shy is shy.

Because it's not easy for me to make small talk, I created a little notebook to carry with me. I'll write down topics—something I read or heard about that's interesting—and I'll study it before I go into a room. Because, when most of us go out, that's when the brain freezes. You stand there and think, "Oh, God, I can't think of anything to say." But if you have your little cheat sheet, you can say to yourself, "I read this and it was kind of interesting; let me throw that out there." And sometimes I'll make conversation out of nothing but the shared moment: "Don't you feel awkward at things like this?" Because most people do. Everybody's wearing a mask. No matter who you are, I understand that what I'm seeing is your game face, and I know that you're just as vulnerable and insecure as I am.

Realizing that is critical, because in life and in business, your relationships with people (whether inherited or acquired, conscious or unconscious) have as much to do with your success as all your professional knowledge.

When I was a student at Brandeis [University] there were about 3,000 students and about 200—maybe 300—black folks. I always knew, because of my upbringing, that I needed to have relationships with people outside my immediate world, but I had mostly black friends in college. If I had it to do again, I would have broadened my horizons, because that's the world in which we're going to be operating.

We just don't have the luxury of hanging out only with each other. White people can go through an entire lifetime and never have to deal with us or think about us, but we can't do that. Somehow we have to be fluent and conversant in both worlds. We have to be able to relate to everybody. Again, we have to step out of our comfort zone.

Thankfully, I had established a relationship with the chaplain of the university. At graduation there were prizes awarded to students who distinguished themselves in specific fields. I got the prize for outstanding student pursuing studies in social work and something like $1500 came with it. I would not have gotten that honor if not for my relationship with him. I'm not saying I didn't deserve it. What I'm saying is that anybody could have gotten that award, but he and I had established a strong relationship and, in the end, everything is relationship generated.

If there are five people who do what you do and have exactly the same credentials, and one person needs to be picked for the social work honor, who do you think will be picked? Whoever is making the choice will pick the person with whom he or she has a relationship; somebody who made him or her feel good, sent a card when he or she was were feeling down. As you go through life, that's how people distinguish themselves. That's how it works.

So if you don't make the move to establish a relationship outside your inner circle where you're most comfortable, no one's going to know about you.

I know that the ability to relate favorably to people may seem like something intangible, but the results are absolutely and totally tangible (it turns contacts into contracts). This has happened in my business over and over again. Believe it: Any rule can be bent, broken, or cease to exist if the rapport is right. Not everyone will end up getting you a new client or a terrific marketing connection, but the people who ultimately gravitate to you will be the conduit through which your success will flow.

I still spend a lot of time with kids in need, and I'll just bring them places because they need to be exposed. Unless they see another side of life, they're going to remain hopeless and dangerous, and it is up to us to do that. They will never know anything else unless we show it to them, but a lot of people just don't care. What they don't realize is that doing something like taking a kid under their wing doesn't just make the child's life better, it changes *their* life. And it's the reason we're here: to hold each other up.

There's a young man who I kind of adopted seven years ago through a mentoring program. I don't have any biological children, but he's lived with me over the years. When he graduated from college last year, I began to understand many of the feelings of pride and separation that parents have. I never would have experienced parenthood without him.

Another thing I try to get across to the kids is that there are no excuses (race, sex, the economy) for not being able to do what you want to do. Everybody's life isn't fair. Realizing that doesn't make your pain any less, but it may help you to put another frame around the picture and see it a little differently. Despite any statistic, you can defy the odds if you want it badly enough.

I draw a lot of inspiration from my family. I wonder about what drive my mother had to be the only one of nine to go to college or even graduate high school. And I marvel at my father who had to leave school in the eighth grade but started a business later in life. I think about what it took for him to keep that going. I draw a lot from all that. I take things from everyone I meet: the good and the bad, the people I respect and those that I don't.

There are too many examples of those who came before us who made it in spite of great odds. But at the same time, you have to keep success in perspective. Focusing on some imagined payoff isn't what gets you there; it's doing your best today, everyday, that moves you forward.

I don't think I've ever really felt like I've "made it." I mean every day there's some kind of acknowledgment or verification of my being accomplished. The phone constantly ringing tells me that. People say that I've done well. My reputation for being a good person and doing good work is solid. And I've had a lot of very, very gratifying moments in this business. But, have I "made it"? I'm not sure what "it" is. You know, you just do what you do and you don't really think about that.

I put this quote up in my office about the four stages of a career: Stage one is, "Who is Terrie Williams?" Stage two is: "Get me Terrie Williams!" Three is: "Get me a Terrie Williams *type*." And four is: "Who is Terrie Williams?"

I had it photocopied and I sent it to a lot of my clients because that's the way the world works, and that's truly the way this business works. Nobody stays on top forever. I keep it up as a reminder.

People say to me, "How come you're so grounded?" or, "I can't believe you returned my phone call." It's because I am *just like you*. And if I lose these [clients] tomorrow and my phone's not ringing, I want you to treat me exactly the way you treat me today. The way you treat people when you're on top is the way you're gonna be treated when the lights go down. And the lights *will* go down at some point.

You know, I do believe that everything happens for a reason; everything falls into place the way it's supposed to. And when X has run its course, then something new will present itself. That's what happened when I left social work, and I know that there are other things for me to do.

I think a lot of people who are successful just did what was in them to do. My business is successful, but real success to me means having balance and peace of mind, and I'm still working on that. That's the more meaningful part of the equation for me.

At the end of the day, I'm a social worker who started my own company without the benefit of the ole boy/ole girl network, and without money or agency or business experience. I am a work in progress. I don't walk on water. I make a lot of mistakes. I just pray a lot, I go the extra mile and I'm staying in the race.

CHAPTER TWENTY-SEVEN

Deborah C. Wright

President and CEO, Carver Federal Savings Bank

On the surface, Debbie Wright seems to have it all: sizzling credentials, an impeccable southern family pedigree, powerful friends—both black and white—and the job she believes is her destiny. The flip side of that coin, though, is that Carver Federal Savings Bank (Carver Bancorp is the holding company) faces daunting challenges, and Wright is in the hot seat to succeed where others have failed.

As bright and blunt as she is warm and well connected, if anyone can revitalize this institution, it's 43-year-old Wright, who sees her role as not merely a job: "For me, it's a mission."

With a background in finance, housing, and New York City government, Wright was president and CEO of the Upper Manhattan Empowerment Zone Development Corporation prior to her Carver appointment. Harlem—Carver's home base—is familiar stomping ground to Wright, who is single, and it holds an emotional tug for her as well.

With $420 million in assets, Carver is the nation's largest African American-operated bank, but it needs deft and visionary management to survive, no less thrive, moving forward. "It will not be easy; that much is clear," she says. "But, make no mistake: We will get it done."

My family is a very classic one in a way. My dad's a minister. His dad was a minister. And his mother's dad was a minister. My mother's father worked in the Boy Scouts for his entire career. My grandparents literally built a church on top of a hill, and we'd spend Thanksgiving as a family, delivering food to the poor. It was very much a family that was externally focused. As my Aunt Marian [Marian Wright Edelman, founder of the Children's Defense Fund] says, public service is the family business.

It was a wonderful way to grow up. Bennettsville, South Carolina was such a comfort zone for me. There was this very tight-knit womb that the whole black community had around us. The expectations were high and there were really no ceilings on those expectations. That clearly helped make me successful—unconsciously so—at least through graduate school. That's when I went in a direction that was sort of at odds with my family's legacy and, as I would find out much later, pretty much at odds with my own internal compass too.

My whole life I thought I was going to be a lawyer. I realized when I was sitting in my Civil Procedure class that first year in law school that my desire to be a lawyer had a lot to do with Aunt Marian.

I was born in 1958 and my aunt was a lawyer at the time in Mississippi. Her life seemed so glamorous to me. She was always protesting some wrong or getting somebody out of jail. I was getting postcards from Russia and Paris, and I thought, "Hey, that sounds good to me!" Frankly, it was just assumed that I was going to be a lawyer. I had a lot of the traits of a successful lawyer: I was articulate, I was good at arguing (since I was arguing all the time), and I was always getting in trouble, but getting A's at the same time. I had even staged a walk-out from my fifth grade class because the school wouldn't lower the flag for Martin Luther King's death. (It landed me in the principal's office, but he did lower the flag.)

It really wasn't until I was sitting in that Civil Procedure class that I realized that being a lawyer was a whole different set of day-to-day activities and a whole different body of thought than I had imagined. I viewed the legal system as an agent for change, given the role of the law during the civil rights era. When I got to Harvard, I saw that although the law could be used as an agent for change, it could also be used to preserve the status quo. I can remember sitting there while the professor lectured about the origins of contracts law or procedural rules such as, "When you get a summons on a Monday you have to respond three days later and it's got to be certified mail . . . ," and I decided this was *not* for me.

That was a crossroads. I went over to the business school and sat in on some classes and thought, "This is great: Real cases about current events, no books, and small classes where the students are learning by talking to each other. I think I'll do this." I had spent a year between college and graduate school at [the investment firm] Goldman Sachs and I thought, "Hey, maybe this is what I'm supposed to do anyway."

So I called home, and I had my plan. I was going to drop out of law school and go to business school. My parents said, "We'll be on the next plane."

I was the first of four kids. I was the typical first. I had the shoebox under the bed with extra cash stashed that everybody borrowed—I was deep into that responsiblity role. So, the way to make it right for everybody (the first-child thing and the female thing is that everybody's got to be comfortable with the decision, right?) was to do both programs, which is what I did.

It's been said that 99 percent of the people who apply to Harvard Law School say they're going to be public interest lawyers, but 99 percent graduate and go to work for Wall Street firms. There is something about human beings just wanting to be a part of a flock. That is a very strong pull, and the way recruiting is organized at graduate schools, it can be very difficult to find a distinctive path.

I wound up in investment banking because I liked finance and I liked a lot of my peers who were going into it. I also felt a natural competitiveness with my peers. I was one of 13 JD/MBAs in my class. Almost everybody was going into either investment banking or consulting. When I look back on it, I didn't really make a choice. I went with the herd.

Very smart people can always figure out a rationale for doing what they're getting ready to do. For me it was, "Oh, I'll be the first woman partner on Wall Street and I can retire at 40, and then I can do all this other stuff I love to do with people, relationships, charities, etc." Little did I know . . . .

My first real job, at [the investment banking firm] First Boston, was the first brick wall I ever hit, and it was very, very tough.

It was the 1980s and investment banking was the place to be. But without a mentor to guide my steps, I had a hard time deciphering the clues. I mean, I got the assignments to go to Pittsburgh while my colleagues were going to L.A. or Paris. There were assignments I worked on for which I didn't get to go to the client meetings at all. I finally figured out that I wasn't going to create some new financial product, nor was my rolodex filled with the names of CFOs in corporate America, and I had to bring one of those assets to the table to be able to do well.

The word *mentor* has become kind of a work thing and a hierarchy thing. Truthfully, when we walk into our work experiences, we carry so many [mentoring] relationships with us, most of which are unrecognizable names, people who aren't even in business, who just had common sense and something valuable to share with you. There had always been people in my life up to that point to whom I could talk and who were, in the truest sense of the word, mentors. At First Boston I never made that connection.

I was working like a dog, staying late nights—sometimes all night—weekends, that whole crazy life. On a day-to-day basis, it was like boot camp. On the surface, it looked fine: the best clothes, going to Europe for vacations, spending money, and doing all the stuff that everybody else with money does. But I was so hollow inside.

The competition was about money, houses, vacations, much of which I couldn't relate to. But I still thought that one day I would just sort of get in gear. Then one event just brought the whole thing crashing down.

Three years into this experience I was preparing to go on vacation to St. Maarten. On the way out I got a call from my mother telling me that my grandmother was ill. We were extremely close. So I called her, and I said, "Look, if you follow doctors' orders, I'll split my vacation and come back through Dallas on the way home." She said that would be great.

So I went away, and on my way back through Atlanta for a plane change my baby sister was at the airport. I said, "What are you doing here?" She said, "I'm going home for the weekend." I said, "You just got to school three weeks ago." (She was at Spelman College.) And she had to tell me, standing there in the airport, that my grandmother had died while I was on vacation. It was just devastating.

When I got back to work the following week, I ran into my boss in the breakfast line and he said, "Well, how was your vacation?" I told him about my grandmother and—I kid you not—that man said to me, "It's a good thing that's behind you now." That's all he said and kept going. It stopped me cold. I said to myself, "Girlfriend, you are in the *wrong* place."

I went home to my folks three weeks later to talk over my predicament, and I remember my father said, "Who are you doing this for? For us? We don't care. You could be a street sweeper as far as we're concerned." My mother said, "We don't even like you like this. We never see you, and you have an attitude when we do see you. Your face is broken out, your hair is falling out. It's nice to get expensive Christmas gifts, but that's no substitute for the Deb we love."

So that was that. And then the hard part began because then I had to figure out who was this person that I didn't even know anymore.

Leaving First Boston without another job was considered risky. Only one friend told me to quit. Everybody else thought I was having an early midlife crisis and I should just go to another division or investment bank. I had no idea what to do. I felt like a failure. But it was an important brick wall to hit, and it happened at a good point in my career, because, truthfully, I just wasn't on a path that was ever going to make me feel successful or happy. It forced me to deal with me.

It also forced me to get on a path on which I could deal with the legacy of my family and find a way to make peace with the fact that I'm a part of something larger than myself. You know, having an incredibly strong and accomplished family legacy is a gift, but it is also a burden and, at times, it's been overwhelming.

After I left First Boston, I did a really interesting thing, which, for me, was unusual, because until then, I had always felt that I had the answers. I called up Harvard's alumni placement office. They had a class about preparing for your future that, of course, I didn't take in school because I *knew* what I was going to do. They suggested that I call the professor who taught that class. I did, and it was really a wonderful experience.

I remember flying up to Boston, talking to him, and taking some personality tests, which I had never done before. When he evaluated them, he said, "What's up with you? I can't even believe you got through First Boston for three years."

He just broke it down for me. Going from category to category, he explained that what I was looking for in a career, based on what I said on paper was almost 180 degrees different from the job I had just left. It didn't help me figure out what I should do, but it did help me to figure out that I'm motivated by people and causes.

That was revealing, but it still didn't solve the question of what to do. I have memories of going to Central Park and sitting there for hours at a time with a yellow pad. I was supposed to be writing down the kinds of things I was interested in. I would leave that park in tears, with nothing on the paper. Finally, I decided to go see some people who I was close to and just talk about ideas.

I went down to Washington and spent some time with my aunt. What bubbled up was senior citizens and housing. Then I spent a couple of days with my congressman at the time, just trailing him to see what that life was like. They gave me people to call, and that started the ball rolling.

It was an interesting time, because people were just so fascinated to meet this woman with three Harvard degrees. The impact of that single factor, Harvard, is remarkable. A woman who was in graduate school when I was in college used to call it "the H-bomb." When somebody asks you a basic question, "Where did you go to school?" and you say, "Harvard," there is no neutral reaction to that. People either hate you or respect you—both way out of proportion to what you deserve. In my case, the response was, "What's the problem? You can do anything you want to do."

I said, "*That's* the problem. It's not what I *can* do. It's what do I *want* to do?"

My aunt sent me to David Rockefeller's daughter to learn about the New York Partnership. She was on vacation, so she sent me to a woman named Ellen Straus, a board member who was acting president at the time. She introduced me to Kathy Wylde, who ran their Housing division. I connected with Ellen and Kathy right away. Both became long-term supporters and mentors.

They called up and said, "Look, we really want you to be here, but the only job we have open is putting together a sales team for a new project we're building in Harlem called Towers on the Park. It only pays $35,000 a year, so we're embarrassed to even tell you about it. But we want to commit to you that if you come, we'll apply to some foundations and try to get it to $60,000." I said, "I'll take it."

They were thrilled, and I was thrilled, and it was one of the best years of my life because I felt like what I was doing mattered to somebody. I was up in Harlem, which was fascinating. My great grandparents had lived there and I remembered so many stories from my dad and others about Harlem in its heyday.

All of a sudden it was, like — Boom! — I was just springing out of bed in the morning. They wouldn't even have had to pay me. I was making $135,000 three years into First Boston. I never spent my bonuses, so I didn't need the money. I just wanted to feel excited about work again. That whole experience put me on a different path. It put finance in a context that I cared about.

There were some awkward moments at first, because I've always been a big planner, and I had a job, but I still didn't have a plan. I remember bumping into a guy I knew at a party. He was very successful at a leveraged buyout firm. I remember this guy coming up to me and saying, "Hey, where are you now?"

I just started cringing and said, "Well, I'm at the New York Partnership." He said, "What's that?"

I told him that it was civic organization headed by corporate CEOs, and that I worked in the Housing division, and the guy paused for a second and then said to me, "Yeah, but what's the deal? What are you *really* going to do? What's this going to *lead* to?" In his mind I had to have a scheme that this fit into. It couldn't possibly be that I was just in Harlem selling some apartments. That just didn't make sense to him.

I said, "No, this is where I am." He sort of looked puzzled and excused himself, and I sat there feeling like I was three feet tall for a minute.

In that period, as I went through a process of redefining what success was, I also came to understand the value of where I came from. Certainly one perspective would be, "She's from Bennettsville, South Carolina, where's that? Podunk, USA," but the biggest heroes in my life were the people I grew up with.

You have to keep track of who you are because otherwise you get lost. My comfort level is about ultimately knowing the value of the people I had the honor of growing up with. From having spent a lot of time with people—rich and poor—who have grown up in situations that look very nice on the outside, but are really very troubled on the inside, I know that there's just no substitute for having an internal compass. I can't take credit for mine. It was a gift from a lot of extraordinary everyday folks. And I don't get flustered around the so-called rich and powerful because I know that at the end of the day, they're just like us.

Slowly but surely, the New York Partnership evolved from a place to which I had escaped, to a place where I started to reconnect to who I was.

The first year I was just happy to be happy, but I did not think for a minute that this was what I was going to do with my life. The second year, I still didn't know, but I knew I wasn't going back to investment banking. I just figured I would sort of bump into the right experience.

That third year is when I said, "Okay, you can't transition forever. You have to be figuring out a plan." And then the [City] Planning Commission just happened. It really was, literally, bumping into somebody at a cocktail party who said, "Gee, the [David] Dinkins administration is looking for some bright young people, and I'm on the search committee, and you should send your resume to the Planning Commission." I didn't think for three seconds that that was going to happen.

When it did, that was very difficult for my boss, an extremely bright woman who was 150 percent committed to the cause. We had gotten very close. On the one hand, she was proud of me; on the other hand, she was bothered by my leaving. I remember her saying, "We invested all of this in you for three years. How could you leave?"

That was very hard to hear, but I said to her, "Look, how many Harvard JD/MBAs do you know who spent three years working 24 hours a day, getting paid $60,000 a year? That's just not the way young people view their careers. We don't stay places 20 years."

We didn't see each other for six months. But then I called her to congratulate her on a grant she had won, and we are very close friends today. That was a real growing experience for me, to kind of step out of myself and realize how a mentor would feel and what she was going through— letting go of a mentee. A lot of times you don't understand those experiences until later. I've had that happen to me subsequently, and it's very hard to say goodbye.

When we were growing up, my dad used to say about different things that would come up, "It's just money." He just had a sort of unspoken ethos about what was important. When I was appointed to the Planning Commission, it paid $22,000, and my parents just laughed. They said, "We can't figure you out at all. You go from $135,000 to $35,000 to $60,000 to $22,000. What's up with you?"

But I feel very instinctual about the job moves that I have made. I haven't actually looked for a job since I left First Boston. Everything that's happened since then has just evolved through relationships or events. That's why I always tell young people that there's no "free" job or experience. You're always being evaluated, whether others acknowledge it or not. And you never know when you'll bump into a former colleague at a pivotal juncture or need a body of knowledge from a prior job.

I went from the Planning Commission to HPD [the Department of Housing Preservation and Development] to the New York Housing Authority to UMEZ [the Upper Manhattan Empowerment Zone]. Each move seemed like the right thing to do at the moment, and each position has been a tremendous growth experience leading to the next. That's hard for a planner, but I'm at a point in my life where I have to just say, hey, I'm not in charge of this completely. There's a lot of it that I can direct, but there's definitely something bigger going on.

The truth is, I wanted this [Carver] job back when I was at the New York Partnership. I told Kathy Wylde then that this would be the perfect place for me to be and I shared some of my vision of what Carver could become. I had come to realize that I wasn't looking for a job, I was looking for a mission. She later heard that the president at the time was looking for someone he could groom as his successor, so, Kathy introduced me to some folks who recommended me for the job.

But the word came back that, because I was a woman, it would never work. The gender thing is very, very deep, and we have trouble talking about it in the black community. It's prevalent in all of our institutions, even the church.

Ultimately getting this job felt great. It felt like a real victory. And now is the right time; I am really ready for it. My Aunt Olive said that I had been preparing my whole life for this position, and it does seem that way in retrospect. All prejudice—whether it's about race, age, or gender—cuts both ways: You can be debilitated by it or you can be empowered by it. I say to [my assistant] Gregory all the time that it's wonderful to be underestimated, because by the time the person who's doing that figures you out, you've already lapped them.

At the same time, I know I wasn't ready before. I had to go through a process—or two, or three—to get here. An elite boot camp was necessary to understand the standard I am now required to translate (from Wall Street to 125th Street, and back). Through time in government and in nonprofit work, I learned the neighborhoods and people that make this city tick—and how to make deals work for everyone. I had no way of knowing it, but these experiences were preparing me for dealing with the here and now.

It's been very challenging here at Carver, as I have moved to remove the senior management team, some of which are men who had been here for 30 years or more. It was very hard. It was like looking at a parent, or an uncle, and saying, "You don't cut it anymore." But if I didn't deal with that, it would hold the institution back, and I can't let that happen.

A few years ago, my brother asked me, "How did you develop that skill to see stuff clearly and just zoom in on whatever needs to get done?" I don't know. I think it's not something you develop, it's just a gift. And it's not something that I really got in touch with until these managerial roles kicked in. But I am very focused on making sure that what gets done is quantifiable. Maybe that's why I'm attracted to situations that are broken—so I can fix them. At the same time, I've learned that that role can be gratifying, but it also makes you a lightening rod.

A few months after I started here, a guy who runs an organization here in Harlem reached me at home at 10 o'clock at night. I had just gotten in from a long day; I was tired. He told me that someone at Carver had put out the rumor that I was replacing men with women because I was gay. Just straight up, they just put that out there. I had to sit down on my couch and say to myself, "Why is my being in this position so threatening?" I don't walk around thinking, I'm a woman—I'm a black woman—and I'm 41 and other people are 61. I'm just doing my job.

To him, I made light of it, and said, "You know, my mother told me to stop and pick up a husband and some children. I guess this is what I get for not following her advice." He laughed and I laughed, but this type of thing is wounding, especially when you're dealing with intense day-to-day challenges and the sacrifices one inevitably makes in accepting this kind of life's work.

I was the MC on a panel of business women at [a meeting of] 100 Black Women, and someone from the audience asked the question, "What sacrifices have you had to make to be successful?" Before I could answer, the panelists said they had done an informal tally at our table, and none of us had children. That blew my mind.

When you're young, and just starting out, people just tell you to go for it. They never tell you about the consequences or the trade-offs, and you're too young to even understand what they are. It just never crossed my mind that I should be thinking of marriage and family back then.

An older friend told me ten years ago that, in a relationship, someone has to decrease so the other can increase. Then, as now, I hope that's not true. Connecting with someone who's as comfortable being himself as he is with allowing me to be myself is important to me. And, if I can tell you with confidence that there's something larger at work regarding my career, then I have to believe the same is true on the personal side.

That's why my prayers each morning are, "God, just make me open to whatever the lesson is so I can get it and get on to the next one."

Index